Arguments about
Animal Ethics

Arguments about Animal Ethics

Edited by
Greg Goodale
and
Jason Edward Black

LEXINGTON BOOKS
A division of
ROWMAN & LITTLEFIELD PUBLISHERS, INC.
Lanham • Boulder • New York • Toronto • Plymouth, UK

Published by Lexington Books
A division of Rowman & Littlefield Publishers, Inc.
A wholly owned subsidary of The Rowman & Littlefield Publishing Group, Inc.
4501 Forbes Boulevard, Suite 200, Lanham, Maryland 20706
http://www.lexingtonbooks.com

Estover Road, Plymouth PL6 7PY, United Kingdom

British Library Cataloguing in Publication Information Available

Library of Congress Cataloging-in-Publication Data

Arguments about animal ethics / edited by Greg Goodale and Jason Edward Black.
    p. cm.
  Includes bibliographical references and index.
  ISBN 978-0-7391-4298-1 (cloth : alk. paper) — ISBN 978-0-7391-4300-1 (electronic)
  1. Animal welfare—Moral and ethical aspects. 2. Animal rights. I. Goodale, Greg, 1966– II. Black, Jason Edward.
  HV4708.A74 2010
  179'.3—dc22

                                                                    2009050526

Printed in the United States of America

Contents

Chapter One

Rhetoric and "Animals"

A Long History and Brief Introduction

Greg Goodale and Jason Edward Black

Rhetorical scholars are trained to understand that when scientists and philosophers claim to make logical arguments, these are not unbiased, purely logical, or the only arguments available for improving the common good. The Nazis exemplified the problem with "logical" arguments when their scientists "proved" the superiority of the Aryan race over the Jewish race. Of course, it is easy enough for those who look back upon the past to see that Nazi science was not unbiased because it was so different from our own. Even in 1937 social critic Kenneth Burke understood that the Nazis were inventing what appeared to be logical arguments to support the contradictory belief that Jews were simultaneously weakening and threatening the German people.[1] But if the science that motivated a nation to do awful acts was ideology rather than truth, and was grounded in arguments that only appeared to be logical, what makes us so sure that our own science is not similarly ideological? What makes us so sure that we have not been lured into a belief that future generations will condemn as immoral? Burke argued metaphorically:

> It is relevant to recall those specialists whose technical training fitted them to become identified with mass killings and experimentally induced sufferings in the concentration camps of National Socialist Germany. Hence, insofar as there are similar temptations in our own society . . . , might we not expect similar motives to lurk about the edges of our sciences . . . ? But liberal apologetics indignantly resists any suggestion that sadistic motives may lurk behind unnecessary animal experiments that cause suffering. The same people who, with reference to the scientific horrors of Hitlerism, admonish against the ingredients of Hitlerite thinking in our own society, will be outraged if you follow out the implications of their own premises, and look for similar temptations among our specialists.[2]

Science and philosophy, with their purportedly "natural" hierarchies, enable the use, exploitation, and killing of nonhuman animals with little moral quandary. These beliefs, for they are not truths in any objective sense, led Burke to wonder about the similarities between the Holocaust and vivisection. Is it any wonder, then, that Charles Patterson wrote an entire book, *Eternal Treblinka: Our Treatment of Animals and the Holocaust*, about the relationship between the Holocaust and the Hecatomb, citing throughout comparisons that survivors of the death camps made between their experience and the experience of other animals.[3] The comparisons made by Burke, Patterson, and Patterson's many witnesses are the first of many rhetorical tactics that readers will encounter in this book, and one that is particularly troubling given our uncertainty over the distinction between humans and other animals. For most readers, it is the trope of the metaphor. However, for some readers, the shared experience of Holocaust victims and animals sent to their slaughter is not metaphorical at all: to them, we are all animals who suffer fear and pain.

The essays in this volume begin to get at the rhetorical practices that surround thousands of years of debate about the relationship between humans and nonhuman animals. These essays look, for example, at how Christian traditions continue to inform secular arguments about managing animals, the practice of science as it dates back to Francis Bacon, and the diversion of interest from argument in the rhetorical sense, where arguers attempt to negotiate toward a solution that benefits all, toward argument in the popular vernacular by which arguers yell at each other without listening. Essayists in this volume critique all sides of the debate, noting how campaigns waged by vegetarian advocates and activist organizations like People for the Ethical Treatment of Animals (PETA) have failed to persuade an audience beyond true believers, and how that organization employs arguments that reify the supremacy of human beings. On the other side of the debate, rhetorics of the food and beverage industry and the biomedical research industry are examined to determine how their messages continue to persuade most Americans even in the face of contrary evidence. Other authors theorize the place of language and whispering in the human/nonhuman animal relationship, the confused meaning of terms like "human" and "animal," and how we persuade ourselves of the need to practice ethics toward other animals.

The discipline of rhetoric as it is practiced in English and communication departments has not yet seen a volume devoted to arguments about animal ethics. To be sure, a few essays on the subject have been published to this point. The granddaddy of the rhetoric of animal ethics essays was published in 1994. Kathryn Olson and Thomas Goodnight's "Entanglements of Consumption" analyzed the participation of animal rights activists in debates about whether or not purchasing and wearing fur is cruel.[4] Though the activists and their opponents depend on enthymemes (arguments that rely on audience's assumptions) and perceive the world in very different ways, they have engaged in the public sphere, and this is a positive signal about our ability to argue over controversial issues. Peter Simonson in his 2001 essay "Social Noise and Segmented Rhythms" argues that the shift from news-oriented events like animal laboratory raids to celebrity-based promotion led directly to the rapid growth of PETA in the late 1980s and early 1990s.[5] Lesli Pace's essay "Image Events and PETA's Anti Fur Campaign" (2005) appears in the footnotes of a number of the chapters in *Arguments about Animal Ethics*, and for good reason.[6] Hers is one of the first essays to adopt rhetorician Kevin DeLuca's notion of the image event—visual arguments that often make the news or find their way into popular culture.[7] Jason Edward Black's essays "Extending the Rights of Personhood, Voice, and Life to Sensate Others" (2003) and "SLAPPs and Social Activism" (2003) have also been influential and will appear in the footnotes of this volume.[8] His articles have laid the groundwork for connecting the rhetoric of animal ethics to a much broader scholarship about rhetoric and social movements. Wendy Atkins-Sayre's essay "Articulating Identity: People for the Ethical Treatment of Animals and the Animal/Human Divide" (2010) examines how PETA's visual rhetoric breaks down the boundaries between humans and nonhuman animals.[9] On the English-rhetoric side of the equation, Mary Trachsel has taken a theoretical route in her 2007 essay "Husserl's Intersubjectivity and the Possibility of Living with Nonhuman Persons," which leads her to rethink theories of mind in a manner that recognizes the consciousness of others broadly defined.[10] And, Patricia Malesh has recently published an essay, "Sharing our Recipes," that employs ethnographic methodologies to understand the relationship between identity and veganism.[11] Finally, Carrie Packwood Freeman, a media studies scholar, has recently published two essays, "Food for Thought" (with Debra Merskin) and "This Little Piggy Went to Press" that examine how the media reifies stereotypes and identities relating to the consumption of meat and tofu.[12] In this volume, she turns to language to deconstruct the words upon which those stereotypes are founded.

Rhetorical scholarship provides a particularly valuable perspective for understanding arguments surrounding the human/nonhuman animal relationship. Those arguments are rarely premised on fact, but rather on long-held assumptions and the effectiveness of many tropes that have not yet been studied in depth. Traditional assumptions concerning the juncture of rhetoric and human/nonhuman animals are thoroughly reflected in Burke's perspective on the relationship. His entire rhetorical program, "symbolic action," is dependent upon the superiority of human animals as "active agents" who use "language as a symbolic means of inducing cooperation in beings that by nature respond to symbols."[13] Vitally, Burke occludes nonhuman animals from languaging forms. Almost in a Cartesian way he denies nonhuman animals any agency as sentient and "thinking" beings; he relegates them instead to what he calls "motion." Motion encompasses only the biological functions of being; it is entrenched in "animality" insomuch as it involves "growth, metabolism, digestion . . . respiration, functions of the various organs . . . and so on."[14] Action, on the other hand, involves ethical considerations because of the use of symbols. To him, only human animals deserve such benefit. In turn, nonhuman animals are glossed as having no purpose or will. Concomitantly, Burke's program prevents human animals from ever entering the so-called natural order again or, in the least, demonstrates how they can never "be . . . animals."[15] So, in his estimation, nonhuman animals have no agency, and human animals sever their ties with nonhuman animals as soon as second-order processing and language enter the equation. Coupled with Burke's insistence that human animals define realities—including the "natural" world—through a hierarchy placing the "other" below human animals as agents, it remains clear that nonhuman animals maintain no rhetorical space in the relationship. Yet he recognizes that he may be wrong as evidenced by the quotation in the first paragraph of this chapter.

Burke's interventions in the 1950s and 1960s were nothing new for rhetorical scholars. Indeed, the relationship between rhetoric and nonhuman animals extends all the way back to Aristotle, who wrote in *Synagôgê* of Korax and Tisias, the first two practitioners of rhetoric.[16] Korax is the ancient Greek word for raven/crow (the Greeks did not distinguish between the two species) and Tisias means egg. As the author who most persuasively argued that "man" is the only speaking animal, Aristotle has long served as the authority on both the human/nonhuman animal boundary and on the practice of rhetoric. But this authority has been, since the dawn of the Age of Science, contradictory because in his writings on nature he suspected that certain kinds of birds, like the raven/crow, were rhetors.[17]

Interestingly, Aristotle's inconsistency has created a rupture in the rhetorical tradition through which the human/nonhuman relationship can be reassessed. Though rhetorical scholars have not yet worked through that entrée, the post–New Rhetoric era (which often spotlights Burke's program as a model) has, at least, reflected a shift in attending to the human/nonhuman relationship. Such a shift is rooted in the social movement turn in rhetorical studies that took hold following rhetorician Leland Griffin's insistence that scholars move away from a single-speaker enterprise where critical interest was focused solely on intent-effects.[18] His call to examine movements generically and processually spawned a series of definitional and methodological debates about social change in rhetorical studies.[19] And, as world revolutions took place in the 1940s and 1950s, and as efforts for liberation in the United States grew between the 1950s and 1970s, the rhetorical dimensions of such change became the centerpiece of rhetorical studies.

Inevitably, critics turned their eyes toward the burgeoning environmental movement and, as an attendant sub-area, animal welfare/rights issues. Rhetorician Christine Oravec, for instance, focused critical attention on environmental preservation, mostly through case studies of national parks and key preservationist figures. Her piece "John Muir, Yosemite, and the Sublime Response: A Study in the Rhetoric of Preservationism" exists as one of the first social change studies to emphasize the holistic connection between human animals and the environmental "sublime," a pathos appeal that functions through ontological linkages, just as arguments in favor of the human/nonhuman animal relationship do.[20] Following suit, rhetorical critics such as Jonathan Lange, M. Jimmie Killingsworth, Jacqueline S. Palmer, Tarla Rai Peterson, Phaedra Pezzullo, and Kevin DeLuca have continued the project of moving the environment to the forefront of social change studies.[21] Their work focuses on a variety of case studies, but common denominators appear to be the issue of "ethics" and both the ways that living/sentient subjects are connected with human animals and the ways that human animals ought to consider these subjects. (Notice the use of the term "subjects" rather than "objects;" the latter term typically occludes ethical considerations in terms of ontology.) The work in animal ethics outlined earlier in this section draws direct influence from these environmental movement and social change studies within the field of rhetoric. Ultimately, the "moves" of earlier scholarship about both environmental rhetoric and animal ethics have become the generative foundations to the important dimensions of the human/nonhuman animal relationship explored in this volume.

RHETORICAL SCHOLARSHIP AND ANIMAL ETHICS

In *Arguments about Animal Ethics* we open with three theoretical essays that ground us in language and self-persuasion. Freeman's essay, "Embracing Humanimality: Deconstructing the Human/Animal Dichotomy," gets us to the root of the problem with the human/nonhuman animal relationship: the words we use that make humans seem distinct. Trachsel's "How to Do Things without Words: Whisperers as Rustic Authorities on Interspecies Dialogue," seeks to get outside the silo of our assumptions to find a common language shared by humans and animals, thus breaking down distinctions. Malesh, then, examines how it is that some are empowered to persuade themselves of the being-ness of nonhuman animals in her essay

"The Battle Within: Understanding the Persuasive Affect of Internal Rhetorics in the Ethical Vegetarian/Vegan Movement."

The next three essays are critiques of animal rights rhetoric. "I'm Too Sexy for Your Movement: An Analysis of the Failure of the Animal Rights Movement to Promote Vegetarianism" by Laura K. Hahn, describes how the animal rights movement, as exemplified by PETA, has failed to reach out beyond the already-persuaded because of messages that distract from a key goal: that humans should not eat meat. Similarly, Brett Lunceford's "PETA and the Rhetoric of Nude Protest" employs DeLuca's notions about "image events" to describe how PETA's nude protests do little more than titillate and offend, while appealing only to the already-persuaded. Jason Edward Black provides a more positive analysis and a potentially powerful rhetorical strategy in his essay "Biting Back at the Empire: The Anti-Greyhound Racing Movement's Decolonizing Rhetoric as a Countermand to the Dog-Racing Industry." Black argues that a focus on postcolonial rhetorics has the potential to recover greyhounds as beings in much the same way that postcolonial scholars have recovered colonial subalterns as agents worthy of concern.

Turning to rhetorics that exploit animals, Greg Goodale, Wendy Atkins-Sayre, and Richard D. Besel and Renee S. Besel examine three industries. Goodale's chapter, titled "The Biomedical Research Industry and the End of Scientific Revolutions" centers the public relations machinery of this massive industry in the context of theories about how scientists are able to change perceptions about nature. Ultimately, he argues that the biomedical research industry prevents a future scientific revolution by taking advantage of assumptions that vivisection is the best way to create new medical treatments. Atkins-Sayre similarly takes on corporate interests in her essay "Protection from 'Animal Rights Lunatics': The Center for Consumer Freedom and Animal Rights Rhetoric," a front that exploits assumptions about the radicalism of vegetarianism and organizations like PETA that advocate for animal rights. Besel and Besel take a different tack in their study of a popular television program. In "*Whale Wars* and the Public Screen: Mediating Animal Ethics in Violent Times," they argue that the image events created by anti-whaling activists are exploited by entertainment executives in a manner that elides the very whales the show is supposedly about.

Finally, *Arguments about Animal Ethics* ends with a hopeful essay about the common ground we share due to humanimal's long history of thinking about the relationship between humans and other animals. Jane Bloodworth Rowe and Sabrina Marsh argue in "Feral Horses: Logos, Pathos and the Definition of Christian Dominion" that both sides in the debate over what to do with horses on the Outer Banks of North Carolina rely on the same tradition—the Christian concept of "man's" dominion—to persuade audiences about managing and protecting these animals. Our attitudes toward other animals are indeed shaped by ancient passages in Aristotle and the Bible.

Rhetorical criticism produces a sense of what is not being addressed and how those issues might be brought into a sphere where discourse and debate become possible again. As the critic Raymie McKerrow informs us, our discourse is limited to those things with which we are aware, by what we assume to be true, and by those we permit to speak.[22] And of course, the rhetoric of those activists who champion "animal" rights, or welfare, or liberation, or abolition, and of those who argue that humans should be permitted to use "animals" must be examined for failures, assumptions, and exploitations if we are ever to have an honest debate about the relationship between humans and other animals.

None of us are without bias. None of us enter into these debates without assumptions that act as truths and prevent us from engaging in a symmetrical dialogue with those who disagree. It is the discipline of Rhetoric, however, that provides us with the opportunity to recognize and reject our assumptions while undermining the false assumptions of others. The first false assumption, then, that we undermine here is the distinction of "man." If we are to have a frank and candid discussion about rights and responsibilities, welfare and liberation, and rhetorical strategies we must first remember that, like the ancient rhetors Korax and Tisias, we too are animals. Thus when we write of *Arguments about Animal Ethics*, we include humans in the category animals.

Part One

RHETORICAL THEORY AT THE HUMAN/NONHUMAN ANIMAL BOUNDARY

Chapter Two

Embracing Humanimality

Deconstructing the
Human/Animal Dichotomy

Carrie Packwood Freeman

Crossing borders or the ends of man I come or surrender to the animal—
to the animal in itself, to the animal in me
and the animal at unease with itself . . .

—Jacques Derrida[1]

Most people do not see themselves as animals, considering that term to refer
to a wholly different category than humankind—there are minerals, plants,
animals, and then there are humans. In almost two decades of advocating for
nonhuman animals (NHAs), I have discovered that the hegemonic distinction between human and animal serves as a primary boundary that constrains
and impedes an average American's consideration of animal rights as a valid
ethical position.[2] A harmonious conversation about animal issues splits at the
point where I, as advocate, compare injustice toward NHAs to that toward
humans. At this point, speciesism comes into play, and I have lost my audience, as the listeners claim that caring about humans' interests takes priority.
This is indicative of the general acceptance of animal *welfare* viewpoints in
favor of better treatment of domesticated and "useful" animals as opposed to
animal *rights* viewpoints that reject the very practice of domestication and
use.[3] Those arguments deployed on behalf of animal rights often lead no-
where absent deconstructing the human/animal dualism that lies at the heart
of speciesism.

As a communications scholar, I seek to define which aspects of this
deconstruction are most useful for animal rights advocacy. I will argue in
this chapter that advocates should prioritize notions of *humanimality*, or
in other words, how humans might rhetorically construct themselves as
animals. Yet my research on popular vegetarian campaigns of U.S. animal

rights organizations finds that when campaigns focused on humans, it was
on their propensity to be *ethical* and *humane* rather than on their animality
or their similarity to NHAs. Campaigns more often focused on the sentience
and suffering of NHAs, particularly seeking to convince the public that
maligned NHA species such as pigs and chickens had similar capabilities
to other NHAs who are more well-liked, such as dogs and primates.[4] This
welfare emphasis is not an effective rhetorical strategy for transforming
discriminatory worldviews about animals as "other."

This reticence for advocates to explicitly construct a sense of humanity's
animality (humanimality) is not surprising, as American society is rhetorically constructed on humanist principles that celebrate humanity's special-
ness and define it in opposition to animality. Thus, in seeking to rhetorically
combat speciesism, how can animal advocates talk about humans and other
animals in ways that are posthumanist?[5] In answering this question, I draw
upon posthumanist scholarship to critically analyze how these humanist
tensions not only affect but also exist within animal rights philosophy itself, likely weakening arguments in favor of animal rights. My goal is to
improve the logical basis upon which this philosophy informs animal rights
advocacy.

I begin by examining how humanist terminology makes it hard to rhetorically avoid speciesism and embrace humanimality. I then analyze the
paradoxes involving animal activists' deployment of humanist adjectives
like *humane* and *ethical*, as well as tensions over whether animal rights
strategies should promote humanity's similarity to other animals or take a
new tack toward embracing diversity among all animals. This involves deconstructing not only the human/animal binary but also the related binaries
of nature/culture and similarity/diversity to unify these dualistic concepts
in strategic ways.

I suggest that animal advocates more humbly represent humans as social
animals who are uniquely prone to excess, explaining the biological need for
humanity's complex ethical systems (in comparison to other social animals)
as opposed to viewing human morality solely as a magnanimous cultural
choice. Animal advocates' efforts to promote humans' ethical treatment of
NHAs, rather than continuing to primarily craft messages saying "they are
like us," should begin to promote the idea that "we are like them" in many
ways that are worth acknowledging. However, the challenge in this focus on
humanimality and expanded notions of identity is to find a way to respect the
diversity represented in the animal world (in groups and individuals) so as
to avoid creating new hierarchies or revised notions of "the animal other." I
therefore conclude by presenting a blended approach as a solution to better
understanding the humanimal/NHA relationship.

THE PROBLEM OF HUMANIST TERMINOLOGY

Inconsistent Definitions of the Term *Animal*

Animal advocates must struggle with using the very central term *animal*. As philosopher Mary Midgley observes, *animal* has two definitions with differing connotations: a "benign" one that includes humans; and a "negative" one that not only excludes humans but also represents what is "unhuman, the anti-human."[6] This links the human/animal and nature/culture dualisms. Similarly, social anthropologist Tim Ingold explains the two opposing conceptualizations of animality as (1) a "domain or kingdom" (which includes humans—a scientific taxonomy that takes into account ecological connections/dependence) and (2) a "condition" (which excludes humans and is "opposed to humanity").[7] In the latter conceptualization, human culture is separated from nature, which is seen as the NHA's domain. This anti-human condition of being an "animal" represents the distinction between "natural" behaviors devoid of values or reasons and the process humans go through to become enculturated and overcome this animality.

Even though humans may understand they are technically part of the animal kingdom, to call a human an *animal* is largely considered an insult. English scholar and animal advocate Joan Dunayer states, "nonhuman animal terms insult humans by invoking a contempt for other species. The very word *animal* conveys opprobrium. *Human*, in contrast, signifies everything worthy."[8] She notes that when someone says "humans *and* animals" they commit a "verbal ruse" denying the benign definition of animal that includes humans in the animal kingdom.[9] The grammatically incorrect yet common phrase "humans and animals" is even used by animal rights campaigns due to a combination of assumptions about the distinction and the connotation of *animal* as an affront to audience members' superior status as humans. Indeed, there is a long history of those in power using NHA labels to belittle human groups for purposes of hierarchizing, marginalizing, and oppressing.[10] Calling a human an *animal* also invokes an implicit belief in the evolution of species that categorizes humans as primates; animal advocates may be unwilling to risk offending religious viewpoints grounded in a humanism that views humans as closer to a divinity than apes, as the evolution versus creationism debate is highly politicized in the United States.

Struggle for Non-Speciesist Terminology

Given the problematic double meaning of the word *animal*, it is challenging to find a non-speciesist term to denote proper respect for NHAs. Other animals could be called *nonhuman animals* (NHAs), as I choose to do in this essay, or *other-than-human animals*, as both of these labels present the benefit of reminding humans that they too are animals; humanimality is fore-grounded every time *nonhuman animal* is invoked. However, these labels still mark them as an "other" in negation to the dominant term *human,* such as *non-white* may imply a racial hierarchy. Activists sometimes refer to NHAs using the term *being*, as in *sentient being* or *living being*, but this still does not carry the weight of *human being* as far as indicating an implicit dignity. Indeed, while the phrase "human dignity" is common, its counterpart, "ani-mal dignity," is rare.

Instead of finding a new term for other animals, humans could redefine themselves by including the word *animal* in their own description, calling themselves *human animals* instead of just *humans* to remind themselves of their mutual status as animals; this may help eliminate the use of the term *animal* as an insult toward humans.[11] Alternately, humans could simply refer to all animals as *persons* and distinguish them, humans included, based on species names when needed. It does, however, seem like some new terms are required to properly denote the new value humans should be placing on what philosopher Jacques Derrida refers to as "the multiplicity of living be-ings" and animals' status as members of one group.[12] Some might find the term *infra-human* too clinical, so perhaps *humanimal* is the best neologism so far proposed, as it reveals that the term *animal* is literally a part of *human*.[13] Advocates should carefully phrase existing words to increase respectfulness toward other animals and foreground how language has been used to covertly privilege humans. But it also seems the creation of new terms is necessary to circumvent the speciesism inherent in a discourse built to reflect the human/ animal dichotomy at the heart of the Western worldview.[14]

Inability to Define Human Borders

In the debate over definitions of *animal,* Derrida prefers to embrace com-plexity instead of homogeneity, emphasizing that there are many differences that could be characterized as "uncrossable borders" among all animals, even among humans. This diversity cannot be reduced to just one definitive border between humans and all other animals: "There is not one opposition between [man] and [non-man]; there are, between different organizational structures of the living being, many fractures, heterogeneities, differential structures."[15] Archaeologist P. J. Ucko echoes this claim that the borderlines are indistinct, even between mammals and other animals: "Contrary to the normal assumption, the borderline between humans and animals, or more specifically between humans, and birds, fish or invertebrates, is anything but obvious, clear and immutable."[16] In fact, Derrida states it was very difficult to identify any trait that is uniquely "proper of [man]" or exclusive to humans, "either because some animals also possess such traits, or because [man] does not possess them as surely as [he] claims."[17] This is reminiscent of philosopher Peter Singer's contention that there are some NHAs who possess more so-called human capabilities than certain humans, such as infants or people with cognitive disabilities.[18]

Other scholars have noted this same futile humanistic struggle for humans to find a line they can draw in the sand based on one uniquely human characteristic. Anthropologist Elizabeth Lawrence, for instance, details the many allegedly "human" traits throughout history that failed to be proven exclusively human, such as: making tools, teaching cultural practices, practicing rituals, having unique personalities, being aware of death, building and transforming nature, creating art, practicing altruism, possessing language, and experiencing wonder.[19] While language-use was once considered a hallmark of humanity, Derrida also acknowledges NHA language. He explains how human language is related to that of other animals through the notion of *différance* (the fluidity and interconnectivity of meaning that relates to and relies upon a myriad of other meaningful concepts):

> I am thinking in particular of the mark in general, of the trace, of iterability, of différance. These possibilities or necessities, without which there would be no language, *are themselves not only human*. It is not a question of covering up ruptures and heterogeneities. I would simply contest that they give rise to a single linear, indivisible, oppositional limit, to a binary opposition between the human and the infra-human. And what I am proposing here should allow us to take into account scientific knowledge about the complexity of "animal languages," genetic coding, all forms of marking within which so called human language, as original as it might be, does not allow us to "cut" once and for all where we would in general like to cut.[20]

For Derrida, the trait of language that might represent this border between species is analogous to a cut in the subject, or who can be defined as a subject and not an object. This cut, designating a sense of which subjects' interests and perspectives matter, can be marked wherever humans choose, and he lobbies for the cut to include NHA languages.

But should philosophers keep looking for a place to cut or even continue asking what makes humans different from other animals? Midgley answers "no" by acknowledging we are all complex beings who share many qualities, so searching for one differentiating factor is reductionist and futile.[21] She proposes that philosophers instead ask what the best thing about human life is and answer it according to traits that other animals may also possess. That concern is important as a start to discursively shifting the scholarly questions and the purpose of constructing these truths so that the answers are productive rather than destructive and enable community as opposed to separation or marginalization. Scholars and advocates should begin to ask how all species are unified and in what ways primary differences can be viewed as strengths.

Defining the Moral Boundary between Species

While there are not distinct divisions separating *all* humans from all other animal species in ways that are morally relevant, philosopher Daniel Elstein contends that the broader categorical concept of *species* is itself a contested and arbitrary social construction.[22] He cites Charles Darwin's belief that *species* was an indefinable category where differences between animals were more a matter of degree than kind. Elstein claims that, although these degrees of difference represent varying gaps between species, there is no clear way to determine how much of a gap is of moral significance.[23] Yet in defining moral significance, Elstein argues that it is a common logical fallacy for people to say that distinctions are based on some physical or biological trait, when it is really *mental* traits that they prioritize. *Physical* traits (such as the ability to mate, DNA similarities, or physical resemblance) do not sufficiently warrant the exploitation or mistreatment of a species, while *mental* traits (such as language use, intelligence, or sentience) form the real basis for why people say species divisions matter morally. In quite a radical idea, Elstein proposes reducing the myriad of animal species down to four different (but not mutually exclusive) "moral species concepts" which are based on an animal's mental ability to (1) plan for the future, (2) experience boredom, (3) suffer pain, and/or (4) feel emotions.[24]

The morally relevant traits specified in animal rights philosophy are broader versions of these mental traits. Consider that Singer claims that sentience is the true moral distinguishing factor, and Tom Regan proposes that beings who are conscious subjects of their lives should be the key concern.[25] These mental traits still necessitate a hierarchy, to some extent, where categories of animals are deemed (by humans) to be sentient and conscious enough to warrant fair treatment as a subject. For example, mammals and birds may qualify while oysters or insects may not. This hierarchy reveals the complications of hegemonic power in the creation of truth.[26] Humans can engage in an ideological struggle to define who counts as morally significant beings, yet it is always humans (and certain groups more than others) who maintain the power to redefine mental traits in ways that could just continue to serve instrumental interests and maintain human privilege. This could even be done under the guise of animal protection, as discourse can continually be constructed and reconstructed to enable a comforting appearance that humans are treating "the other" morally.

Human society especially privileges the mental trait of morality—a "civilized" trait that is generally assumed to be a unique product of human culture rather than other animal societies or nature. The next section explores how animal advocacy rhetoric could fulfill its need to appeal to morality (perhaps including the notion of being "humane" toward other animals) without reinforcing the problematic nature/culture and human/animal divides.

ETHICALITY AND THE NATURE/CULTURE AND HUMAN/ANIMAL BINARIES

Rhetoric and the Misunderstanding of Violence

As the so-called humane species, a paradox exists in the lofty, humanist moral values humans claim to have (and to which animal activists appeal) and the way that "human kindness" is often not reflected in humans' actual relations with other animals. These actions seem largely based on self-interested rather than altruistic values. Dunayer suggests the word *humanity* is both speciesist and unjustified, as it implies that kindness is an inherent part of each human's nature, yet many examples can be given of individual humans failing to show compassion. She also critiqued the common use of the phrase *human kindness,* as if the two words naturally fit together, whereas the term *animal kindness* seems foreign and senseless to the ear.[27]

Because humans have a high opinion of their moral values in comparison to the supposed lack in other species, if they had to bear witness to or admit the harm they actually cause other animals (such as in factory farming), it would propagate cognitive dissonance. Derrida predicts that the "industrial, scientific, technical violence" humans impose on NHAs must and will change, albeit over centuries, because it will become "more and more discredited" and "less and less tolerable" as it becomes visible.[28] Further emphasizing visibility and perceptions, he believes a driving force of this change is that this violence "will not fail to have profound reverberations (conscious and unconscious) on the image humans have of themselves."[29] Thus he asks interviewer Elisabeth Roudinesco, "If you were actually placed every day before the spectacle of this industrial slaughter, what would you do?" Roudinesco replies that she would not eat meat anymore and would live somewhere else, because she prefers not to see it.[30] This answer illustrates a point Derrida makes about humanity's need to avoid acknowledging the violence: "No one can deny seriously, or for very long, that men do all they can in order to dissimulate this cruelty or to hide it from themselves, in order to organize on a global scale the forgetting or misunderstanding of this violence."[31] This rhetorical denial of daily violence and oppression assumes that humans' collective mistreatment and murder of other species causes guilt; therefore, *visibility* of violence is to be avoided in both images and words, requiring careful framing of the way humans view their interactions with other animals.

The "misunderstanding" of violence is practiced rhetorically through strategic use of the word *murder*. One way humans avoid feeling guilty, according to Dunayer, is to construct the notion that "unjustified killing is murder only if the victim is human." She claims humans "prefer to couch nonhuman exploitation and murder in culinary, recreational, and other nonmoralistic terms."[32] Ecofeminist Carol Adams also acknowledges humans' rhetorical tricks meant to deny oppression and violence in food choices. She argues that terms like *meat* and *veal* create an "absent referent" where the individual NHA victim of oppression as well as the human perpetrator are purposely removed from the concept.[33] But what is the benefit of hiding this abuse if humans seek to truly be "humane?" According to Dunayer, "Speciesism is a lie, and it *requires* a language of lies to survive. Currently, our language denies the harm that humans routinely inflict on other animals; linguistically, both the victims and the perpetrators have disappeared."[34] The answer, then, is that it satisfies a psychological need to believe oneself to be *humane*, and the need for this positive self-perception likely takes privilege over actually doing the hard work of living up to one's morals.

This reveals the complexity of the humanist tension in relation to animal ethics, since these scholars must conceive of humans as *being* a moral species to presume people need to deceive themselves linguistically in order to continue being speciesist, yet paradoxically state humans are *not* inherently moral enough to live up to the term *humane*. As I analyze this circularity, the human claim of morality begins to look as if it might be a façade for arrogance in which language (like the very term *humane*) is used as the veneer. Yet animal ethics and advocacy rely upon the idea that if activists rhetorically challenge people to acknowledge the harm they cause other animals, it *would* activate an innate morality. While people's improved behavior might be enacted primarily for purposes of egoism and self-esteem, the advocacy rhetoric reveals a belief that altruism should also be a motivating factor.

The Paradox of Humane-kind

I argue that the notion of human morality results in a conflict for animal advocacy where the very idea that humans should treat NHAs better may be humanist. In other words, promoting an essentialist and superior view of the human being may privilege humans with a certain ethical status presumably not found in other animals (hence the word *human* as the basis for the word *humane*). Because animal advocates claim that species differences are more of degree than kind, I contend that if they were to be truly morally consistent instead of supporting an implicit paternalism or dominionism toward other animals, they would have to expect all other animals to have ethical standards and responsibilities too (albeit based on the animal's individual capacities and free will and not necessarily a contractarian notion of exact reciprocity). This poses a rhetorical conundrum over how to call for human ethical behavior without eliciting elitist notions of "humanity" in opposition to an implied brute animality. But when it comes to the supposedly humanist moral standards, if society conceives of these principles as deriving from nature and not just human culture, then it logically follows that morality might also naturally apply to many social animal species.

Recent research contends that social species *do* have general expectations for cooperative and moral behavior within their group. Animal ethologist Marc Bekoff and philosopher Jessica Pierce find that humans are not the only animal to develop morality and justice, as other social animals practice fairness, empathy, altruism, and trust in their own ways with varying levels of complexity.[35] These scholars coined the term *animal morality* to describe the pro-social behaviors that they believe are a product of both biological and socio-cultural factors. They describe morality as specific to each species and note that individual animal behavior may vary in how well each chooses to observe these group standards, indicating animals exhibit a sense of free will and are not just guided by instinct.

The claim that humans are not the only moral animal could be left at that. However, I will additionally explore the idea of a "natural" ethic that applies to individuals of most animal species, transcending the notion of morality being limited to the culture of social or "higher" animals and its implication that humans must therefore be the highest and most moral animal due to their choice to privilege cultural rather than natural tendencies. As nature and culture conflate here, I examine human ethics by deconstructing it within the nature/culture dualism.

The Nature versus Culture Debate in Ethics for Humanity

Consider that human ethics generally value the compassionate tendency of humans to protect the weak or innocent, such as children, from predation and exploitation by the strong. This protection from exploitation is the basis of social justice movements, and on the surface it appears to be in opposition to the harshness of a simplistic "survival of the fittest" view of nature.[36]

Yet, humans' ethical prohibition against causing harm is legally limited to harm *in excess* of what is necessary for one's survival (consider self-defense arguments in murder trials or in justifying war). This is a principle in line with what other animals practice in nature that ensures ecological balance. Despite ethical standards, clearly many humans do practice exploitation of the weak, often to excess (consider child pornography, slave labor, factory farming, greenhouse gas emissions, genocide/extinction, etc.). In fact, at the risk of essentializing, I argue that the one relevant trait that does distinguish the human species from most other animal species is its ability to do most things (both good and bad, productive and destructive) to *excess* of what is necessary for survival.

Throughout history, philosophers have acknowledged humans' propensity for excess and have discussed this tendency in both positive and negative terms. For example, Aristotle noted that humans could be the most wicked, cruel, lustful, and gluttonous beings imaginable.[37] Neoplatonist philosopher Porphyry believed animals are sentient, rational beings who "likewise have vices, and are envious; though their bad qualities are not so widely extended as in men: for their vices are of a lighter nature than those of men."[38] English philosopher Thomas Hobbes, too, said that language allows humans to benefit from society and laws, but that humans can also use speech for misdeeds, like lying and teaching bad behavior, so that "[man] errs more widely and dangerously than can other animals." Hobbes posited that humans are also more destructive for unjust reasons than other animals: "So just as swords and guns, the weapons of [men], surpass the weapons of [brute] animals (horns, teeth, and stings), so [man] surpasseth in rapacity and cruelty the wolves, bears, and snakes that are not rapacious unless hungry and not cruel unless provoked, whereas [man] is famished even by future hunger."[39] Implying that there are also natural guidelines outside *human* ethical systems, Michel de Montaigne argued, "animals are much more self-controlled than we are, and keep with greater moderation within the limits that Nature has prescribed."[40]

As humans seek to move beyond natural limits, they create additional choices that lead to excess. German philosopher Johann Herder blamed this on humans' sense of free will: "whilst animals on the whole remain true to the qualities of their kind, man alone has made a goddess of choice in place of necessity."[41] French philosopher Jean-Jacques Rousseau admired humans' free will to resist instinct and choose behaviors, specifically behaviors that lead to self-improvement. But to Rousseau this free will was also the "source of all human misfortunes" which "producing in different ages his discoveries and his errors, his vices and his virtues, makes him at length a tyrant both over himself and over nature."[42] Rhetorician Kenneth Burke described a human as one who is corrupted by his/her pursuit of perfection to ascend in hierarchies and is given to excess in this pursuit; Burke especially noted humans' excessive use of symbols and tools.[43]

Feminist scholar Rosalind Coward argues that humans' excess created hierarchies and social inequalities at an unnatural level, while "in animal societies there's a startling absence of complex accumulation and unequal distribution of resources."[44] The source of humanity's excess can be traced back to the advent of agriculture.[45] The domestication of animals about 11,000 years ago transitioned many human beings to a more sedentary, agricultural way of life. Agricultural surpluses created divisions of wealth. In order to protect this wealth, patriarchal warrior cultures developed, creating oppressive systems of control such as slavery and imperialism. While forager societies often viewed other animals with wonder, respect, and partnership (not that some of these societies did not cause extinction or suffering), herder/agrarian societies were more likely to disempower animals in order to control and demystify them. Thus, many societies came to view domesticated animals as commodities and wild animals as competition and pests.

If humans are characterized by excess, which can lead to both comfort and poverty, charity and harm, then an ethical system becomes socially and ecologically necessary for purposes of restraint. Western philosophers have often lauded humans' ability to think abstractly, because it leads to free will, which leads to the ability to control and choose behaviors. Control was implied to be a positive ability to demonstrate restraint in the face of both the "sins" of excess choice in a human society and a supposed animal instinct born from nature.[46] Ancient Western philosophers valued temperance and restraint as ethical virtues, including restraint in food choices.[47] Yet, while humans have the ability to individually show restraint in the face of choice, some claim humans, as a whole, excessively decrease choice in environmentally problematic ways. Modern environmental philosopher J. Baird Callicott calls humans "devolutionizers" for the mass extinctions they cause, and food writer Michael Pollan claims that humans are "homogenizers" who use science to simplify natural complexity, such as with monoculture crops that decrease natural diversity.[48]

Environmental philosophers often credit human ethics to biology and evolution, arguing that ethical behavior is natural, and what is natural is, therefore, good. Aldo Leopold conceives of ethics as biological, where there is naturally a "limitation on freedom of action in the struggle for existence."[49] Callicott believes this was influenced by Darwin's evolutionary theories of humans as social animals that need to create kinship. He contends that ethics would have preceded reason in humans' evolutionary process, because humans needed to have complex linguistic skills that came from being social, and being social requires some limitations on individual freedoms. Darwin, as well as philosophers David Hume and Adam Smith, all thought that ethics rested on feelings and sentiments, which were found in the animal kingdom.[50] Darwin said that natural selection privileges those individuals with feelings, as they would be more likely to produce offspring who behave in socially acceptable ways. This echoes sociobiological theories that cooperation is more natural than competition among highly social animals, such as humans.[51] Thus Callicott argues that nature is not immoral, as "intelligent moral behavior is natural behavior."[52] Philosopher Holmes Rolston also argues for a *natural* ethic where right is determined by an ability to sustain life rather than just sustaining pleasure.[53] He argues the is/ought principle, usually seen as specious, can make sense in nature because as humans use science or experience to describe how nature functions and explore nature's intricate relationships and harmony, they discover that what *is* often or frequently is what *ought* to be. It is, then, hard to know where facts end and values begin.

I contend that because the human practice of exploiting or harming other animals *to excess* goes against harmonious or ecological principles often found in nature, that humans' ethical system of promoting compassion and protective justice *is* actually largely based on "natural" principles: both the principle of *cooperation* to garner social support and the principle of *moderation* for ecological balance. I believe our fundamental ethical principles are, or should be, based on the idea of taking only what we need for our basic survival, complementing the principles of deep ecology, with any excess acts of harm constituting exploitation and a breach of ethics.[54]

Ultimately, this moderation is what most other animals (not just social animals) already practice, making all animals equally subject to these same ethical guidelines; this notion of equality avoids the humanist tendency to imply that humans should be kind to other animals because humans are ethically superior beings. So I argue that while humans can admit that their ethical system may be highly complex and impressive when compared to that of other animals, this high level of sophistication appears to be necessary to restrain humanity's special propensity for excessive harm. Therefore, when advocates promote animal rights on ethical grounds, they should avoid the word "humane" and take care not to insinuate that all ethical principles are limited to the realm of humanity or that the human animal is more advanced. Perpetuating a construction of the human species as "humane-kind" might unintentionally reinforce the problematic human/animal dualism and related notions of human superiority that lead to not only discrimination against NHAs but also condescending notions of paternalistic stewardship.

One tension in the conclusion above is that it might imply that animal rights should be garnered by emphasizing the *likeness* between human and nonhuman animal traits, in this case a capacity for ethical behavior. Applied more broadly, if one admits that humans or other animal species might generally exhibit more "positive" traits (as in a morally relevant mental trait) than other animals, does that imply some animals are more worthy of rights or fair treatment than others who are different, particularly disadvantaging those who are less like humans? The next section will explore this concern that the likeness model, popular in social justice rhetoric, is ultimately humanist and therefore self-defeating in combating speciesism.

DILEMMAS OVER WHETHER ANIMAL RIGHTS STRATEGIES SHOULD PROMOTE SIMILARITY OR DIVERSITY

Contradictions between Animal Rights and Humanism in Promoting Similarity

Inconsistencies associated with humanism and animal advocacy rhetoric cause some posthumanist scholars to critique the philosophical basis of animal rights, while they remain sympathetic to the need to end modern institutionalized violence toward NHAs. Critical theorist William J. T. Mitchell advises posthumanists to study humanism as essential to a critique of speciesism: "'Speciesism' is ritually invoked in the denigration of others as animals while evoking a prejudice that is so deep and 'natural' that we can scarcely imagine human life without it. The very idea of speciesism, then, requires some conception of 'the posthuman,' an idea that makes sense, obviously, only in its dialectical relation with the long and unfinished reflection on species being that goes by name of humanism."[55] An analysis of humanism fits with the contention that a focus on humanimality and an interrogation of human hegemony—and not just the mistreatment of the animal "other"—should become central to animal activism.

But in considering animal rights philosophy, Derrida contends that animal rights is a flawed concept so long as it models itself after a juridical concept of human rights, as the notion of human rights is based on a humanist "post-Cartesian human subjectivity" that has led to the very oppression that animal activists seek to end. Derrida writes: "Consequently, to confer or to recognize rights for 'animals' is a surreptitious or implicit way of confirming a certain interpretation of the human subject, which itself will have been the very lever of the worst violence carried out against nonhuman living beings."[56] He claims that rights are so conflated with humanism that they cannot serve as the basis for ending NHA exploitation. This is why, even as critical as he is of industrialized exploitation, he writes about animal rights from the perspective of an outsider: "I have sympathy (and I insist on that word) for those who revolt: against the war declared on so many animals."[57] In merely expressing "sympathy" for activists' desires to challenge violence, he clarifies his doubts about the efficacy of activist communication strategies that rely upon an implicit humanism and a legal notion of rights.

The theories posed by the most prominent animal ethics philosophers, Singer and Regan, could be considered humanist in their focus on how NHAs are similar to humans.[58] Taking this stance, Cary Wolfe notes the irony that animal rights' anthropocentrism ends up "effacing the very difference of the animal other that it sought to respect."[59] It is true that the tensions between the priorities of similarity and difference are essential to the paradox present within animal rights. Thus feminist scholars Lynda Birke and Luciana Parisi find that, "The tension between our similarity and our difference from other animals, moreover, informs much of the political and philosophical tension around debates on animal rights."[60] To clarify a misconception, Ingold states it is not anthropocentric to show how a particular human trait, even a positive one, is unique to the human species, as every species is also likely to have something unique about it. It *is* anthropocentric, however, to compare nonhumans to humans and expect NHAs to have the same capacities before respect is granted, which is something that some animal ethics philosophers do.[61]

This anthropocentrism is especially explicit in animal ethicist Paola Cavalieri and Peter Singer's *Great Ape Project*, in which they propose that nonhuman primates serve as a bridge species who deserve to have their rights recognized before other animal species because of apes' similarities to humans.[62] But on a broader scale, even the suggestion that there are few, or no, traits that humans possess that are not also possessed by at least some other animal species is also anthropocentric, albeit more implicitly.[63]

However, before chastising animal rights philosophers and activists for implicitly promoting humanism, one might determine whether the activists' line of argumentation is based more on the desire to *build nonhumans up* in the "noble" likeness of humanity (expanding humanity to include other animals) or based more on the desire to *knock humans down* off their self-constructed pedestal, encouraging them to embrace, instead of shun, their innate animality (expanding animality to include humans). The issue is really a matter of directionality, and I argue the distinction between the two approaches is key. The latter approach of encouraging humans to embrace their animality is less humanist and therefore more morally tenable to posthumanist scholars. But, strategically, it is less commonly used, presumably for the utilitarian reason that it more directly challenges current ideologies about human supremacy and comes across as more threatening to the status and esteem of the very humans who must be convinced. While advocacy that focuses on humanimality might have more philosophical veracity, I recognize that on the level of media sound bite in a commercially dominated public sphere, it may fail to resonate with the American public in meaningful ways, and thus takes more rhetorical skill to construct.

Embracing Human Animality

In thinking long-term, if animal activists fail to convince humans to respect their animality instead of despise it, humans may never treat other animals with appropriate respect. Philosopher Giorgio Agamben notes that humanity is currently based on how much humans control the animal within themselves, as Western metaphysics defines humanity in opposition to animality.[64] This relates to a politics of excluding someone who must still simultaneously be included. The animal is held in an ambiguous space that is both external and internal, where he/she is subject to exile and death without remorse.

Consider the human practice of eating the bodies of other animals. Philosopher David Wood surmises it is less about sustenance than it is about humans' need to demonstrate control, control not only over other animals but more importantly over the animal within themselves.[65] Legal scholar Lee Hall theorizes that meat-eating reveals insecurity, resulting in humans' need to demonstrate power over nature and maintain an image of themselves as predators and not as vulnerable prey.[66] To overcome this fear-based suppression of our animality, the human practice of needless killing of NHAs must be defined as murder (as it would with unjustified killing of humans) or else the animal will always be "the other" instead of ourselves.

Rather than just averring that humanimality is personal to viewing oneself as an animal, it can also be social in terms of viewing one's species as part of the Earth's animal collective. Philosopher Gary Steiner proposes that humans be conceived as members of a greater planetary *community* in which they have moral obligations toward all other sentient beings as fellow kin, regardless of those beings' rational ability to reciprocate or advocate in a human justice system.[67] Steiner describes the predominant rights-based animal protection approach as too reliant on liberal, rationalist rhetoric grounded in anthropocentrism, leading activists to stretch the truth of NHA capabilities for rationality. Thus Steiner critiques the similarity model when deployed in individualistic terms. Instead, he highlights the broader notion of *kinship*, saying "what is lacking is the underlying sense of dwelling alongside animals in a cosmic whole which transcends us and within which we must struggle to find our proper place," which supports a more humble and holistic view of humans as fellow animals.[68]

Another approach to privileging humanimality is through recognizing that wisdom (a valued mental trait) can be obtained via the body by all animals in ways that are not limited to a human-centered rationality reliant on a limited,

linguistic or phonetic notion of language. David Abram, an environmental phe-
nomenologist, suggests deconstructing the mind/body dualism that parallels the
human/animal and subject/object dualisms by privileging the *body* as a source
of communicative knowledge.[69] Abram encourages humans to begin to reaffirm
their bodies and physical senses as a communicative site of gaining wisdom
about the entire natural world instead of just relying on human symbolic communication and limiting knowledge to anthropocentric realms. By embracing
the "primitive" sensual communication most humans have lost, they would
expand their knowledge by beginning to relearn and value what other species
are communicating.[70] If the body were not viewed as separate from, and inferior
to, the mind, then humans would not use the supposed superiority of the human
mind's ability to abstractly reason as an excuse to reduce other life to mere
bodies devoid of wisdom. In this view, the body, even that of NHAs, should be
enlivened as a subject rather than enervated by being reduced to an object.

Abram's view is useful for redefining intelligence in a non-anthropocentric
sense and associating it with all animals, thereby increasing humans' appre-
ciation for the wisdom that can be gained from "reading" the world in ways
more common to NHA or "primitive" culture than industrialized human culture. This could also restrain activists from claiming that NHAs are "voiceless," encouraging an acknowledgment that NHA communication is silenced
in one sense and often unheard or misinterpreted in another. To recognize
the NHA voice, activists should attempt to include NHA communication in
advocacy campaigns.

Asking humans to begin to respect the body's wisdom and to embrace their
animality is perhaps a philosophically rigorous approach to promoting animal
rights, but it is not as pragmatic as the humanist approach of simply proving
that many NHAs are similar to humans. The latter recognizes that because
people place a high value on supposedly human traits (such as intelligence,
kindness, emotional sensitivity, symbolic communication, education, artistic
talent, and spirituality), it is only reasonable that animal activists appeal to
the fact that NHAs also *share* some of these traits when trying to convince
humans to have higher respect for NHAs.[71] Therefore, Derrida's and Wolfe's
suggestion that animal rights philosophies should be less humanist and should
avoid this human rights or "likeness" model of social justice is unsettling and
challenging to conventional activist wisdom about achieving social progress
for oppressed groups.

Promoting Difference and Diversity

A philosophical problem with the tactic of emphasizing that NHAs share
many valued "human" traits is that it runs the risk of reducing other animals
to lesser categories of "sub-humans." Wolfe explains that different species

cannot be expected to possess "qualities, potentials, or abilities that are real-ized to their *fullest* in human beings."[72] This could leave NHAs forever stuck in the role of diminished or immature humans, just as humans would always be a diminished version of cats, chimpanzees, birds, fish, or any other species, and just as women were once considered diminished forms of men.[73] Activists and philosophers may also find it counterproductive to insinuate that NHAs are close to being humans but are just *under-developed*. Dunayer posits that, from an evolutionary perspective, species should not be ranked as more or less "primitive" against the benchmark of humans serving as the "advanced" species. She clarifies, "species don't evolve toward greater *humanness,* but toward greater *adaptiveness* in their ecological niche," which is reflected in the fact that Darwin did not believe in ranking species as higher or lower.[74]

The case against promoting similarities (whether it be by expanding human-ity or animality in either direction) leads to the somewhat counterintuitive argu-ment of promoting *differences* in order to gain equality for other animals. On the surface this flies in the face of reason, since their differences from humans have been highlighted as an excuse to discriminate against them. However, toward this goal, an acknowledgment of difference does not have to equate with an admission of inferiority.[75] While other species are different, they are by no means failed or lesser versions of humans. In exploring the idea of embrac-ing differences, it is useful to acknowledge that the advanced stages of some human social justice movements in the United States have also moved in this direction, as they now promote diversity. The problem that the earlier human rights approach had in gaining equality by emphasizing the similarities between human groups (i.e. men and women, whites and blacks, or heterosexuals and homosexuals) was that the historically oppressed groups were then forced to assimilate into the dominant group's world and live by the standards set by white, Western, heterosexual males. Just as many activists in the civil rights movement do not advocate for complete colorblindness, under the premise that it would wipe out some distinguishing and valued cultural traits and generally disrespects difference, so too the animal rights movement should not expect people to be blind to the many splendid cultural and biological variances among animals. Animal activists should ask people to respect these differences. Diver-sity in both human society and the natural world is not limited to groups or spe-cies but applies to *individuals* within groups/species as well, or else it promotes reductionist biological essentialism.[76]

CONCLUSION: BLENDING SIMILARITY AND DIVERSITY

Ultimately, I propose the best position to these dilemmas is a blended one that embraces both the fundamental commonalities that provide kinship in a broad sense and the specific differences that provide diversity in an individual sense. While people may come to value NHAs and respect diversity, the concern is that they will still prioritize fellow humans over other animal species if they do not see some similarity that connects all animals and gives them a reason to value other species just as they value their own species. Consider Steiner's suggestion that "we must learn to identify with animals, to see ourselves in them and them in ourselves, in order to appreciate their plight and their prospects" as part of his proposal for conceptually expanding humanity's moral community and identity to include other animals as kin.[77]

As a shared trait, or what Burke called a "consubstantial" unifying trait that creates mutual identity, I suggest that Regan's idea of being a conscious "subject of a life" may be the best option; subjective consciousness is broad enough to include many animal species yet still allow for diversity within and among species.[78] It could be compared to the consubstantial trait of *personhood* that has allowed for equality among races, genders, and ethnicities, while still allowing for diversity. Singer's notion of sentience is quite similar and could also work, as long as the focus expands beyond concerns over bodily suffering and emphasizes individual *life* and personhood. Perhaps if animal rights campaigns encouraged people to embrace diversity and their own animality it would mitigate some of the problematic humanism inherent in building on a human rights model.

The ideas of critical theorists Gilles Deleuze and Félix Guattari seem to support this notion of blending human-animal relations, as they argue that animals serve to rupture notions of identity and sameness.[79] In their article "Becoming Animal," they use the Nietzschean idea of "becoming over being" to emphasize animal-becoming as a way to free humanity from its humanistic straightjacket. Deleuze and Guattari privilege notions of expansion, multiplicity, mutuality, heterogeneity, and rhizomes over straitjackets like classification, identification, essentialism, and linear progression. Becoming is considered "real," as it contains difference and acknowledges how everything is implicated in everything else. Similarly, zoologist and philosopher Donna Haraway prefers to see humans as "becoming with" animals: "I am who I become with companion species, who and which make a mess out of categories in the making of kin and kind."[80] This complicates traditional notions of identity by saying it is something determined primarily by our *relations with* other animals.

The ideas of these scholars pose an even larger rhetorical test than do my previous discussions of combating speciesism, as they challenge *how* we think rather than *what* we think. Instead of just asking people to incorporate the animal other into a new and expanded identity of fellow conscious beings, as I have in this chapter, this scholarship asks people to understand themselves outside a defining notion of "self." Rather they should understand themselves more openly via their dynamic relationships with all beings. Hopefully, scholars undertake the challenge to demonstrate how notions of "becoming over being" might inform a radically different and truly posthumanist advocacy rhetoric. Overall, there is great value in advocates undertaking the challenge of embracing the deconstructive principles of diversity, difference, and complexity. But to avoid total relativism, their rhetoric must maintain some sense of unity and kinship that respects ethical standards based on overarching principles, like avoiding unnecessary harm and valuing sentience. This encourages humanities scholars (and/or activists) to admit that natural tendencies and ecological principles have some merit and that there is a "humanity" in what was once thought to be a separate realm of nature.

Rather than primarily talking about NHAs, animal advocates must rhetorically problematize the fragile borders of humanity and species through deconstruction of speciesist language so that humanimals begin to feel pride in their animality. This requires transformation of language to reconstruct new identities, because humanimals will likely experience instability from the deconstruction of deep-seated binaries that once provided familiar and stable boundaries. Therefore, to put the humanimal at ease with itself, advocates and scholars must construct the posthuman in ways that blend the retention of moral integrity and rights with the introduction of a humbler and more integrated place among fellow beings who all must live sustainably within nature's ethic.

Chapter Three

How to Do Things without Words

Whisperers as Rustic Authorities on Interspecies Dialogue

Mary Trachsel

In a series of lectures published as *How to Do Things with Words*, J. L. Austin demonstrates that the primary function of human words is not to name the world but to contract the relationships and orchestrate the social actions that structure human community. Human language is human social behavior, Austin tells us, and can be analyzed in pragmatic terms as "speech acts," the things we *do* with words.[1] We rely so heavily on words to do the work of building and maintaining community that we can scarcely imagine sustained, complicated, or meaningful communication without them. While we recognize paralinguistic communication systems such as body language, we tend to see them as preliminaries or supplements to verbal language, not as alternatives to words.

At the same time that words have the power to extend and solidify human community, they also work to estrange humans from nonhuman animals. From Aristotle's pronouncement that "rational speech" distinguishes humans from other animals, through René Descartes' denial of nonhuman selves because animals cannot speak about their mental experiences, to Noam Chomsky's description of language as a biological apparatus that uniquely characterizes human minds, language has made other animals unrecognizable to us as speaking subjects. Rhetorician Kenneth Burke describes our linguistic estrangement from other animals as a departure from the realm of non-reflective, non-deliberative animal "motion" into the intentional, symbolic realm of human "action." Burke, who joins Austin in regarding language as action, further defines verbal language as a uniquely human "species of action" that typifies us as "the symbol-using animal."[2]

Our reluctance to recognize wordless animals as speaking subjects stems largely from our reverence for words as the hallmark of human mind, a species of mind that is not merely unique but also, because of its uniqueness, intellectually *advantaged* over other minds. Human language, according to cognitive philosopher Daniel Dennett, deserves credit for the *sapiens* in *Homo sapiens*: "There is no step more uplifting, more explosive, more momentous in the history of mind design than the invention of language. When *Homo sapiens* became the beneficiary of this invention, the species stepped into a slingshot that has launched it far beyond all other earthly species in the power to look ahead and reflect."[3] Dennett claims the advantage language confers on humans is not simply *more* brainpower—it is a different *kind* of brain altogether—one that sets us apart from the crowd of other species on earth: "Perhaps the kind of mind you get when you add language to it is so different from the kind of mind you can have without language that calling them both minds is a mistake."[4] Dennett speaks for many who dismiss claims of mental connections between humans and other species as mere stories, imaginative departures from the empirical ground of science. He exposes the human inclination to fabricate communion with nonhuman minds in an account of his meeting with the robot Cog, an artificial intelligence model that replicates human communicative behaviors such as visual tracking and facial focus. As one of Cog's designers, Dennett was fully aware of the artificiality of Cog's intelligence, yet he reports that even he was tempted to attribute sentience and intentionality to Cog, as he experienced the sensation of being in the company of another mind.[5]

It is easy to dismiss the notion of keeping rather than parting company with other animals as the stuff of fables, a fond delusion, a romantic yearning, or an anthropomorphic projection of our languaged voices onto dumb animals. The title of linguist Stephen R. Anderson's book, *Dr. Doolittle's Delusion: Animals and the Uniqueness of Human Language*, captures prevailing academic discomfort with stories of talking animals and the humans who claim to understand them.[6] It is one thing to observe that some domesticated animals can learn to attach meaning to human words, particularly when these are uttered as commands; it is quite another to claim that we can actually engage other animals in dialogues spoken in languages not entirely our own. Those who, like Dr. Doolittle, claim that animals are talking back to them in these alleged dialogues are subject to charges of anthropomorphic ventriloquism—projecting their own subjectivities onto animals to sustain an illusion of nonhuman intentionality.

Rustic stereotypes of humans who are "naturally" in tune with other animals suggest that one way to avoid the delusion of interspecies ventriloquism is to hold silent and listen closely for the voices of others. Henry Wadsworth Longfellow's American literary homage to the so-called noble savage, *The Song of Hiawatha*, attributes Hiawatha's ability to converse with birds and animals to his rapt attention at the doorway of his grandmother's wigwam, listening to the voices of the wind and trees and other songs of Nature.[7] From these singing voices Hiawatha learns the languages of the birds and animals and makes them his own. A similar rapt attention to other-than-human voices is the starting point of feminist Josephine Donovan's dialogic version of care-based animal ethics in the final essay of *The Feminist Care Tradition in Animal Ethics*. Donovan asserts that *listening* to other animals' voices is a necessary first step in the process of recognizing other species as full-fledged members of the moral community.[8] The kind of listening Donovan has in mind is intently focused on language-learning but finds language in a wide variety of voices beyond those of humankind. Listening for other species' voices, she explains, requires us to intensify and expand the array of communication channels we normally use for human conversations. Listening like this, straining to hear voices that may lack sound as well as words, requires an enhanced understanding of what counts as listening and speaking and of what counts as attention and intent.

Rhetorical theory has already proposed models of human communication centered in the task of paying heightened attention to the intentions of other "speakers" without assuming the primacy of human speech or language. Eric King Watts, for instance, argues that a more inclusive notion of "voice" is required if we are to expand our capacities to listen and to speak. In addition to Ferdinand de Saussure's twofold linguistic definition of voice in the symbolic realm of *langue* (language) and the sound/action realm of *parole* (speaking), Watts conceptualizes voice in social terms, as "a relational phenomenon" that coordinates subjects in dialogues of mutual "answerability."[9] To hear and comprehend voices in this relational sense, Watts explains, is to participate in the ethical and emotional bonds of communal subjectivity. At the dialogic heart of this social identity is a responsive interplay of assertion and recognition that envelops both self and other in "meetings of the mind and heart."[10] In presenting voice as the relationship of *You* and *I* as a particular *We*, Watts defines listening as openness to the other's knowability or need for acknowledgment, and thus he includes listening as an essential component of voice. Michael J. Hyde similarly advocates a rhetoric grounded in openness to others, even when those others lack voices that speak in words. Hyde traces the concept of extra-verbal listening to Emmanuel Levinas's theory of conscience, which directs attention not to the words or the audible voice of the other, but to the human face, which can "speak without uttering a word."[11]

But Donovan seeks practical rather than theoretical guidance in learning to engage other animals in authentic dialogue, and so she directs us to science, specifically the science known as ethology, whose practitioners observe and interpret human and other animals' "language behaviors" as indicators of social cognition. Ethologists want to understand the shared qualities of brain and mind that enable organisms to create and maintain social alliances, share resources, coordinate travel, forage or hunt cooperatively, reproduce, and survive.[12] My own inquiry into the possibilities of interspecies dialogues takes up Donovan's suggestion that a practical understanding of such dialogues can be learned from ethologists' methods of deciphering the behavioral codes of other species. I argue, however, that the rhetorical limitations of scientific observation, specifically its methodological demand for the separation of observing human subject and observed animal object, create an additional need for something other than scientific authority. I direct my search for such authorities outside of academe, to communities where human and nonhuman animal lives are densely interwoven. In such environments, "rustic authorities"—whose expertise derives from working experience without the necessity of academic training—model and teach a pragmatic array of human-animal communication methods. Potential rustic teachers include shamans, hunters, herders, farmers, pest exterminators, pet owners, animal keepers, trainers, and caregivers. What might such practical authorities contribute to academic understanding of other animals' communication behaviors? Could they help us recognize other animals as speaking subjects? What wisdom might they offer about establishing and maintaining ethical relationships with individuals of other species?

My search for pragmatic guidance in conducting interspecies dialogues assumes a moral premise shared by environmental and care-based animal ethics, namely that caring and respectful relationships with members of other species are morally desirable goals. The particular rustic authorities I turn to here are animal handlers associated with a folk tradition known as *whispering*. While there is much discussion among animal handlers and their critics about the "true" nature of whispering, the term generally denotes animal-handling methods that subscribe to the virtues of intimacy, respect, soft-spokenness, and nonviolence. Historically, observers as well as practitioners of animal whispering have attributed the quietude of their methods to *languages* shared with other animals. As in human negotiations, whisperers maintain, speech acts—even those without words—can deflect and prevent acts of violence between species, preserving peaceful coexistence. In light of such claims that whispering offers an ethical as well as a rhetorical model of interspecies communication, I look to animal whisperers for both practical and moral guidance in recognizing other animals as subjects and engaging them in dialogic conversations. In particular, the pedagogical discourse of whisperers advocates both an ethic and a rhetoric of interspecies dialogue that opens with an exchange of receptive attention. Such dialogues combine openness to the embodied presence of the other and projective identification with the other. To relational human communication models grounded in Levinasian acknowledgment of the other, the whispering paradigm adds an unquestioning readiness to attribute intentional identity across the species divide that our own words have so powerfully constructed.

THE CALL FOR A DIALOGICAL ETHIC
OF CARE FOR OTHER ANIMALS

In the final essay of *The Feminist Care Tradition in Animal Ethics*, Donovan calls for "a dialogical ethic of care for the treatment of animals" to correct the paternalism of care-based ethics that restrict nonhuman animals to the ranks of voiceless moral patients or victims whose voices have been silenced by our own. If we want to conduct interspecies dialogues, Donovan writes, we must "learn to read the languages of the natural world," thereby coming to recognize other animals as "speaking subjects rather than merely objects of our speaking."[13] The language-learning process Donovan recommends begins with disciplined listening, an *attentiveness* to other animals that is grounded in "attitudes and aptitudes such as openness, receptivity, empathy, sensitivity and imagination."[14] Because the languages to be learned by paying this kind of attention lack words as we know them, meeting this language-learning challenge requires us to develop enhanced listening skills for discerning meaningful intentions behind wordless cries, postures, gestures, movements, facial expressions, odors, touches, and behaviors.

Like many other essays in the collection, Donovan's care-based approach to animal ethics departs from the rhetoric of animal rights by embracing partial and non-rational identifications with nonhuman animals. Instead of regarding animals en masse, or as species representatives, an ethic of care finds moral significance in particular relationships between individual human and nonhuman subjects. Like the commonplace about learning foreign tongues (*If you want to learn a language, fall in love with someone who speaks it*), ethics of care endorse the instructional value of intimate dyadic engagement. Just as engaged and purposeful attention to a foreign other fosters foreign language learning, foreign language learning promotes engaged and purposeful attention to a foreign other. At its moral best, Donovan explains, this purposeful desire to know another assumes the shape of care: "by paying attention to, by studying, what is signified, one comes to know, to care about the signifier."[15] A caring stance toward other animals, according to Donovan, develops only out of a familiarity with them as individual subjects of "unique needs and wishes," and this familiarity in turn depends upon relationships of embodied presence.[16]

The distance between Donovan's dialogic ideal of care-based animal ethics and the justice-based tradition of animal rights is illustrated by a story philosopher Peter Singer tells in his introduction to *Animal Liberation*.[17] The antagonist is a carnivorous party guest who professes her love for animals. Pointing out the logical and moral contradictions between the guest's words and her deeds, Singer asserts the alternative position he shares with his wife, both non-lovers of animals who respect animal lives as ends in themselves, quite apart from human emotional needs and desires. When Singer and his wife report that they have no pets, their fellow guest is confused and asks for clarification, "But you *are* interested in animals, aren't you, Mr. Singer?" Singer explains that he and his wife are "not inordinately fond of dogs, cats or horses in the way that many people are." They are "not especially 'interested in' animals," and they "certainly do not 'love' them," but they are committed to certain moral principles. They oppose the "arbitrary discrimination" of human chauvinism and advocate "the prevention of suffering," regardless of the sufferer's species. To them, nonhuman animals are "independent sentient beings," not pets or instruments of human ends like "the pig whose flesh was now in our hostess's sandwiches."[18] Singer's principled abstraction from the embodied presence that is so essential to Donovan's care ethics reminds us of the distancing capacity Burke ascribes to human language as a medium for constructing a symbolic reality that transcends "the paper-thin line of our own particular lives," conferring on humans the power to escape from the immediacy and pathos of embodied perception.[19]

Replacing concrete, personal relationships (people and their pets) with abstract, impersonal ones (moral agents and patients), Singer advocates an impartial and dispassionate approach to animal ethics consistent with broad academic distrust of emotionality, corporality, and nonverbal expression. He explains that he did not write *Animal Liberation* for people whose regard for nonhuman animals is behaviorally expressed by "stroking a cat or feeding the birds in the garden," and he rejects human fondness for other animals on the grounds that it trivializes his moral concerns. His refusal to be known as an "animal lover" arises from an understanding of love as an infantilizing force that precludes "serious political and moral discussion" of human-animal relationships. When it comes to human rights, he explains, no one would suggest it is necessary to "love" members of silenced minorities or to see them as "cute and cuddly."[20]

Perhaps a similar desire to avoid charges of nonacademic sentimentality or naiveté prevents Donovan from recounting her own personally experienced, nonverbal dialogues with other animals. Indeed, though the contributors to *The Feminist Care Tradition in Animal Ethics* generally agree that unique and affectively charged relationships between particular humans and other animals are morally central to care-based animal ethics, none actually presents first-person relationship stories as a grounding for ethical theory or political action. Epistemological suspicion of emotional identification with other animals is not the only reason personal relationship stories rarely provide the theoretical grounds for animal ethics, however. Donovan implies that as an academic field, ethics has so estranged humanity from animality that moral philosophers simply do not know how to pay ethically disciplined attention to other animals or enter into dialogues with them. Institutional settings for academic theorizing are typically devoid of nonhuman animals, and philosophers are trained to value and produce knowledge in verbal form, separating and elevating humanity's languaged rationality from other ways of knowing. The Western philosophical tradition, Donovan implies, leaves ethicists unprepared to deploy the full range of sensory, emotional, and cognitive faculties required for interspecies dialogues.[21]

ETHOLOGISTS AND ETHNOGRAPHERS

Despite powerful academic conventions of human estrangement from other animals, Donovan maintains that dialogic relationships are possible if we adopt the methods of ethologists to gain "intellectual understanding" of nonhuman animal languages.[22] Using anthropological field-observation methods, ethology arose in Europe and Japan in the first half of the twentieth century, when the attention of American biologists was increasingly absorbed by laboratory science. Konrad Lorenz, a founder of the field, defined ethology as an ethically leveling, comparative discipline that regards humans and other animals alike as Darwinian subjects of their own social behaviors. Animal behaviors, human and otherwise, can therefore be studied as evolutionary survival strategies shaped by interactions between organisms and their environments. Social animals, whose individual survival is dependent on social organization, can be studied in terms of the communication strategies they use to build and maintain social structures, whether these be families, tribes, herds, packs, flocks, swarms, or pods.[23] Intraspecies communication, what we might call the native language of a social species, certainly dominates the communicative behavior of many animals, human or otherwise, but interspecies communication may also be important, even if only in the antagonistic dialogues of predator and prey.

Grounded in the grand narrative of biological evolution, ethology has historically embraced narrative as a valid form of knowledge. Lorenz's own writings—for instance, his account in *On Aggression* of the graylag goslings who "imprinted" on Lorenz himself from the moment of hatching and thereafter followed him as though he were their mother—illustrate the anecdotal style that reflects the discipline's narrative core.[24] A naturalist whose backyard was the Vienna Woods and whose house and garden were filled with domestic animals and tamed wildlife, Lorenz framed his studies of intra- and interspecies communication within "narratives of relationship," the kind of stories Margaret Urban Walker describes as starting points for moral understanding.[25] As Lorenz's popular science texts reveal, the ethologist's understanding of animal behavior comes first and foremost from intimate relationships with other animals. To an outsider, as Lorenz knew well, such relationships might appear extraordinary or even magical, but to insiders, the individuals involved in the relationship's dialogic exchange, they are quite literally common knowledge.

King Solomon's Ring, a book whose title refers to a legendary ring that enabled Solomon to understand other animals' language, opens with Lorenz's assertion that unaided by magic, he can understand and communicate with other species. "I am not joking by any means," Lorenz assures his readers, explaining that all social animals employ some sort of "signal code" with its own "vocabulary" and that "by knowing the 'vocabulary' of some highly social species of beast or bird it is often possible to attain to an astonishing intimacy and mutual understanding."[26] He insists that the stories in *King Solomon's Ring* adhere strictly to "scientific fact," telling of relationships that admit empirical scrutiny and scientific explanation. A commitment to scientific knowledge coupled with a desire to communicate this knowledge to a general readership is, for Lorenz, an act of professional ethics. "Why should not the comparative ethologist who makes it his business to know animals more thoroughly than anybody else, tell stories about their private lives?" he asks. "Every scientist should, after all, regard it as his duty to tell the public, in a generally intelligible way, about what he is doing."[27] Lorenz sought to fulfill his moral obligations to share his professional knowledge with the general public by writing several works of popular science; in addition to *King Solomon's Ring*, the best known of these is *Man Meets Dog*, in which an account of the co-evolution of *Homo sapiens* and *Canis familiaris* is liberally punctuated with Lorenz's whimsical drawings and stories of the dogs that have participated in his family's history.

Although Lorenz and fellow ethologists Karl von Frisch and Nikolaas Tinbergen were awarded the Nobel Prize in Medicine in 1973 for their studies of animal behavior, ethology has struggled for acceptance as a legitimate scientific discipline, especially when ethologists turn their attention to the cognitive behaviors we describe in humans as "subjectivity" or "intentionality" or "consciousness" or "mind." As present-day ethologists Colin Allen and Marc Bekoff explain in *Species of Mind*, objections to cognitive ethology usually take some form of denial that nonhuman animals have minds, or that their minds are comprehensible to humans. Such denials usually preface warnings that reports of animal subjectivity are tainted by emotional identification, distorted by anthropomorphism, or weakened by data collection methods that lack scientific rigor.[28]

In response to these criticisms, today's ethologists employ various methods to empirically substantiate their translations of animal language behavior. In "Dialog with Black Box: Using Information Theory to Study Animal Language Behavior," Zhanna Reznikova reports on two such methods. First, double-blind experiments test the abilities of apes, dolphins, and parrots to communicate with humans using "intermediary languages" of gestures, lexigrams, or vocalizations approximating human speech. Second, mechanical simulation—for example, robotic simulation of honeybee dances and recorded playback of vervet monkey calls—is used to test the validity of direct decodings of message content. Reznikova predicts that information theory, born of computer science, will further improve animal behavior studies' capacity to measure animal consciousness in experimental problem-solving situations. This approach demands prior identification and isolation of the communicative channels available for use and strict control of the information available for transmission. In measuring the amount of information lost in the processes of encoding and decoding, information theory posits individual communicators, whether human or animal or machine, as separate nodes within a communication system. Such an approach requires that communication events be artificially limited, not only in the amounts and kinds of information available for transmission but also in the sources of interference with data transfer.[29]

Demands for scientific proof that animal language is an objective reality suppress the interspecies relationship narratives that Lorenz understood as key to interpreting animals' communicative behaviors. When regarding these behaviors from the perspective of science, human observers do not engage animals in dialogue so much as measure their capacities to communicate in terms we can discern and decode. Cultural geographer Hayden Lorimer describes this suppression of jointly negotiated interspecies understandings as a "zoological diminution of animal experience," a methodological shortcoming he tries to correct with enhanced scientific observation that engages "fuller sensory participation" in environments populated by other species."[30] Lorimer defines his methodology in "Herding Memories of Humans and Animals" as a convergence of ethology and ethnography that reveals the interspecies production of landscape. Examining a site where reindeer were reintroduced to northern Scotland in 1952, Lorimer reports that human-reindeer dialogue is mediated by shared experiences and memories of place; the social meanings of landmarks and pathways at his research site, he writes, can only be apprehended through an interspecies understanding of "the social" as "relations between herders and herd."[31]

Lorimer laments that academic attempts at "connective accounts of the human-nonhuman" typically produce "anaemic" theoretical results.[32] His own geography of northern Scotland counters theoretical anemia with infusions of rustic authority in the form of reindeer herders' first-person narratives of herder-herd relationships. Consulting rustic authorities for advice about conducting interspecies relationships is also a method recommended by religious studies scholar Gerald Harvey, author of *Animism: Respecting the Living World*.[33] Studying with shamans in animist cultures leads Harvey to seek "richer conversations and dialogues" with "other than human minds."[34] A starting point for these enriched conversations in academe, according to Harvey, is a serious discussion between "animists and those academics who respect them" and "animals and those academics who are respectful of them."[35] In these discussions, animists can advise academics on "appropriate etiquette and protocols" for communicating with other species.[36] Harvey admits, however, that prospects for such discussions are dim because few academics occupy either camp, given academic skepticism about the existence of nonhuman minds and scientific dismissal of animism as a false and culturally primitive worldview.

Meanwhile, outside of academe, in the realm of popular or folk culture, rustic authorities are largely unhampered by such barriers to dialogue. As practitioners of human-animal communication, animal herders, hunters, and handlers enjoy considerable epistemological freedom and accordingly offer direct and unapologetic methodological advice about keeping company with other animals. Although their communication tactics and the ends to which they apply them are undeniably marked by professional interests and therefore subject to moral scrutiny, ethical theory in search of pragmatic guidance in the conduct of interspecies dialogues should not dismiss out of hand rustic instruction in how to do things with other animals without the help of words.

ANIMAL WHISPERERS AS RUSTIC AUTHORITIES ON INTERSPECIES DIALOGUE

Suspicions that ethological studies of animal subjectivity lack scientific rigor go hand in hand with concerns about the discipline's ties to folk psychology. As Allen and Bekoff explain, scientists are inclined to regard the questions that trigger cognitive ethologists' investigations of animal minds as the naïve inquiries of folk psychology. Discursive relics of ancient human understanding of mental phenomena, these inquiries assume categories dismissed by eliminativists who argue that primitive ideas must inevitably yield to the advance of modern science and are therefore "very unlikely to have a useful scientific life."[37]

When science is so carefully distinguished from folk wisdom, it is surprising to find the folk tradition of "horse whispering" held up as a model for experimental analyses of animal behavior. In "The Man Who Listens to Behavior: Folk Wisdom and Behavior Analysis from a Real Horse Whisperer," Valeri Farmer-Dougan and James Dougan argue that horse trainers like Monty Roberts, best-selling author of *The Man Who Listens to Horses*, employ handling techniques that belie a "deep understanding of behavioral principles" despite the practitioner's lack of formal education in behavioral science.[38] They focus particularly on Roberts' understanding of language as socially functional behavior and underscore the dialogic quality of his training method, in which "the behavior of the horse and the behavior of the trainer serve both as reinforcer and discriminative stimulus for the other member of the dyad."[39] This interspecies dialogue, conducted in a behavioral language Roberts calls Equus, requires us to learn the communication system natural to the horse, thereby joining the horse's "linguistic community" rather than requiring the horse to join ours.[40] An analysis of Roberts' training philosophy and methods convinces Farmer-Dougan and Dougan that behaviorists like themselves should "recognize that instances of folk wisdom can provide fertile ground for demonstrating the efficacy of behavioral principles."[41] Like Lorimer and Harvey, they appeal to rustic authority in a search for enhanced scientific observation, and like Donovan they embrace the possibility of interspecies dialogue by expanding the definition of language to include nonverbal, relational behaviors such as stroking a cat or feeding birds in the garden. From Roberts they have learned that Equus is a spatial rather than aural language, its primary units consisting of bodily postures, touches, movements, and directional orientations instead of words.

Although he was one of the inspirations for Nicholas Evans' popular novel, *The Horse Whisperer*, Roberts describes his work as "listening" rather than whispering to horses, stressing receptive attention to the horse's "voice": "*A good trainer can hear a horse speak to him. A great trainer can hear him whisper.*"[42] While "whispering" originally referred to a quiet method of horse training, its meaning has since broadened in popular use, and the term now serves to describe communication between humans and individuals of many species, including dogs, cats, cattle, pigs, deer, apes, and marine mammals. In this essay "whispering" refers to training and handling methods described as learning and using the behavioral languages of other animals to facilitate dialogic exchanges. Some animal handlers embrace the actual title of "whisperer"; dog trainers Paul Owens and Cesar Millan, for instance, both refer to themselves as "dog whisperers," and Temple Grandin tells of a student who self-identifies as a "kitty whisperer."[43] Some are described as whisperers by others; Grandin is sometimes called a "cattle whisperer," and she uses that term to describe a stockman named Bud Williams.[44] Others describe their training methods not as whispering but as "listening" (Monty Roberts and Jan Fennel), "talking" or "speaking" (Henry Blake, Barbara Woodhouse, Stanley Coren, Bash Dibra), or "translating" (Temple Grandin).[45] These professional whisperers keep intimate company with other animals and share the belief that these species employ their own *languages*, which we humans can learn if we pay close attention.

If the ethical objective of whispering is nonviolence, the whisperer's methodology for accomplishing this goal is attentiveness, recognition of subjectivity, and empathic response, all proceeding from an immediate and embodied presence, which Hyde, following Levinas, refers to as "proximity."[46] Whispering begins with intense observation of a particular animal, combined with a belief that the animal is a center of intentionality that can be understood and reckoned with. The dialogue that emerges from this starting point develops as an ongoing interspecies relationship that whisperers may refer to as a human-animal "partnership" forged of mutual expectations and responsibilities.[47]

While a few contemporary whisperers hold academic credentials in behavioral science, most do not. Most acknowledge the importance of non-rational and nonverbal ways of knowing and tend to insist that emotional identification as well as "instincts" or "feelings" must accompany objective observation. This reliance on affective and relational understanding complicates verbal articulation of whispering methods. Blake, for instance, prescribes an empathic dialogue in which the human assumes the body and mind of the horse: "to understand a horse you must become a horse, you must think like a horse and act like a horse."[48] Blake, who uses terms like "ESP" and "mental telepathy" to describe this mode of empathic understanding, acknowledges that his approach does not easily accommodate "orthodox research," explaining, "it is difficult to be analytical at the same time as trying to think and react as the animals do."[49] Robert Miller and Rick Lamb make a similar point about leaders of the "natural horsemanship revolution" that began in the 1970s in the American West. Describing the approaches of trainers like Roberts, Miller and Lamb report, "What they felt, what they knew, and what they did with horses could not be easily put into words. Every horse was different, every person was different, every day was different."[50] The reliance on "feeling" and the focus on horses as individuals rather than species representatives make contemporary horse whisperers' methods impossible to codify in the unambiguous language of science, because they reject the empirical divide between observing human subjects and observed animal subjects. Instead, they assume the relational or dialogic identities of humans and horses in the company of one another. Attributing their dialogic expertise to intangible sources of knowledge that defy verbal description, modern horse whisperers distinguish themselves as rustic authorities who operate outside Western science and philosophy.

To an academic audience, the language whisperers use to describe their skill is likely to seem cryptic or romantic. When horseman Ray Hunt advises his adherents that "[t]he right feel and timing bring you the balance" and tells them to "[t]hink right down to the ground" and "[r]ide with life in your body," academic readers may well complain that his recommendations are ambiguous and imprecise.[51] Similarly, when horse and dog trainer Woodhouse asserts that conversations with other animals "must be based upon a great love, a great desire to be real friends with the animal," academic readers will likely object to the emotionality of her approach, to her ready acceptance of the unproven reality of interspecies friendships.[52] Probably even more uncomfortable for academic readers is dog whisperer Owens' recollection of a mystical childhood experience of "infinite, unbridled joy" that he later understood as a flash of insight into the evil of violent and coercive dog-training methods. When Owens subsequently frames his approach in spiritual terms as "part of a journey toward wholeness," a reader trained to expect rational, empirically grounded explanations of experience is apt to squirm at the romantic teleology of such a description.[53]

Even a whisperer as unafraid of romantic discourse as Owens, however, does not reject the contributions of science, and it is important to frame the rustic authority of whisperers as a complement rather than an alternative to scientific authority. Owens describes his methods as an effort "to link intuitive and scientific methodology, all under the spiritual vehicle of nonviolence."[54] While he explicitly rejects "cold, scientific training lessons," he nevertheless describes the alignment of his own methods with "sound behavioral principles," explaining that "in the application of science, rooted in compassion and awareness . . . spiritual and behavioral evolution takes place."[55] This desire to blend rational and irrational ways of knowing in animal-training practices is common among contemporary whisperers, perhaps reflecting a desire to establish credibility in the modern world while retaining connections to a legendary past.

The original whisperer is often identified as an eighteenth-century, uneducated, impoverished, Irish horse trainer named Dan Sullivan, whose handling method was so mysteriously quiet that he had only to whisper in a vicious horse's ear to make the animal tame and cooperative.[56] In fact, however, the connection between whispering and horse training long preceded Sullivan in a public ritual performed by members of the Secret Society of Horsemen, a trade guild that arose in northeast Scotland in the late middle ages and eventually spread to England, North America, and Australia. Veterinarian and historian Russell Lyon reports that the horseman's craft and trade blossomed in the eighteenth and nineteenth centuries, when a convergence of developments in plow design, horse breeding practices, and demand for agricultural products increased the need for effective management of horses, then still the primary source of power in agriculture. According to Lyon, by the middle of the nineteenth century in the British Isles, the Horseman's Society was so powerful that "no farmer could work his fields without a horseman who was a member of the Society."[57]

The Horsemen safeguarded their professional secrets with private and public rituals, including initiatory trials, a special handshake, and a secret phrase. Among the public advertisements for the society was the Horseman's practice upon first meeting a new horse assigned to his care of standing close with a hand on the horse's muzzle while whispering the Society's secret phrase into its ear. Other public demonstrations of a Horseman's special powers included leading horses home from auction without ropes or halters and driving them in the fields without bits, bridles, or reins. The real secret of the Horsemen's ability to communicate with horses, according to Lyon, was olfactory stimulation. To bond with a new horse, for instance, a Horseman fed it an oatcake laced with scented herbs (to banish the previous handler's scent) and saturated with the new Horseman's sweat (a replacement scent). This and other secret recipes made use of the heightened olfactory sensitivity of the horse, an animal subject to flight and reliant on nose as well as eyes and ears for early detection of danger.

The public ruse of controlling horses by whispering words in their ears ironically protected the Horseman's secrets of wordless communication. Though contemporary horse whisperers like Roberts describe their mode of communication as a language of space and movement rather than smells, both old and new whisperers have understood the importance of communication on the horse's own terms. Beyond agreeing on the need to learn the native language of the horse, according to Lyon, old and new whisperers are even more deeply united by a common ethic of nonviolence rooted in attitudes of kindness, compassion, love, and respect for horses.[58] This ethic infused the secret phrase of the Horsemen's Society, "both as one."[59] According to Lyon's informants, the phrase signified "total empathy between horse and man," an ideal Horsemen considered unattainable without kindness.[60] Among the initiates' secret oaths was a promise never to mistreat a horse or allow another person to treat a horse badly. As novice Horsemen advanced in the Society, they learned methods of meeting the "three principles of a horse"—action, attraction and attention—with the "three principles of a horseman"—

patience, perseverance, and good temper.[61] In negotiating such meetings, Lyon writes, the horsemen's "secret" was best captured in the advice given by an old whisperer to new member, "Be kind to them, laddie, an' they'll do anything for you."[62]

For most animal whisperers today, kindness is methodologically essential, but is only a part of the complex interspecies relationship-building process that is their trade. Unconstrained by scientific skepticism, their relationships with the animals they handle and train begin with assent to nonhuman subjectivity. Dennett has called this starting place "the intentional stance," meaning "the strategy of interpreting the behavior of an entity (person, animal, or artifact) by treating it *as if* it were a rational agent whose 'actions' are governed by 'choices' informed by 'beliefs' and 'desires.'"[63] Dennett explains his scare quotes as an acknowledgment that his terms for consciousness come from folk psychology, not academic discourse. But such distinctions do not concern most whisperers. For instance, in explaining what it takes to be a good stockperson, Grandin observes, "you have to recognize that an animal is a conscious being that has feelings, and some people don't want to think of animals that way. This is true of researchers and veterinarians as well as stockpeople."[64] Including academically trained researchers and veterinarians along with stockpeople for their refusal to acknowledge animal subjectivity, Grandin implies that academic credentials like her own are not sufficient preparation for conducting the kinds of dialogues that have earned her a reputation as an animal whisperer.

Whisperers complain that failure to recognize animal subjectivity leads to a multitude of sins. Grandin, for example, objects to researchers' myopic reduction of animals to mechanized biological systems made up of chemical parts and urges scientists instead to "look at the whole animal" in order to understand its motivations and interpret its behavioral signals.[65] Roberts points to his own father as an example of a stockman who regarded horses not as chemical systems but as machinery, a perspective that justified cruel and insensitive handling techniques. Roberts recalls his father telling him, "A horse is a dangerous machine, and you'd be wise to remember that. You hurt them—or they'll hurt you."[66] While Grandin emphasizes the empirical distortions of scientific specialization, Roberts is primarily concerned with the moral failures that result from refusal to recognize animals as centers of subjectivity. Both object to the mechanization of nonhuman animals, their reduction to systems and machinery devoid of intentionality and sentient responsiveness.

As their autobiographies attest, most whisperers adopt an intentional stance toward animals in early childhood, often in rustic settings where human and animal populations intermingle freely, uninhibited by cultural distinctions between humans and animals that are inculcated through formal education. Roberts, for instance, tells of being raised on a rodeo competition grounds and from infancy being carried on horseback by his mother as she taught riding lessons. "Well before I could walk," he recalls, "horse geography was as familiar to me as the human kind."[67] Woodhouse, who begins *Talking to Animals* with the statement, "I should have been born in a stable," recounts early memories of petting wild deer in the woods behind her home and says of herself as a young child, "I already lived in my mind in the world of animals."[68] Henry Blake reports, "My earliest memories are of horses rather than people, and horses rather than places or people have represented the milestones of my life."[69] Like Roberts, Woodhouse and Blake claim their own animality via interspecies relationships that contribute powerfully to their own identities. Likewise, Millan in recalling his rural Mexican childhood when he was known as *el perrero* (the dog boy) explains that his identification with dogs grew from a desire to know them as subjects of minds: "The only place I really wanted to be was among the animals. From as early as I can remember, I loved to spend hours walking with them or just silently watching them, trying to figure out how their wild minds worked."[70] The untutored boyhood belief that these "wild minds" are knowable through behaviors characterizes Millan the dog whisperer as a rustic or natural-born rather than formally trained ethologist.

For whisperers, attentiveness to other animals develops out of close and prolonged observation into the discovery of another species' wordless language. A vivid account of this process comes from Roberts' recollection of the wild mustang herd he watched in the Nevada wilderness as a young teen. Roberts was particularly intrigued by the "dialogue" he observed between the lead mare and a socially transgressive colt. Recalling an exchange that later became the basis for his own "joining up" technique with untamed horses, Roberts describes his discovery of the wordless language he calls Equus: "As I watched the mare's training procedures with this adolescent and others, I began to understand the language she used, and it was exciting to recognize the exact sequence of signals that would pass between her and the younger horses. It really was a language—predictable, discernible, and effective."[71] Roberts' pragmatic definition of language as a recognizable system for negotiating relationships and achieving social effects opens up the possibility of interspecies dialogues without the use of words.

Learning the native languages of other species, however, requires an initial period of receptive language learning when the human subject must keep a respectful and attentive silence, remaining open to a nonhuman animal's assertions of self. For Roberts, it was only after this stage of the learning process, when he quietly observed horses' body language from afar and eavesdropped on their conversations within the herd, that he began to realize he could use Equus productively to *speak* as well as *listen* to horses: "Perhaps, it occurred to me, I could use the same silent system of communication myself. If I understood how to do it, I could effectively cross over the boundary between human (the ultimate fight animal) and horse (the flight animal). Using their language, their system of communication, I could create a strong bond of trust. I would achieve cross-species communication."[72] As every social animal speaks its own species of language, whisperers like Dibra, Grandin, and Woodhouse, who work with multiple species, have to become multilingual. Regardless of species, however, the ability to comprehend and speak animal languages gives whisperers of all kinds an alternative to cruel and violent training methods, as language enables a trainer to substitute speech acts for acts of violence, soliciting willing cooperation rather than forcing compliance.

In using other species' languages, whisperers therefore favor the speech acts of "gentle persuasion"—*requests, suggestions,* and *invitations*—over *commands* and *threats.* Roberts writes that a central tenet of his philosophy is that "a rider or trainer should never say to a horse, 'You *must*.' Instead, the horse should be invited to perform because, 'I would like you to.'"[73] Blake gives similar advice: "Instead of saying, 'You damn well have got to do what I tell you to do,' we say 'let's do this,' or 'let's do that.'"[74] Fennel, whose methods emulate Roberts', describes the guiding acts of training as "request" and "reward," explaining, "I use the word 'request' rather than 'command' advisedly because what we are talking about here is a two-way street. Always remember, we are trying to create a situation where the dog is doing things of its own free will."[75] Dog whisperer Owens similarly reports, "I don't use the word 'command,' which infers that something negative will happen if the dog doesn't 'perform.' Instead, I believe raising a dog nonviolently involves *asking* for behaviors." Malcolm Gladwell writes of dog whisperer Millan's body language, "there is no commanding, only soliciting."[76]

Although they reject force and command-based handling, whisperers acknowledge the inevitable dynamics of dominance and submission in relationships with other animals. Whispering ethics accepts Yi-Fu Tuan's premise in *Dominance and Affection* that unequal power relationships are not necessarily morally objectionable. Tuan argues that although power certainly can be abused in ways that are cruel, exploitive, and devoid of affection, power does not inevitably lead to these abuses; it may choose the alternative channels of attention and care. In relationships with other animals, Tuan observes, dominance combined with affection produces pets instead of victims.[77] Sociologist Leslie Irvine maintains that affectionate and respectful dominance may also characterize relationships with animals more accurately described as *companions* than pets: "Whereas a pet must please and entertain a human 'master,' a companion animal has a guardian or caretaker who acknowledges the animal as one whose ways of being in the world are radically different but still worthy of respect."[78] For whisperers, respect is a matter of acknowledging and caring about the interests of the animal subject rather than according it equal "rights" within a democratic framework. Dominance and inequality, although anathema to the human ideal of democracy, hold survival value in the social organizations of many species, and adopting the perspectives of other animals means appreciating how their interests are defined by those social structures. Science writer Meg Daly Olmert notes that for wolves and their evolutionary descendents, "belonging to a family is more important than their rank in the family," while horses are "desperately social" and ready to surrender their freedom to be part of a herd.[79] For such animals, dominance hierarchies provide social stability, reduce the dangers of solitude, and eliminate the need for continual fighting over resources such as food, territory, and mates.

In whispering philosophy, then, dominance often equates with leadership, not cruelty, exploitation, or enslavement.[80] The first step toward assuming benign leadership is to demonstrate respect for the animal's point of view, and this assumes a prior willingness to learn the animal's native language as a nonviolent means of establishing and maintaining leadership without instilling fear. Miller and Lamb explain that the whisperer's initial conversation with a horse in training ideally lays the groundwork for a relationship in which the horse submits willingly to human leadership. At the outset, the whisperer assumes the role of "benevolent dictator," but as the relationship grows in trust, the human's position shifts to something akin to the "senior partner" in a relationship of nearly equal distribution of power, characterized by "*complete respect devoid of fear.*"[81] Because the social organization of horses in the wild is a dominance hierarchy headed by leaders who look after the survival of herd members, horses are predisposed to 'hook on' and submit to individuals who inspire confidence. As Miller and Lamb put it, the offer a human can make, of care and protection in exchange for absolute obedience, is "just the kind of deal [a horse] looks for his whole life."[82]

Like horse whisperers, dog and livestock whisperers promote human leadership through gentle persuasion rather than force, keying their persuasive efforts to the social expectations of the given species. For this reason, Millan advises people to consider dogs first as animals, then as dogs, then as breeds, and finally as named individuals. As a species, dogs derive their social expectations from den-dwelling, predatory ancestors whose lives were organized not by the herd but by the family pack. In Millan's terms, dogs negotiate their positions in the pack through a "language of energy." As descendents of creatures whose survival depended upon cooperative hunting, dogs recognize leadership as calm-assertive energy, and when they are confident in their leaders, they do not simply *submit* but do so willingly, as calm and confident leadership gives them the psychological "balance" of freedom from fear.[83]

THE RUSTIC RHETORIC OF WHISPERING: WORDLESS DIALOGUES OF ATTENTION AND INTENT

Like animal whisperers, Donovan proposes dialogic interspecies relationships in which speech acts can constrain and deflect acts of violation. In support of her assertion that serious dialogues with other animals are not only desirable but also empirically possible, Donovan's appeal to the authority of ethologists effectively shifts human-nonhuman animal communication from the realm of romantic legends about King Solomon, Hiawatha, Dr. Doolittle, and Tom Sullivan and away from the personal testimonies of fond pet-owners to the solid academic terrain of science. Donovan's invocation of science joins Singer's care to separate himself from "animal lovers," Lorimer's elaborate *apologia* for his rustic authorities, and Harvey's gloomy predictions about the possibility of animist-mediated dialogues between animals and academics; all express a similar distrust of nonacademic authority, a guardedness against "romance" in its various guises of emotional vulnerability, childish fantasy, or rustic naïveté. Myths of animal charmers and of fools who are charmed by animals pose a threat to serious, scholarly consideration of nonhuman animal communication, trailing all the deceptions, distortions, and ambiguities of legend and romance.

But whisperers are largely unperturbed by these narrative associations with their craft. In the whispering tradition, professional knowledge and romance are relatively free to overlap and blend via academically forbidden channels. The mystique of the animal-charmer actually advanced the social and economic prospects of the original horse whisperers, and the same holds true for the animal whisperers of today. Their autobiographical stories of animal-saturated childhoods often preface their claims to exceptional gifts as adult animal-communication experts. Dibra's *Catspeak*, for example, proclaims his "legendary" ability to talk with animals and cites his international fame as the official trainer of Hollywood celebrities, both animal and human. Woodhouse invites identification with Saint Francis when she describes as "blessed" people who communicate well with other animals.[84] Roberts embraces the romantic genre of relationship stories when he describes his trade secret as a "special affinity" born of his "life obsession with horses."[85] Fennel distills the gift of communicating with animals to the gift of speaking in tongues, describing linguistic expertise like her own as "confidence" in speaking "the ancient language that has been lost."[86] Cultivating a reputation for extraordinary, even paranormal communication powers is a way for contemporary whisperers to create and maintain a clientele in a contemporary, urbanized culture that is increasingly coming to value nonhuman animals as family members who provide companionship and emotional support.[87]

But unlike the original whisperers, who jealously cultivated the mystical ethos of the animal charmer, today's whisperers are more likely to be public educators like Lorenz, who seek to transmit their professional knowledge to other human beings, not to guard it from them. When divulging their trade secrets to the public, whisperers often explain their pedagogical mission in the relational terms of care. Roberts, for example, in dedicating his book to "Equus: the flight animal," writes of his desire to correct the ethical failure of non-recognition across the species divide, asserting that "we owe this species an apology for causing it to endure our lack of understanding for thousands of years."[88] The moral objective of his pedagogy is to set these interspecies relationships to rights, and the method he proposes for bridging the gap between his own personal feelings and public understanding is nonverbal language learning. Equipped with an understanding of Equus, Roberts announces his "immense" moral ambition as a teacher, to "change the way humans relate to horses."[89]

Regardless of the species they converse with, whisperers who accept the moral responsibilities of public education assent to the task of demystifying their special gifts and making their methods transparent to the uninitiated masses. Coren, after agreeing with Lorenz that, "the 'magic' in Solomon's ring . . . is hidden in *science*," describes his knowledge base as a blend of linguistics and behavioral science.[90] Like Roberts, Coren assumes the professional responsibilities of a language teacher, but instead of lessons in Equus, he offers to help readers learn the language he calls "Doggish." As a guide to recognizing Doggish words and understanding their combination into intentional phrases, Coren provides "A Visual Glossary and Doggish Phrasebook" of canine postures, gestures, facial expressions, and vocalizations. Such reference guides are common fare in whisperers' pedagogical publications. Blake, for instance, offers a "dictionary of horse language" consisting of 47 phrases, some of them divided into "sub-messages," with a key to equine inflections of context, purpose, and degree of imperative. Dibra presents drawings and a chart of "The Body Language of Cats" that keys feline social intentions to signals of body, ears, eyes, mouth, tail, vocalization, and whiskers.[91]

Assuming rustic authority to teach the codes and protocols of dialogues with speaking subjects from other species, whisperers prescribe an ethical rhetoric of receptivity and connection that is not averse to proximity, pathos, or partiality. Like behavioral scientists, they instruct us first to observe carefully, paying close and silent attention to animal others. But unlike scientists, whisperers prescribe a receptive stance that is by no means disinterested or entirely rational; instead it is inflected by automatic assent to the subjectivity of the other. In Dennett's terms, whisperers prescribe "the intentional stance" as a necessary opening to dialogues with other animals, encouraging us to listen "as if" other animals will speak to us with communicative intent. For our part, the stance entails the *intent to understand* the sense of other animals' speech. In the absence of words to negotiate interspecies relationships of mutual intentionality, whisperers advise that we look to nonverbal signs of communicative intent, seeking language in touches, odors, gestures, movements, tones, pitches, vocal qualities, muscular tension, posture, facial expression, and gaze.

These physical and sensory language channels enable dialogic exchange only in the embodied present. For whisperers, extending our sense of the social to include other animals literally means keeping company with them in the here and now, engaging in a mode of recognition that is essentially unburdened by demands for empirical verification or theoretical justification. While many whisperers undoubtedly understand and concur with scientific accounts of animal communication, and just as many surely agree with Singer's principled objections to animal suffering, they arrive at these conclusions through a relational rhetoric that resembles Watts' and a nonverbal rhetoric that shares much with Hyde's. Their approach to nonhuman animals can be distilled to a pragmatism that is interested and embodied rather than detached and verbally abstracted; their goal is to establish functional, nonviolent interspecies relationships rather than to protect the rights of autonomous individuals. Whispering logic is therefore dyadic as well as dialogic, because it arises from the proximate and partial social context of intimate interspecies relationships, relationships of you and me together in the here and now.

Keeping intimate company with other animals in whispering terms is at once rustic science—employing enhanced, multisensory observation of animal others—and rustic morality—prescribing a relational ethic that grants subjective agency to voices speaking in other-than-human languages. Accepting physicality, emotionality, relational identity, and other elements of romance as enhancements rather than distortions of observation of other animals, whisperers advocate the use of any sensory or extrasensory channel that can deliver information about the other. But beyond offering a version of the "enhanced scientific observation" Lorimer called for, whispering prescribes a morality recognizable as care. As moralists, whisperers do not simply condemn animal suffering by assuming a pacifist stance against violence toward other animals; they enact that stance in dialogues of nonverbal behaviors, including the cognitive behaviors of paying attention, granting intentional subjectivity, and caring to communicate. In our own intraspecies dialogues, we tend to regard these nonverbal behaviors as preliminary to speech and not as speech itself. But if we expand our conceptual understandings of voice beyond human speech, and language beyond words, as whisperers urge us to do, then these cognitive behaviors emerge as the opening speech acts of interspecies dialogues, plotting a rhetorical route of escape from the prison house of words and into the company of nonhuman animals.

Chapter Four

The Battle Within

Understanding the Persuasive Affect of Internal Rhetorics in the Ethical Vegetarian/Vegan Movement

Patricia Malesh

This morning I awoke to find an e-mail from Eli in my inbox. The subject line was simple—"maybe I will go vegan." The body of the e-mail was a slightly blurry photo of a pink-nosed cow craning her neck to plant a sloppy lick up the jaw and along the cheek of a woman in her forties, her eyes closed and her smile wide and toothy. Eli's been a good friend for over a year and, during that time, we've had many conversations about my decision to go vegan and my evolving, decade-long commitment to the lifestyle. He had been a card-carrying vegetarian once, when he lived in a Buddhist community where this was expected; he left both communities behind long ago. Though respectful and sympathetic—he never minds substituting tofu and soymilk for cream and paneer when we head to Sherpa's for saag—Eli has never been convinced by my lifestyle. He worries about nutrition (. . . *he got awfully skinny when he was vegetarian*), his past experience suggests vegan living is simply too much work (. . . *he's never really been into cooking*), and he has other commitments that he does not want to be distracted from (. . . *as a social worker, he prefers advocating for people to advocating for animals*). But when that blurry cow leaned close, like a nascent lover, and her quarry received her as such, Eli was opened to, and taken by, a rhetoric far greater than any I could wield—unspoken, unconscious, unhuman—and he was much more susceptible to it.

Ethical vegetarians/vegans (EVVs) can and should be understood as members of a socio-cultural movement that challenges and attempts to dismantle the cultural ritual of meat-eating. As such, its rhetoric, often found in narrative form, offers insights into the relationship among identity formation, socio-cultural norms, and resistance.[1] Like the rhetoric of the mainstream civil rights movement and feminist movements, that of EVV can be understood as attempting to "[call] America to its moral self" by blurring distinctions between personal and collective identity, disrupting cultural (as well as political

53

and economic) hegemonies, and highlighting moral conflict and social justice through rhetorics of oppression.[2] More importantly, the study of EVV rhetoric makes transparent the relationship between rhetoric and morality in a climate of deconstruction in which, according to theorist Jean Nienkamp, "the very possibility of moral agency is being called into question by various postmodern conceptions of subjectivity."[3] Despite this, ethical vegetarians literally embody their rhetoric and exhibit their morality.

Positioning subjectivity as a consequence of self-directed rhetoric is common practice within movement studies. The making of resistant, post-structural, malleable subjectivity has been framed by Michael Warner as counterpublic activity, theorized by Richard Gregg and Charles Stewart as an Ego Function of movement activity, and partitioned by Alberto Melucci as the defining feature of collective identity in new social movements.[4] These theories help illuminate the auto-constitutive function of vegetarian rhetoric and conversion narratives as tools that EVVs use to establish a positive, alt-cultural, collective identity. However, they are less helpful for explaining the prevalence of animals as rhetors within these narratives. Eli's cow—the affect of her rhetoric as apparent as it is unconscious—holds moral and rhetorical agency. But that agency likely originates from within Eli as he struggles to make sense of the internal dissonance he's experiencing between his learned socio-cultural values and his inherited physiological response.

In previous work, I analyze the rhetorical dimensions of personal narratives as interactive instruments for making and sharing meaning that create experience rather than recount it. Specifically, I extend and theorize vegetarian and vegan "stories of becoming" as epistemological constructs that help EVVs make sense of their decision to pull away from meat-eating as the dominant culture of consumption, justify this decision to others, and potentially persuade others to do the same.[5] In this chapter, I investigate and theorize the persuasive effect of internal and embodied rhetorics in the EVV movement. Specifically, I examine how such rhetorics ascribe or recognize animal agency and, in doing so, justify personal challenges to normative perceptions of animals as food.

For a better understanding of the episto-rhetorical process through which humans ascribe animals with agency, I turn primarily to Nienkamp's explication of internal rhetoric and social theorist Michel Foucault's analysis of Socratic *parrhesia*—the speaking of truth to power broadly defined—as both precursor to and necessary for rhetoric aimed at others. Nienkamp contributes to the literature on self-directed rhetoric and subjectivity by framing internal rhetoric as a "rhetorically negotiated conception of the self and moral agency [that takes] into account biological *and* cultural, conscious *and* unconscious influences on who we are, what we believe, and what we do."[6] Her description of internal rhetorics makes overt the mental processes through which EVVs determine and interrogate subjectivity. Nienkamp offers a rhetorical theory of the unconscious capable of exposing animal agency as a defense that EVVs employ to justify their subjectivity as morally warranted.[7] Such framing is more useful than that of Melucci and Warner—who argue subjectivity is self-organized and conscious respectively. And Gregg and Stewart—who examine (1) how acts of dissent help individuals and collectives in self-directed movements assert their agency, and (2) how advocates in other-directed movements reinforce their already exalted self-perception. Such internal deliberation as a form of self-knowledge makes possible what Foucault labels *parrhesia*—the philosophical practice of resistance through "altering one's belief or opinion" and also "changing one's style of life, one's relation to others, and one's relation to oneself."[8] The study of these psychological battles can expand communication scholars' perceptions of what counts as rhetoric to include dialectics of personal interaction, human-animal among them, that take place beyond the public sphere and beyond discourse. In these encounters, poststructual identification is a consequence of internal rhetorics and ripe with socio-transformative potential. Put simply, the study of the ethical vegetarians'/vegans' internal rhetorics exposes how individuals embody their rhetoric to become agents of change.

Using as primary texts ethical vegetarian/vegan narratives that frame animals as rhetorical agents, I conduct this analysis in two parts. First, I make a case for combining Nienkamp's theory of internal rhetorics—as "the persuasive tactics we use on ourselves"—with Foucault's analysis of Socratic *parrhesia*—as dangerous free speech through which individuals establish a harmonic relationship between their beliefs and their actions—to establish a causal relationship between internal rhetoric and possibilities for *parrhesia*. Second, I illustrate how this causal relationship unfolds in the ethical vegetarian/vegan movement by unpacking the gestalt realizations—in this case abrupt epiphanies that unveil an ethics of consumption—that sponsor personal transformation as socio-cultural resistance.[9] These realizations, brought about by human/animal and human/food/animal interactions, illustrate the rhetorical self as a *location* for the practice of rhetoric, rather than as an agent of or audience for rhetoric.[10] In other words, the study of EVV identification processes makes overt the rhetorical dimensions of cognition and embodiment.

THE BATTLE WITHIN: UNDERSTANDING THE SOCIO-CULTURAL AFFECT OF INTERNAL RHETORICS

In this section, I outline Nienkamp's case for internal rhetorics as a precursor to and requisite for *parrhesia*. I do so in order to position the ethical vegetarian/vegan movement as a hybrid of self-directed and other-directed movements through which participants come to embody the movement.[11] Because such agency requires individuals and collectives to live in contrast to accepted habits of consumption in order to expose these practices as immoral and ignorant of truth, I argue that internal rhetorics enable EVVs to speak truth to power and, in the process, restructure dominant social logic by embodying an alternative to it.

Internal rhetorics—rhetorics that exist as facets of the mind in dialogue with itself—are responsible for self-persuasion and necessary for socio-cultural dissent. In *Internal Rhetorics*, Nienkamp traces evolutions in the ways that rhetoricians understand self-persuasion and its relationship to external rhetorics whose audiences include both rhetor and the rhetor's community. As preparation for her discussion of internal rhetorics, Nienkamp integrates perspectives of rhetoric in general that range from canonical versions that treat rhetoric as the learned, deliberate, and public art of "craft[ing] persuasive language in a public setting" through Socratic frames that treat thinking as a conversation "which the soul has with itself" to Burkean claims that rhetoric is a process of identification rather than persuasion.[12] Working from this expansive view of rhetoric as the "*function* of all language and symbol use" that "pervades and conditions our human existence," she reframes the study of rhetoric as a study of *rhetorical effect*. This framing positions people as both audience for as well as producers of rhetoric and, in doing so, makes possible perceptions of animals as rhetors, a phenomenon I return to and explicate in the next section.[13]

These internal rhetorics challenge traditional distinctions between aspects of identity that bifurcate the personal from the collective, the rhetor from the audience, and the epistemological from the moral.[14] Nienkamp fuses rhetorical theory with psychology to expose the complexities of identity whereby "the self" is neither reducible to nor independent of social construct. She defines internal rhetorics as situations of self-persuasion, different from external rhetorics in *scene* rather than *essence*—a Burkean terministic screen that acts as "a lens through which to study mental activity rather than a reference to a particular kind of mental activity."[15] Internal rhetorics, then, are both a precursor to, as well as a necessary element of, rhetorics directed at external audiences.

One such rhetoric that is heavily reliant on internal rhetorics and equally efficacious in sponsoring them is the Greco-Roman concept of *parrhesia*. Foucault resurrects *parrhesia* in contemporary thought in his lectures on *Fearless Speech*.[16] In these lectures, he traces changes in the meaning and application of *parrhesia*—the frank disclosure of one's beliefs, understood as truth, in situations where the *parrhesiastes* faces ridicule and punishment from those in power. While parrhesiastic speech was originally understood within "the framework of public life," its use and usefulness migrated to include "the context of community life," "the context of individual personal relationships," as well as self scrutiny/self-examination as *scenes* for *parrhesia*.[17] The *essence* of the term remains unchanged as willful, dangerous honesty that can only be spoken by individuals (and groups) whose actions, or lifestyles, are consistent with their beliefs and morals. Understood as such, *parrhesia* is a valuable rhetorical device through which subjugated populations can speak on their own behalf and validate their lived experiences in the hopes of eliminating the dominant ideologies that govern their potential agency. In order to speak their mind freely, however, *parrhesiastes* must first understand it themselves. As deliberations between conflicting truths, internal rhetorics make such self-knowledge possible, including the knowledge of self-as-social agent. *Parrhesia*, then, is the practice of first speaking truth to oneself and next speaking truth to others.

Like other rhetorics, the internal rhetorics that structure "the self" are deliberations between rhetors and audiences who seek to integrate personal appetites with socio-cultural ways of knowing in order to challenge, adjust, and/or reinforce either or both. Internal rhetorics are worth examining because they expose these roles of rhetor and audience as always multiple and competing, since they migrate through different aspects of self in order to dialogue with one another. This is the primary means through which post-structural selves-in-society are constructed. As "the rhetorical function of thought," internal rhetorics form "the interstices of human life—between action and reflection, wisdom and speech, reason and the appetites."[18] Consequently, the rhetorical self is not a unified self but rather a collective self marked by postmodern fragmentation in both experience and action. According to Nienkamp, understanding the self as rhetorical means that, "[w]e are no longer black boxes either producing or receiving discourse, but complex agents that take in cultural and direct rhetorics; reject, manipulate, or swallow them whole; and re-create or respond to them in personal utterances and actions, intentional or not."[19] Characterized as the process of discerning appropriate courses of action, internal rhetorics are *the action of thought* and, as such, have both intrapersonal (epistemological) and interpersonal (moral and ethical) affect.

For this reason, a theory of internal rhetoric is useful for those studying processes of identification as social movement activity of which *parrhesia* is an example. Social movement theorists schooled in continental approaches to sociology argue post-structural self-identification is the epicenter of socio-cultural change. These scholars work to theorize culture both as a product of those in power and as a source of resistance for those without.[20] The movements they study, woven into the fabric of everyday life, exist as what Melucci calls "a network of small groups" who struggle for authority over symbolic codes, identity claims, and representation.[21] Since New Social Movements rely on post-structural, self-selected individual and collective sources of identity—such as ethnicity, gender, sexuality, and dietary ethics—these movements "requir[e] personal involvement in experiencing and practicing cultural innovation."[22] For EVVs, personal involvement literally translates into embodied rhetoric.

Because ethical vegetarians/vegans identify and are identified, often negatively, by their socially unsanctioned habits of consumption *in addition to* their advocacy for others, they complicate accepted perceptions of how subjectivity is constituted through processes of identification by agents of social change. In his work with social movements, Stewart advances Gregg's ego function of protest rhetoric as a version of internal rhetorics, epistemic in nature. In Gregg's original argument, he describes the ego function of protest as "*constituting* selfhood through expression" that is essentially self-directed, meaning that the audience for protest rhetoric is the protesters themselves.[23] The ego function of such rhetoric is self-empowerment. Stewart extends the ego function to include movements that are not "self-directed" but rather that seek to change conditions for an "other."[24] In these movements, the ego function is not a matter of self-empowerment so much as a means of celebrating and enhancing the moral superiority participants already feel. Despite these contrasts, the question that drives Gregg and Stewart to theorize an ego function of movement praxis is the same one that guides Nienkamp in her exploration of internal rhetorics and me in my analysis of EVV: How does agency develop within the self as a precursor to and catalyst for the types of interpersonal interaction that lead to social change?

The ego function, as a characteristic of both self-directed and other-directed movements, is helpful but insufficient for explaining the internal rhetorics of ethical vegetarians/vegans as agents of social change. EVV rhetoric indicates the movement as other-directed. In most cases, animal advocacy is an organic component of EVV. When it is not, animal advocacy is replaced by eco-advocacy. Whether advocacy is on behalf of animals or the environment, it takes place on behalf of a literally and metaphorically voiceless "other." Such rhetoric saturates EVV movement praxis that is conducted through offense rather than defense, whereas participants act as attackers instead of attacked.[25] Self-positioned as saviors in a battle against evil-doers, animal rights activists and environmentalists do not suffer their identification. However, EVVs are not synonymous with nor reducible to animal rights activists.

Since EVVs choose to *identify and live* in contrast to social norms, they are vulnerable to and suffer from personal critique. Such critique—the effect of which on movement participants is subordination within society that leads to feelings of victimhood and oppression—situates EVVs as members of a self-directed movement. Stewart describes these self-directed movements as "created, led, and populated primarily by those who perceive themselves to be dispossessed" as they struggle "primarily for personal freedom, equality, justice, and rights."[26] Participants struggle, amidst critique and persecution, to justify and affirm their lived experience as valuable. In such movements, participants become agents of change by embracing their identity and building communities around it, rather than lamenting it. The degree of success that disenfranchised populations have in their struggle to convince themselves and others of their self-worth hinges on their ability to isolate and name the shared situation that unites them and distinguishes them from others.

Ethical vegetarians/vegans establish a collective identity, a subjectivity, as a hybrid of self- and other-directed movements. Whereas EVVs are themselves subjugated because they have chosen to resist the dominant culture of consumption, they do so on moral grounds as advocates for animals or the environment. In this respect, the internal rhetoric that makes agency possible for EVVs is neither wholly contingent on empowerment nor solely activated by a perception of moral superiority. EVVs do struggle, on personal as well as interpersonal platforms, to self-identify and self-define their praxis, an ego function of self-directed movements but not other-directed ones. However, EVVs also position themselves as "moral crusaders who [speak] and [write] of sacred quests to assist others, challenge evil forces, and bring about a better world for all," an ego function of other-directed movements, but not self-directed.[27] It is in search of a theory of internal rhetorics that subsumes these contrasts in order to describe more accurately the ways in which select EVVs find their own rhetorical agency by ascribing some to animals. For this reason, I return to Nienkamp's interpretation of the rhetoric we use on ourselves rather than adopting Stewart's heuristic of the ego function in self- and other-directed movements as a catalyst for *parrhesia*.

Internal rhetorics, as framed by Nienkamp, function epistemologically by enabling self-knowledge and self-definition as distinct from, but heavily influenced by, collective ways of knowing. This intrapersonal function of internal rhetorics constitutes as well as characterizes the psyche and provides a "frame of reference for the consciousness of the self."[28] Nienkamp terms this vein of internal rhetorics *primary*, because it is pervasive, often unconscious, yet discerning. Because primary internal rhetoric "does more than passively echo the cultural voices around us, . . . [by] actively select[ing] and adjust[ing] these voices according to personal history and circumstance," it births agency and exposes "each human being [as] a site of both rhetorical dissension *and* concerted rhetorical action."[29] When humans face situations that create dissonance between internalized ideologies and other aspects of personality that, for one reason or another, gravitate towards conflicting ideologies, primary internal rhetoric becomes a "mechanism through which new voices are incorporated into the rhetorical self."[30] In other words, this primary, epistemological, and ontological strain of internal rhetoric ignites social change by exposing norms as partisan, rather than factual, and, in doing so, sponsoring ethical awakenings that disrupt and/or adjust identity affiliations.[31] Such truth-knowing is a precursor to the truth-telling that characterizes *parrhesia*.

Parrhesiastes, those who engage in the dangerous activity of testifying unpopular morals, must first come to understand and adopt those morals before then can advocate for others to do so. As practice for communication, thinking is "an internalized 'conversation of gestures,' patterned after the social communication that the individual has experienced from others."[32] It "call[s] forth attitudes or actions in the self according to the anticipated responses of others," trying ethos and argument on for fit behind closed doors before parading them for others.[33] Nienkamp frames this more conscious internal rhetoric as *cultivated*, rather than primary, since the rhetorical self recognizes that these private deliberations about morality will ultimately be judged for verité by outside audiences.[34] This cultivated internal rhetoric illustrates how the rhetorical self applies internalized social discourses as it constructs and/ or alters personal and collective identity. When competing moralities face one another as "inner voices" that are housed within a heterogeneous psyche that "depends on and is crucial to" socio-cultural frames, individuals become agents on a spectrum of conservation and reformation.[35]

This has happened historically, according to Foucault, when individuals have engaged in *parrhesia* as a philosophical activity through which competing moralities, dressed as truths, cause individuals to examine their beliefs against their actions. Just as internal rhetorics are precursor to and necessary for rhetoric aimed at others, *parrhesia* can and does attend to the care of the self before, during, and after it engages with others. Courageousness as an essential trait of a *parrhesiastes*—a truth-teller who is recognizable by the harmonious relationship she maintains between her logos (what she thinks) and her bios (what she does)—first appears as the courage to know one's self. It then becomes the courage to speak one's self.[36] In its most profound form, *parrhesia* is the ability to recognize one's self as knowing truth and the courage to speak that truth to others who not only have yet to accept it but who also have the power to deny it.

Primary and cultivated internal rhetorics, as sponsors of *parrhesia*, illustrate how identification processes are both producer and product of rhetoric. Studying them helps rhetoricians "explain how we act and are acted upon in the shifting contexts of our lives" and, from this, theorize "a framework for thinking about how complex—and even divided—socially constructed selves have moral agency in an ideologically saturated world."[37] This is key in instances where people "react" to, rather than "swallow," cultural norms by adopting unpopular, non-dominant moral positions. In such cases, the possibility for parrhesiastic rhetoric becomes available.

The study of internal rhetorics, then, exposes identity formation as a process of persuasion that is most readily accessible in agents of social change and the activities that shape them. Such theorizing makes for a compelling case that rhetoricians should invest more heavily, and overtly, in mapping internal rhetorics as the process and the consequence of social change. One way to do this is to employ internal rhetorics as a heuristic for gleaning how animal agency is manufactured to justify EVV as a counter-cultural ethic and lifestyle. As self-persuasion that occurs between the different facets of the mind in conjunction with and/or prior to rhetoric crafted for public audiences, internal rhetorics makes possible animal agency. And animal agency gives EVVs the courage to speak parrhesiastically. Rather than claiming that animals become rhetorical agents, however, I position individuals as susceptible to and audiences for animal rhetorics. I argue that animals are given rhetorical agency by individuals and groups who seek to justify—to self, to intimates, and to society—their culturally abnormal ethics and activity in order to incite internal deliberations that may lead to adjustments in the beliefs and actions of their audiences.

ANIMALS AS RHETORICIANS,
RHETORICIANS AS AUDIENCE

Framed as self-deliberation, internal rhetorics expose the ethical vegetarian/vegan movement as a self-/other-directed hybrid movement characterized by appeals to empathy that emerge within parrhesiastic narratives of human-animal interaction. The ways that individuals, through varying degrees of consciousness, create and recognize animal agency expose negotiations of subjectivity that take place *within individuals*. Claiming that animals exert rhetorical influence over certain humans allows movement participants to justify their actions to themselves and others as they pull away from dominant socio-cultural ideologies and values (like meat-eating) in favor of less sanctioned ethical paradigms (like vegetarianism/veganism). In this section, I detail empathy as a rhetorical strategy that EVVs use to position animals as subjects and, as such, inappropriate for consumption. Specifically, I examine how EVVs make animals overt as the referent of meat, expose animals as capable of suffering and affection, and anthropomophize animals as rhetoricians and agents of change. Throughout my analysis, I argue that EVVs who share stories of human-animal interactions become *parrhesiastes* in the process by encouraging internal deliberations that, ideally, change the beliefs and behaviors of their audiences.

This process begins when the animal origin of the food meat is made apparent. When animals are made overt as the sources of meat, the disconnect between animal as being and animal as food is mended. In *The Sexual Politics of Meat*, animal ethicist Carol Adams explicates the process whereby animals are unveiled as the "absent referent" of meat.[38] In her assessment, terminology used by the meat industry obscures the "being" of food animals whereby "animals in name and body are made absent *as animals* for meat to exist."[39] In the language of butchering, animals become "biomachines" and "food-processing units" while slaughterhouses become rendering plants and dissecting equipment become "protein harvesters" and "converting machines."[40] American vernaculars further distance meat from its constituents:

> Animals are made absent through language that renames dead bodies before consumers participate in eating them. Our culture further mystifies the term "meat" with gastronomic language, so we do not conjure dead, butchered animals, but cuisine. . . . After death, cows become roast beef, steak, hamburger; pigs become pork, bacon, sausage. Since objects are possessions they cannot have possessions; thus, we say "leg of lamb" not a "lamb's leg." . . . Without its referent point of the slaughtered, bleeding, butchered animal, meat becomes a free-floating image.[41]

Such discursive adjustments complement industry packaging practices— boneless chicken, ground beef, sliced ham—that erase the lineage of meat. This reframing is for the benefit of internal rhetorics that work to maintain a continuity of self-in-society. It neutralizes potential conflicts between inclination and ideology by casting habits of consumption outside the domain of the ethical. When individuals enter situations in which referent and existent collide, however, these same internal rhetorics face strong challenges in the form of an ethics of eating.

Often ethical vegetarians/vegans detail an encounter between self and animal as the moment in which they become aware that meat is made of animal. In these narratives—their "stories of becoming"—people credit interactions with animals for sponsoring "gestalt realizations" that prompt their conversion to EVV. The following examples, gathered from a printed collection of narratives, a single-authored manuscript, and a poster quoting Paul Mc-Cartney taped to a kiosk in downtown Boulder, Colorado, illustrate what this looks like when EVVs consciously address multiple audiences.

> I was driving down a country road in Chesapeake, Virginia when I passed a field of grazing cows. I looked over at them and thought, "You don't have to worry

about me, I would never hurt you." *And that's when it happened*—I became a vegetarian.[42]

When I was seven years old, I went to the 1964 World's Fair in New York. . . . I remember going to see the Borden exhibit and being totally fascinated with Elsie the Cow—being a city kid, I'd rarely get a chance to see a live cow! The next day (a Sunday) my mom made dinner for everyone and she placed a platter down in the middle of the table. I asked her what the "red stuff" was and she told me it was blood from the roast beef. My uncle, always the joker, said, "Remember Elsie? That's either her or one of her family members!" Well, I screamed and yelled and carried on as children do and quit eating red meat. . . . When I became a teenager, the chicken and fish went.[43]

In these examples, the narrators are moved to EVV when their experience of free-roaming, contented cows disrupts the narrative of meat-as-other-than-animal. These experiences are marked by affection and are echoed in Eli's response above. The next two examples are quite different in their orientation but manufacture the same results.

The shot I saw was of a dying calf, looking right into the camera. I felt as if this animal, who was rapidly bleeding to death as the film rolled, were looking directly at me. I left the room deeply shaken.[44]

Many years ago, I was fishing, and as I was reeling in the poor fish, I realized, "I am killing him—all for the passing pleasure it brings me." *And something inside me clicked.* I realized as I watched him fight for breath, that his life was as important to him as mine is to me.[45]

In these examples, the narrators are struck by the suffering of animals and, as agents of this suffering—second- and firsthand respectively, they feel guilt. Whether it is through compassion or guilt, the narrators in the above accounts come to awareness through their interactions with animals.

Together these stories make overt animals as the source of meat, but they also position animals as rhetors capable of causing humans to reflect on their beliefs and actions. And while the narrators position animals as rhetorical agents who are capable of "look[ing] directly at" them, fighting for breath, and being familial, these same narrators frame themselves as locations of deliberation. Their encounters with animals caused these narrators to "feel" and "realize" until "something *inside [of them]* clicked." If this something is understood as a product of internal rhetorics, then what appears to be a gestalt moment is actually a process through which personal experience challenges engrained enculturation and, in doing so, produces a situated response that is capable of restructuring thought.

Since much of the persuasiveness of these encounters comes from the firsthand experience of narrators as they interact with animals, they are less effective in sponsoring internal rhetorics in those who hear them as after-the-fact accounts. This phenomenon is captured, albeit satirically, in an episode of *The Simpsons* titled "Lisa, the Vegetarian." After interacting with a lamb at a petting zoo, Lisa finds herself envisioning her lamb chop returning to its rightful owner as she sits down to eat it. When she expresses her discomfort with eating the same species of animal that she felt such affection for only hours earlier, she is met with disdain and dismissal by the rest of her family. When Lisa says, "I can't eat this. I can't eat a poor little lamb," Homer replies "Lisa, get ahold of yourself. This is lamb, not *a* lamb." After her refusal to eat *a* lamb, Lisa is plagued with visions of meat separating from its animal and landing in its edible form on a plate as Marge suggests that she eat "chicken breast," "rump roast," or "hot dogs" instead. When she furthers her own inquisition by announcing that she cannot stand the thought of eating any animal again, the conversation tacitly acknowledges the rhetorical power of the "absent referent":

> HOMER: Wait a minute, wait a minute, wait, wait, wait. Lisa, honey, are you saying you're never going to eat any animals again?! What about bacon?
> LISA: No.
> HOMER: Ham?
> LISA: No.
> HOMER: Pork chops?
> LISA: Dad! Those all come from the same animal!
> HOMER: Ho, ho. Yeah, right, Lisa. A wonderful, *magical* animal.[46]

Lisa's experience mirrors the actual testimonials above, but it also highlights internal rhetoric as a testing ground for rhetoric whose final audience is external and whose goal is social change. What Lisa is fighting against in the above interaction is not simply Homer's ignorance of where his "meat" comes from, but society's as well. Euphemistic disassociation norms meat-eating within American culture so much so that retellings of experiences where animals become the overt referent of meat are limited in their rhetorical power.

When a human interacts with a food animal as an animal, still whole and sentient, the dissidence between the reality of meat and the semantic and symbolic representation of it becomes evident. Animal rhetoric is necessarily embodied and, as such, is an amalgamation of internal and external rhetorics as well as self- and other-directed advocacies. Though I've focused primarily on internal rhetorics as thought thus far, deliberations between internalized ideology and instinct/experiential ways of knowing convene in the body. Nienkamp describes the body as the location of rhetoric when she argues that "[o]ur physical beings—with their assigned cultural values—thus join other cultural rhetoric and personal history in shaping and reshaping rhetorical selves."[47] As the "agora" or "contributing scene" for internal rhetoric, the body is the platform for reason, a mental phenomenon that carries over from thinking to speaking and that is unchanged by the accompanying shift in audience.[48] A product of materiality and "assigned cultural values," the body is also a location of rhetoric. This is true of animals just as it is true for sentient rhetors. The cultural significance (or insignificance) that we assign bodies informs the assumptions we make about what happens within them.

Once food animals are reunited with their bodies and, as a result, with the ability to suffer, a situation emerges that causes incongruency between some individuals' innate emotional responses and their internalized social values.[49] The various faculties of the self must then deliberate and negotiate an appropriate response, one born of compassion. This is the first step in ascribing animals with agency and harkens back to philosopher Jeremy Bentham's influential argument on behalf of nonhuman animals in which he states, "the question is not, Can they reason? nor, Can they talk? but Can they Suffer?"[50] Compassion and sympathy, then, work at the crossroads of emotion and reason, but personal experience with suffering is necessary to turn sympathy into empathy. When humans who have themselves experienced suffering as both a material and emotional condition recognize parallels between their experience and those of food animals, they are more likely to be empathetic. Many accounts exist in which Holocaust survivors liken their experience in concentration camps to the experience of animals on factory farms. Alex Hershalf, a Holocaust survivor and animal rights activist, makes this comparison directly in his "story of becoming":

> My experiences in the Warsaw Ghetto during the Holocaust had a profound impact on my subsequent life choices. . . . In particular, my experiences in the Nazi Holocaust allowed me to empathize with the condition of farm animals in today's factory farms, auction yards, and slaughterhouses. I know first-hand what it is like to be treated like a worthless object, to be hunted by the killers of my family and friends, to wonder each day if I will see the next sunrise, to be crammed in a cattle car on the way to slaughter.[51]

Other examples can be found in Charles Patterson's book *Eternal Treblinka: Our Treatment of Animals and the Holocaust*.[52] In his book, Patterson does for victims of the Holocaust what Upton Sinclair did in *The Jungle* for slaughterhouse workers nearly a century earlier—detail similarities between their visceral experiences and the experiences of food animals powerful enough to sponsor internal rhetorics that challenge meat-eating as beyond the consideration of ethics.[53]

Not all encounters in which EVVs map their experience of suffering onto the suffering of food animals are as logic-driven as Holocaust and slaughter-house comparisons. In the following example, reason and emotion intersect as a result of personal, situational happenstance rather than systematized and collective experience. This account, posted on a public blog, offers a glimpse of internal rhetorics at work, even when the subjects of change fail to realize or articulate animal agency and empathy as catalysts for change.

> It was 28 years ago today, on 18th August 1981 that I became a vegetarian. I'd been toying with the idea for a while, and was starting to think I wanted to do it. I was at home on the day in question eating one of those little frozen pizzas with ham, cheese and mushroom for lunch, when the phone rang. It was a friend, calling to tell me that a trip to the local swimming pool by two of our closest friends, Mark and Joe, had ended in tragedy. Joe had drowned, aged 16. We never found out how or why it had happened, but the shock of the news brought home to me the fact that meat on your plate is the dead flesh of what used to be a living thing. It's not why I became a vegetarian, but it's how it happened.[54]

In all of these testimonials, the narrators attribute their conversions to vegetarianism, consciously and unconsciously, to empathy and their empathy to a visceral experience that disrupted emotional-ideological compatibility in their rhetorical selves. In such instances, the narrators become advocates for "the other" and participants in an apparently other-directed movement.

The rhetorical power of compassion and empathy has not gone unnoticed by groups and organizations intent on sponsoring internal rhetorics whose effect on their host is adherence to vegetarianism, despite its status as a socially unsanctioned ethic. Such groups as People for the Ethical Treatment of Animals (PETA) and Farm Sanctuary take encounters between individuals and animals, like the excerpts that pepper this chapter, and package them into more generic narratives so that their appeal is less dependent on personal experience and more dependent on the primary, epistemological strain of internal rhetoric that exposes norms as partisan and animals as capable of suffering. The most common narrative that is told and retold by organizations that advocate EVV is the "story of the downed animal." Pamphlets, newsletters, websites, posters, and other forms of sponsored literature commonly display photos of visibly and seriously injured animals—unable to stand, often bloody—accompanied by a story that details the animal's near-death experience. In Farm Sanctuary literature, the most commonly recited story is the one that brought the organization into being, the story of Hilda the Sheep. According to Gene and Lorri Bauston, co-founders of the sanctuary, they stumbled across Hilda in 1986 on the "deadpile" in a stockyard. To Gene and

Lorri, who rescued her, Hilda is a symbol of the hidden injustices of factory farming and a testimony to an individual's ability to make a difference.

While Hilda's story offers hope and promotes compassion by showing individuals their own power for direct action and the need for such action, PETA's most common "downed animal" story employs compassion as a steppingstone to anger and anger as an impetus for action. PETA's "The Story that Will Change Your Life" begins with a photo of a downed cow staring helplessly into the camera. The narrative that follows details her story.

> The truck carrying this cow was unloaded at Walton Stockyards in Kentucky on a September morning. After the other animals were removed from the truck, she was left behind, unable to move. The stockyard workers beat and kicked her in the face, ribs and back. They used the customary electric prods in her ear to try to get her out of the truck, but still she did not move. The workers then tied a rope around her neck, tied the other end to a post in the ground, and drove the truck away. The cow was dragged along the floor of the truck and fell to the ground, landing with both hind legs and her pelvis broken. She remained in this state until 7:30 that evening.
>
> The cow lay in the hot sun crying out for the first three hours. Periodically, when she urinated or defecated, she used her front legs to drag herself along the gravel roadway to a clean spot. She also tried to crawl to a shaded area but could not move far enough. Altogether she managed to crawl a painful 13-14 yards. The stockyard employees would not allow her any drinking water; the only drinking water she received was given to her by Jessie Pierce, a local animal rights activist, who had been contacted by a woman who witnessed the incident.[55]

The story continues until 7:30 p.m., when a local butcher arrived and shot her, later purchasing the corpse for $307.50. In this account, the focalized participants are the cow and Pierce. While one acts as a symbol of the inhumanity of the meat production and those associated with it, the other acts as good Samaritan and movement advocate. The third important character in the drama of the downed cow is the butcher, who exhibits both a callous ability to kill and greed for his due, the flesh of the animal he killed. This story first appeared in PETA literature in 1986 in the *PETA NEWS*, the precursor to the *Vegetarian Times*. It has since been reprinted in full-color leaflet form, on Goveg.com, and other PETA materials. These accounts, as praxis of both the animal rights movement and the ethical vegetarian/vegan movement, suggest that EVVs are speaking on behalf of an "other." However, the reason that EVVs occupy this role is because personal circumstance has led each narrator to dissolve distinctions between others and intimates. In the above "stories of becoming" and "stories of the downed animal," narrators embrace animals as companions in their struggle for agency, rather than or in addition to positioning animals as victims—as dissimilar to the narrators and their loved ones—in need of saving. Movement participants use these stories not only to advocate for animals but also to justify their own identifications, beliefs, and practices.

Because EVVs literally embody their rhetoric in challenge to meat-eating as a dominant culture of consumption, they experience subjugation and struggle to justify, affirm, and advocate for their self-selected, socially unsanctioned identity. In moments and situations when they "out" themselves or are "outed" by others, EVVs become *parrhesistes* if and when they accept their identification as ethical vegetarians/vegans. Such identification is an act of courage, since the praxis of EVV calls accepted perceptions of animals as food into question and ethicizes habits of consumption. Not all who subscribe to EVV, however, are comfortable having to justify their existence. This discomfort is most apparent in moments when they are called upon to be *parrhesiastes*.

Such a moment—when an ethical vegetarian is called upon to become a *parrhesiastes* and is reluctant to assume this responsibility—is captured in a scene from the film *American Splendor*.[56] The film chronicles the life of bitter Cleveland comic book writer Harvey Pekar. It is a dark look at Harvey's struggle to overcome lifelong disappointment with circumstance. One scene in the film details his first dinner date with his future wife, Joyce. As they look over the menu, Harvey's choice to be a vegetarian unwittingly drives the conversation.

> HARVEY: A lot of meat on this menu.
> JOYCE: You're a vegetarian?
> HARVEY: Kinda, ya know, I mean, ever since I got a pet cat, you know, I've had trouble eating animals.
> JOYCE: Yeah, I support and identify with groups like PETA, but unfortunately, I'm a self-diagnosed anemic. Also, I have all these food allergies to vegetables which give me serious intestinal distress. I guess I have a lot of borderline health disorders that limit me politically when it comes to eating.

This encounter captures a common exchange among vegetarians and meat-eaters and points out a fundamental, if often tacit, understanding about the ethics of eating. Dietary choices, which are mostly understood as intensely personal decisions, reflect cultures of consumption. In this exchange, Harvey struggles to articulate his commitment to a vegetarian lifestyle without alienating or challenging his companion. Nonetheless, Joyce's attempt to justify her decision to be a meat-eater suggests that she interprets Harvey's personal commitment to vegetarianism as a judgment on her decision not to be.

Intentionally or otherwise, in his interaction with Joyce, Harvey represents a community of vegetarians who share a similar ethical commitment, making his decision to be a vegetarian both personal and social. Regardless of whether or not he expects others to adopt his perspective, his choice to live as a vegetarian challenges meat-eaters, like Joyce, to take responsibility for their dietary choices and exposes an implicit ethics of eating. Harvey's decision, then, has inherent rhetorical value and forces him to assume the role of *parrhesiastes*. In other words, although he may not be employing it as a strategy, his vegetarianism is nonetheless understood as both a confrontation to meat-eating as a social convention and with those who subscribe to it.

This phenomenon accounts for the popularity of internal deliberations in which humans interrogate the ethics of meat-eating but, in the end, reject EVV as a lifestyle and praxis. If humans accept an ethics of eating that necessarily leads to a socially unsanctioned and permanent change in their behavior, then they must live as perpetual *parrhesiastes*—frank speakers tasked with disclosing their beliefs, which they interpret as truth, in situations where they face ridicule and punishment from those in power. For those who make distinctions between living as an EVV and advocating EVV as a social movement, *parrhesia* is an uncomfortable consequence that requires courage. If humans do not experience situations through which animals are made overt as the referent of meat and as capable of suffering, affection, and in extreme cases sentience, the incentive to become *parrhesiastes*—to identify as and become EVV—is greatly reduced.

Such bravery is easier, however, for individuals who already feel empowered on some level within society when they decide to "out" themselves as EVVs. In his song "Meat is Murder," Morrissey, lead singer of the English post-punk band The Smiths, takes on the distinction between the suffering of humans and the suffering of animals in the hope of erasing it. In the first verse, Morrissey likens the sounds of animals in anguish to human sounds, "Heifer whines could be human cries/Closer comes the screaming knife," a theme he returns to in his final line when he laments ". . . and who hears when animals cry?" Once this relationship is established, Morrissey makes present animals as the referent for meat in the very moments when their animality is made more distant: "the calf that you carve with a smile/Is murder/And the turkey you festively slice/Is murder . . . The flesh you so fancifully fry/The meat in your mouth/As you savour the flavour/Of murder." In these lines, and in his refrain that ends with "death for no reason is murder," Morrissey unites killing an animal with killing a human linguistically by categorizing both as "murder," a *conscious* act of *life*-taking. By doing so, Morrissey assumes the role of a *parrhesiastes* whose critical preaching seeks audience with all who will listen in order to "enabl[e] [the] philosophical themes about one's way of life to become popular, i.e., to come to the attention of people who [stand] outside the philosophical elect," or, in this case, EVV culture.[57] He does so, perhaps, to inspire internal rhetorics that call into question accepted behaviors by challenging the logic that makes them so.

Such challenges are inherently acts of dissent and are treated as such by cultural gatekeepers—consciously and unconsciously. Because those who subscribe to EVV as an ethic and lifestyle refute socio-cultural norms in the process, they are often challenged (by those who don't as cultural gatekeepers) to justify or rationalize their perspective. In anticipation of this, I have argued that rhetors often develop narratives that ascribe animal agency ex post facto in order to justify their alternative, culturally unendorsed ethics and the symbolic action that these ethics produce.[58] This leaves open the possibility that, as Nienkamp suggests, the reasons and rationalizations that people give "[do] not influence the actual decision, but [are] intended to influence public opinion to be favorable of that decision" after the fact.[59] If this is true, case studies of internal rhetorics at work, like this one, are key for understanding how and why humans react as they do to social norms.

I continue to explicate ethical vegetarianism/veganism as a reaction to an ideology of meat-eating by further developing my analysis of empathy as a rhetoric. While compassion and sympathy certainly lend rhetorical agency to animals, these tools of perception are more effective as rhetorics if they lead to empathy. EEVs attempt to initiate this process not only by making animals overt as the referent of meat and, in doing so, reuniting food animals with their inherent ability to suffer but also by positioning animals as agents of and recipients for affection as well as attributing them sentience. When this happens, the practice of vegetarianism becomes a movement characterized by personal abstention and systematized advocacy. Having detailed above how EVVs expose meat as animal and animal as victim, I now turn to affection— both the affection that humans feel for animals and the affection that animals show humans—as a source of ascribed animal agency.

Representing animals as capable of affection as well as suffering is important because the former is not always enough to sponsor EVV. Making a case for the ethical treatment of animals based on their ability to suffer ties humans' responsibility to the treatment of animals while they are alive, not to the immorality of killing and consuming them. In other words, rhetorics of animal suffering make a case for the humane treatment of food animals, but they do not *necessarily* make the case for vegetarianism. Author, activist, and career academic Temple Grandin, and those who support her work, embody this apparent contradiction. Grandin has garnered international acclaim, as well as disdain, as a consultant to livestock processors who seek to improve the conditions of animals from rearing through rendering. She is also autistic, which she credits with helping her experience the world like an animal as "a place of fear without emotion where your thoughts come to you in pictures rather than in words."[60] As a consultant and public figure, she sincerely presents herself as an advocate for animals. She is not, however, a vegetarian. In her book, *Thinking in Pictures*, she justifies her decision by appealing to reified social norms, "Often I get asked if I am a vegetarian. I eat meat, because I believe that a totally vegan diet, in which all animal products are eliminated, is unnatural."[61] Though she positions herself as empathetic, relating to animals more so than humans, she stops short of claiming that they are capable of *emotion*. This distinction allows her to silence the internal rhetorics that suggest there is an ethic to eating that she is violating and circumvent any parrhesiastic responsibility. If she can reduce the physical suffering of food animals, the classic utilitarian argument for vegetarianism, then she can feel morally justified in her continued choice to consume animals. Those who subscribe to EVV, however, expand notions of suffering to include emotional as well as material welfare. Positioning animals as agents of affection is a common way of reaffirming EVV as an ethical necessity.

Narratives that argue animals are capable of the emotion of affection, both giving and receiving, sponsor deliberations about the ethics of eating within individuals that lead to vegetarianism. Such narratives often detail interactions between individuals and their pets that lead their authors to realize that food animals experience equitable forms of affection. The following two conversion narratives illustrate how individuals experience this moment of awareness:

> I also vividly remember the day my grandmother brought a chicken to the house. Innocently, I believed he was going to be a pet but, when he grew older and stronger, he was served to us for lunch. . . . In my mind, I was unable to associate this *living creature* that spent lots of time with me with the dish that was served on the table.[62]

> I realized meat was a living, breathing creature when I was five. I had been given a lamb as a pet. I named her Cinderella and she was my love. One day, when she was grown, I couldn't find her at all. I don't know what they told me, but when I was served my dinner I knew it was Cinderella. Of course, I didn't eat it and to this day I've never eaten *anyone*.[63]

In both examples, the narrators show food animals the type of affection that is usually set aside for companion animals like dogs and cats. By doing so, the narrators suggest that food animals are as worthy as pets of the affection they receive.

However, being worthy of receiving affection is not as strong a rhetoric as positioning animals as agents of affection. In her "story of becoming," unlikely vegetarian Elizabeth Ferrari details the internal rhetorics—brought about by human-animal interaction that challenged the ideologies she internalized as the child of a meat-producer—that caused her to reconsider animals as food:

> My father owned a 'meat packing plant.' . . . Always having 'pets' in my life, I began to wonder how I could eat animals and then choose to live with others. What made the ones I lived with more special than the ones I was eating? As I went through life, I continued to have more creatures live in my home. I think the idea that when you live with them [*sic*], you see a completely different creature than the ones that are killed for food. This is not because there is a difference, but because they are living in close quarters with you and you come to see that they have the same sentient feelings as we humans. They have *their own language*, and they are *intelligent enough that they can understand what we say*. They understand our feelings and when we are happy or sad. They love unconditionally. . . . I think everyone has to come to that place where they begin to feel these creatures' pain . . . to make the connection. Without this, I can't imagine that people will give up eating meat.[64]

Ferrari's narrative exposes the reason that so many "stories of becoming" involve human-animal interactions in which animals are represented as possessing rhetorical subjectivity. Such interactions facilitate internal deliberations capable of exposing meat-eating as a choice rather than a reality, one that, despite social sanctioning, also happens to be unethical. In her narrative, Ferrari also argues for animal subjectivity by suggesting that these creatures are cognate in that "they have their own language, and they are intelligent enough that they can understand what we say." Such framing is crucial for countering the popular philosophical and cultural argument that sentience is required for ethical consideration.

Sentience, and language as its determining gesture, have traditionally been demarcated as human traits and justification for the "othering" of animals. Even Nienkamp, quoting nineteenth-century rhetorician Richard Whately here, uses language as an indicator of rhetorical agency: "the most important function of language for human beings (as opposed to 'Brutes') is 'as an *instrument of thought*—a system of General-Signs, without which the Reasoning-process could not be conducted.'"[65] By framing internal rhetorics as internalized social voices, conversations, inner dialogues, and self-talk, in addition to framing the study of rhetoric in general as analyzing "the rhetorical *function* of all language," Nienkamp bars nonhuman animals from the domain of rhetoric. Arguments to the contrary have been unconvincing, so much so that Bentham's premise, "But can they Suffer," is lauded by animal rights activists as circumventing this bothersome affront.[66] Even Peter Singer, widely recognized as the father of the U.S. animal rights movement, grounds his argument in *Animal Liberation* in Bentham's utilitarian rhetoric.[67] It follows, then, that narratives imbuing animals with language have the most potential to cast them as rhetorical agents.

However, as was previously mentioned, such arguments are difficult. They appear most often as exaggerations that infiltrate internal rhetorics through humor. Dana Lyons's song "Cows with Guns," later adapted into cartoon form for the book of the same name and currently available as a YouTube animated short, TotallyTom's award-winning animated short *MadCow*, and the animated Web-based video series *The Meatrix*, are among the most popular exaggerations. In "Cows with Guns," Lyons tells the tale of Cow-Tse-Tongue, a revolutionary "veal" who studies Che Guevara and leads a nearly ill-fated revolt on the way to the slaughterhouse, only to be rescued in the last possible moment when, "*the order was given to turn cows to whoppers / enforced by the might of ten thousand coppers / but on the horizon / surrounding the shoppers / came the deafening roar of chickens in choppers.*"[68] Their battle call, repeated again and again as the chorus, is "we will fight for bovine freedom and hold our large heads high. We will run free with the buffalo or die.[69] Throughout, Lyons suggests that cows share many basic desires and needs with humans, including abilities to read, reason, and inspire.

They can also get angry. Tom McKeon, a Web animator and filmmaker known as "TotallyTom," made use of this in his animated short *Mad Cow*. Less than two minutes long, this short is a rant addressed at humans and orated by a very, very mad cow:

Fuck you and the horse you rode in on! Yeah, that's right. I said, FUCK YOU. You stupid hairless monkey, Mr. Opposable Thumbs. What do you think, a cow's place is just stand in the field, eat fucking grass, get rained on, and wait for the pneumatic hammer? Hmm? HMM? We are supposed to just sit around in silent anguish as farmers all over the world play with our wives' tits and milk them dry? THAT MILK IS FOR MY BABY, YOU ASSHOLE! What would you do if I came over to your bedroom every morning, stuck a vacuum hose on your wife's nipples and turned the Hoover on? Hmm? HMM? What then? Yeah, well, you'd have my ass cut into steaks so fast, you couldn't even choke out the words "pass the A1" before I was sizzlin' and on your plate! Yeah, I'm mad! I'm the maddest fucking cow you've ever seen, you ten toed freak! You have fucked with the wrong bovine, my friend. You know that milk you had on your cereal this morning? I pissed in it! PASTEURIZE THAT, BITCH! I'm not even going to tell you what I did to the sour cream.[70]

A result of what he considers *inhumane*—and therefore inappropriate—treatment, the mad cow's anger sponsors his parrhesiastic outburst. He is aware that his audience has the power to turn him "into steak." Nonetheless, he speaks truth to power in the face of death and, in doing so, is courageous.

The Meatrix also ascribes animals' agency through personification by representing them as not only capable of, but also prone to, acts of courage. Its purpose is to dissolve the boundary between animal and human like the film *The Matrix* did with the boundary between human and machine.[71] In the original *Meatrix*, the most widely distributed animated short of the series (which now includes *The Meatrix*, *The Meatrix II*, and *The Meatrix II½*), Leo, a pig who lives his life on a small family farm, is approached by Moopheus, a black trench coat–clad cow in dark glasses who offers Leo the chance to see the truth by taking the "red pill" or staying ignorant by taking the "blue pill," not unlike their counterparts in *The Matrix*.[72] According to Moopheus, the Meatrix is "the story we tell ourselves about where our meat and animal products come from." Leo, who opts for the red pill, is then transplanted into a factory farm hog containment facility and educated about the "truth behind our food." After seeing "the truth," Leo joins the resistance as familiar music and special effects evoke the storyline of the original film and the righteousness of its resistance.[73] Following the animated short, viewers are offered numerous links with more information about the harmful effects of factory farming, including animal cruelty, antibiotic resistant germs, massive pollution, and destroyed communities.

By channeling a film that interrogates what it means to be human, a common theme that science fiction aficionados accept, *The Meatrix* appeals to an audience that is already prepared to be flexible with the perimeters around agency, whether this agency takes the form of Hal, the manipulative computer from *2001: A Space Odyssey*; Six, the seductive cylon from *Battlestar Galactica*; or Moopheus, the Laurence Fishburne of livestock. In the case of *The Meatrix*, Leo's decision to learn and help others learn the truth serves as a model for humans who speak out on behalf of "others." It is possible, then, to argue that Leo is framed as a *parrhesiastes* by movement participants and advocates as a means of sponsoring similar acts of courage in the humans that follow his story.

These anthropomorphic accounts, though humorous, can work with other narratives that represent animals as compassionate, affectionate, aggravated, and capable of suffering to cement animal agency as a construct of internal rhetorics. Once the possibility of animal agency is entertained by the internal rhetorics of the heterogeneous human psyche, they have no choice but to acknowledge this possibility and negotiate its significance. And while animal rhetorics are neither solely responsible for an individual's conversion to ethical vegetarianism (since they are always filtered through the intersection of personal experience and socialization), nor do they guarantee adjustments of any kind to an individual's beliefs or actions for the same reason, they evidence the complex processes through which individuals persuade themselves.

These processes, characterized by the effects they have on identity, illuminate how individuals become *parrhesiastes* and, in doing so, agents of personal and socio-cultural change.

IMPLICATIONS FOR SOCIAL CHANGE

By examining the epistemological and ethical functions of internal rhetorics as they occur in particular situations, rhetoricians can theorize the ways in which individuals 1) internalize social norms, 2) integrate ideology with reason and emotion, 3) situate self in and differentiate self from the collective, and in doing so, 4) challenge and adjust dominant social norms. By explicating ethical vegetarianism/veganism as a case study of the process and affect of internal rhetorics, as well as the ideological imprints that manifest through embodied rhetorics, I have described how rhetorical selfhood emerges through processes of identification. Personal and social change results from rhetors' abilities to justify their perspectives by framing them in language and experience that their audience accepts, sponsoring internal deliberations between the different faculties of the self, and creating situations that demand compassion, empathy, affection, identification, and advocacy. Because an individual can, as Nienkamp suggests, "either mold her behavior to fit [social] norms or, as Burke has suggested earlier, rationalize behavior that does not quite meet the external standard," she holds within her the key to social reform as well as the agency to unlock it.[74] Internal rhetorics of EVV, then, perform within and encourage parrhesiastic self-disclosure by individuals who position morality as an offspring of truth and who establish an ethos of self-worth by embodying their ethics.

An ethos capable of socio-epistemo-ethical restructuring, however, is forged in the fire of fear, in moments when claiming an unpopular identity is an act of courage in a cultural climate where the political is personal and the personal is punishable. As rhetoricians, we spend most of our time studying collectivities as the perpetrators and recipients of the "infinitely ramifying characteristics of discourse" in an epoch when rhetoric is "the condition of our existence."[75] By exposing the auto-rhetorical elements of conversion and identification within the EVV movement, I have offered an explanation for the process through which animals become rhetors, one in which animals are imbued with rhetorical agency by humans. Whether this happens subconsciously, as a catalyst for restructuring personal ethics in contrast to social norms, or consciously, as intentional movement rhetoric produced to catalyze the former, it is born of the very human desire to influence the cultural and moral contexts in which we all live—human and animal alike.

However, as the above analysis illustrates, there is much to be learned beyond the ethical vegetarian/vegan movement by studying internal rhetorics as vehicles for self-persuasion and necessary ingredients in embodied ethos. If the rhetorics we use on ourselves are indeed both epistemological and ideological in nature, as I have argued here, these rhetorics have implications for any study of *identity as an act of persuasion*. This includes the study of publics and counterpublics as well as their more aggressive cousins, social movements—both self-directed and other-directed. It also has implications for studies of performance and religion, academics and activism, and community engagement and globalization. In essence, the study of internal and embodied rhetorics is the study of identity—how it forms and how it fights. As such, it places all of our theorizing about aspects of self-in-community squarely within the confines of rhetoric and rhetoric within the confines of self.

Part Two

CRITIQUES OF
ANIMAL ETHICS RHETORIC

Chapter Five

I'm Too Sexy for Your Movement

An Analysis of the Failure of the Animal Rights Movement to Promote Vegetarianism

Laura K. Hahn

Invented by the New York Radical Women, the phrase "the personal is political" emerged as the rallying cry of the Second Wave women's movement in the 1960s. Feminist poet and essayist Katha Pollitt explains,

> The personal is political was a way of saying that what looked like individual experiences with little social resonance and certainly no political importance— rape, sexual harassment, you doing the vacuuming while your husband reads the paper—were all part of a general pattern of male dominance and female subordination.[1]

The solution was to be found in political action—feminism.[2] If we extend this logic to everyday personal practices, such as eating, we could argue that what we eat—or do not eat—is also a political statement. For example, the practice of "eating organic" offers consumers the luxury of affirming, seeing, and tasting the politics of their plate. As Michael Pollan, author of *The Omnivore's Dilemma* and *In Defense of Food*, explains, in the beginning "organic's rejection of agricultural chemicals was also a rejection of the war machine" as the same companies that made pesticides also manufactured napalm used in the war in Vietnam. Thus, "eating organic . . . married the personal to the political."[3]

A vegetarian lifestyle arguably offers the same gratification of seeing (or not seeing, as in the absence of animal products) people's politics on their plates, feet (vegan shoes), or in the bathroom (cruelty-free bath products). Yet, despite recent trends, and in particular increasing empathy toward animals, the personal politics of vegetarian lifestyles have not found a broader place in the public politic surrounding food. Even with the dramatic rise in natural food stores and vegetarian foods (veggie burgers, veggie dogs,

Tofurky), which makes shopping for a vegetarian diet easier than ever, the question remains, why haven't more people adopted this diet, and more importantly this perspective?

As the chapters in this volume attest, the goals and interests of the animal rights movement are vast. From hunting, to animals held in captivity, to animal experimentation, to becoming ingredients for shampoo, animal rights activists advocate on many fronts to cease the use of nonhuman animals. However, the use of animals for food comprises 97 percent of animal deaths caused by humans.[4] Thus, this is an apt moment to examine the culinary and nutritional landscape to ascertain reasons why vegetarianism has failed to become a mainstream dietary choice. Why has the animal rights movement failed to promote vegetarianism as other 1960s advocacy movements successfully forwarded environmentalism, feminism, and organic foods? How has the animal rights movement failed to integrate its ideological underpinnings with the larger discussion—or obsession—that Americans have with their relationship to food? This essay examines the rhetoric of the animal rights movement, as exemplified by People for the Ethical Treatment of Animals (PETA), to uncover its failures in promoting vegetarianism.

Although there have been a few legislative improvements in conditions for farm animals, there has been very little change in "farming" practices. In 2008 California voters passed Proposition 2, a new state statute that prohibits the confinement of animals on factory farms. In 2006 voters in Arizona passed Proposition 204, which prohibited calf and pig confinement crates. While *New York Times* editorialist Nicholas Kristoff cites these recent ballot victories as evidence that "animal rights are now firmly on the mainstream ethical agenda," evidence suggests otherwise.[5] These ballot initiatives certainly represent a few, literal steps for animals in that they can now turn around in their cages, but ultimately they reaffirm a welfare, as opposed to a rights, position.

The rights and welfare positions are the two major divisions among the larger animal protection movement that encompasses "all efforts to prevent cruelty, improve humane treatment, reduce stress and strain, and monitor research with animals."[6] The differences between the rights and welfare positions include those of strategy, philosophy, and goals.

Supporters of a welfare position believe in and work toward the elimination of animal cruelty, while maintaining that humans have the right to humanely use nonhuman animals for research, entertainment, consumer goods, and food. From this view, nonhuman animals should be free from unnecessary pain and suffering, but they should not be granted rights. Strategies of welfare groups include education and legal reform. Countering that view, the animal rights position claims that humans do not have the right to use nonhuman animals regardless of how well they are treated, because animals are sentient beings they have inherent value and the right not to be used by humans. Strategies of this arm of the movement extend beyond education and outreach to include large media campaigns, direct action, and in a tiny minority of cases, the liberation of animals from factories, laboratories, and puppy mills.

The distinctions between the welfare and rights movements are highlighted by understanding their rhetoric. The former is content to work within the status quo; the latter claims to promote a radical agenda (but as we shall see, it does not). The former "occurs when the agitators accept the value system of the establishment but dispute the benefits or power within that value system."[7] Radical deviance, the kind that PETA claims it partakes in, "occurs when the agitators dispute the value system itself and seek to change it or replace it with a competing value system."[8] So, the welfarist accepts that animals will continue to be used as food, but wants them in comfortable cages (as seen in the passage of Proposition 2). The animal rightist disputes the use of animals in any form and instead adopts a vegan diet. The popular PETA slogan, "animals are not ours to eat, wear or experiment on" exemplifies this position. However, PETA's campaigns do not promote this position; rather, their messages reify the status quo.

For the purpose of this essay, I examine animal rights texts, particularly those created by PETA, that exemplify how this supposedly radical arm of the animal protection movement has failed to advance a vegetarian agenda. They have distracted audiences' attention away from the vegetarian message in favor of titillation, challenges to commercial hypocrisies, and by accepting and reifying the status quo like their animal welfare cousins. To situate this argument in context, I first describe and contrast the current vegetarian population alongside the increase in meat consumption and the recent growth of natural food stores in the United States. Next I look at animal rights slogans, two animal rights publications, *Vegetarian Times* and *VegNews*, and three recent PETA commercials. Descriptions of these texts are followed by a discussion of the rhetorical significance of these messages (again focusing on PETA campaigns) for the animal rights agenda as it applies to promoting vegetarianism.

VEGETARIANISM AND MEAT CONSUMPTION

Summarizing a variety of surveys about the vegetarian population, sociologist Donna Maurer argues there has been little increase in the U.S. vegetarian population in the last three decades.[9] According to the Humane Research Council (HRC), as of 2008 there are between 2.8 and 3.6 million adult vegetarians in the United States. The Harris Interactive Service Bureau shows only 3.2 percent, or 7.3 million U.S. adults follow a vegetarian diet.[10] HRC's executive director Che Green explains, as "one to three percent of the entire population, vegans and vegetarians are a blip on the demographic radar. Statistically speaking, we're below the margin of error for most surveys."[11] The majority of vegetarians are white, educated, female, middle class, and young: 59 percent are female, 41 percent are male, 42 percent are between 18 and 34 years old, 40.6 percent are between 35 to 54, and 17.4 percent are over 55.[12] For those who follow a vegetarian lifestyle, 57.1 percent have followed it for more than 10 years, 18 percent for 5 to 10 years, 10.8 percent for 2 to 5 years, and 14.1 percent for less than 2 years.[13] Those small numbers at the bottom end of the time scale indicate either very slow growth or no growth in vegetarianism at all.

Typically people eat a vegetarian diet for one of two reasons: health concerns and ethical issues.[14] Motivation matters when it comes to the question of how likely people stick to the diet. A vegetarian motivated by health reasons is less likely to adhere to the diet and more likely to succumb to social pressures to eat meat, make "exceptions" for special events or holidays, or give up the vegetarian diet for other kinds of health-related diets. A vegetarian who is motivated by ethical concerns is more likely to stick to the diet and feel something akin to being a force for a "greater good." These people are also more likely to become vegans and participate in other animal rights actions.[15]

While some may select a vegetarian diet for economic reasons, Maurer explains that people of fewer economic means rarely become vegetarians by choice. Because "the capacity to purchase unlimited quantities of meat is associated with higher socioeconomic status," if one's financial situation improves they generally increase their food spending on meat.[16] In essence "[p]eople from lower income groups rarely become vegetarians before they acquire the capacity to purchase all of the meat (i.e., status) they want" as meat consumption elevates one's standing on the ladder of socioeconomic success.[17]

Looking at the relationship between diet and self-concept among vegetarians in the middle class, in 1981 sociologists Kurt Back and Margaret Glasgow found that food choices reveal distinct identities. According to the sociologists, "vegetarians define themselves negatively and create strong boundaries against the general society."[18] As we will see, this identity formation is no longer so strongly bounded thirty years later. Vegetarians, as part of the middle class, have less interest and motivation than those from lower socioeconomic groups "in holding onto meat's generally accepted status as a representation of power, prestige and strength."[19] If status can be demonstrated in one's professional and social lives, then perhaps there is no need to assert it on the plate. For those of the middle and upper-middle classes, the individual choice of a vegetarian diet could be a strategy to "differentiate themselves from other social groups."[20] With the plethora of choices about food and diet, "modern people in rich societies have reached a stage of satiety, of exhaustion with 'choice,' that sometimes makes them want to have something they can reject."[21] Vegetarian diets provide an easy, clear-cut set of boundaries about what not to eat. Yet, as I will discuss later, if the practice of eating a vegetarian diet remains in the private sphere, as a lifestyle choice, rather than expressed as a public and political position, then the movement's growth is limited. A public presence is needed to encourage others to become vegetarians, provide a sense of collective identity, and encourage business owners to cater to the vegetarian population.

Arguably, food often helps consumers project an identity and social location as it offers two strategies for communication: solidarity and separation.[22] Food solidifies by bringing people together in a common activity: eating. The global popularity of restaurants, cafés, and bars all attest to the fact that we like to eat and drink with others. Secondly, food separates by marking our individual or group identity (ethnicity, religion, class, gender) depending on what restaurants we frequent and what foods we purchase. Thus many vegetarians "use diet as a form of self expression and creativity."[23] Moreover, food can simultaneously be used to solidify and separate. Jews, for example, may eat kosher food as a way of linking them with historical traditions and peoples while separating themselves from non-Jewish peoples. Similarly, in solidarity with nonhuman animals, vegetarians may separate themselves from the carnivores at the table.

In addition to the cultural, class, and sensory reasons for eating meat, also understandable is that in many parts of the country meat is one of few readily available protein sources. Yet with the influx of natural food stores, vegetarian foods are now readily available even in most rural areas. Since the once counterculture ideals of organic eating and environmentalism have been incorporated into current mainstream practices (e.g., Whole Foods Supermarkets, organic sections in major supermarket chains, recycled cups at Starbucks, and so on) these philosophies and these practices have gone mainstream. At present, the market for organic products is growing at 17–20 percent per year and is now the fastest growing segment of the American food marketplace.[24] By comparison, the conventional food market is growing at 2–3 percent per year.[25] The ultimate rise in popularity and sales of organic food has depended on retail outlets willing to introduce, market, advertise, and deliver the products to a broad consumer base that extended well beyond the counterculture. In 1980 there were only 6 natural food stores in the United

States In 2003, organic foods were sold in 20,000 natural food stores and 73 percent of conventional grocery stores.[26]

Despite the options, the vegetarian population has remained stagnant, and Americans are eating more meat than at any other time in history.[27] In 1957 the average person ate 141 pounds of meat per year, with that number increasing over the past half-century: 165 pounds in 1967, 175.9 pounds in 1977, 179.08 pounds in 1987, 182.24 pounds in 1997, and 196.47 pounds in 2007. For the animals, this translates into over 10 billion deaths in 2003, up from 5 billion in 1980 and 1 billion in 1940.[28]

Looking at the rise of meat consumption alongside the stable numbers of vegetarians, Erik Marcus concludes the modern animal protection movement, the overarching movement that includes animal welfare, animal rights, animal liberation, and animal abolition efforts, has failed in its three most important tasks: "increasing the percentage of Americans who are vegetarians or vegan, encouraging nonvegetarians to reduce their consumption of meat, diary products, and eggs; [and] diminishing the suffering of farm animals."[29] This failure of vegetarianism to prosper alongside the rapid growth and availability of natural food stores (where vegetarian options are readily available) is puzzling.

WHY NOT VEGETARIANISM: A RHETORICAL ANALYSIS

The major media appeals of the vegetarian arm of the animal rights movement have been twofold: cruelty and sex.[30] Images of cruelty displayed on posters, T-shirts, and videos include the beating of a nonhuman animal over the head, crowded cages, and dismembered bodies. The second major campaign strategy, largely orchestrated by the leading animal rights organization—PeTA—is that of the sexy vegetarian. The focus of my analysis examines the sexy vegetarian, which includes stereotypically "hot" celebrities such as *Playboy* models engaging in titillating acts, often with vegetables.

Given that women still do the bulk of the grocery shopping, it follows that women should be the target audience for vegetarian campaigns.[31] Yet, because the images of the "sexy vegetarian" are constructed from the male gaze, as we shall see, and because such images are "an invitation for women to consider their own appearances in comparison to the protester rather than an opportunity to reflect on the plight of animals," the female consumer becomes an object without agency in the animal rights campaigns.[32] If viewers are to make the logical leap that eating vegetarian will help them lose weight and look like these women, then that health information, alongside the ethical appeal, needs to be an explicit part of the argument, rather than an implicit plea.[33] But the messages coming out of animal rights organizations and ethical consumer groups appear to be designed for an entirely different purpose.

Filling the rhetorical function of solidification—uniting followers "to create a sense of community that may be vital to the success of the movement"—slogans, T-shirts, and bumper stickers are sites of expression for the sexy vegetarian.[34] Perhaps the most famous effort to tie vegetarianism to sex while creating a positive identity was the bumper sticker: "Vegetarians Taste Better." On PETA's CafePress website one can still order merchandise that reads, "Vegetarians Make Better Lovers" or "I am too Sexy to be Cruel to Animals." Often, however, the message is not about that 97 percent of animal cruelty that occurs in the form of meat-eating, but rather much smaller elements of the animal rights problem. From AnimalRightsStuff.com, for example, one can obtain buttons that read, "Real Women Fake It" printed over a leopard fur graphic. Also for sale are women's T-shirts such as "Nice Girls Fake It" (printed in large text across the chest) followed by "Real fur hurts animals" (printed in a smaller font). Another proclaims, "Whips and Chains belong in the Bedroom" (in large text across the chest) followed by "not the circus. Boycott Ringling Brothers" (in a smaller font).

Marketing to teens and college students, the website peta2, takes a similar approach. It claims to be "the largest youth animal rights group in the world—maybe even the universe."[35] A women's T-shirt that is for sale from the site reads, "Breasts Not Animal Tests." The product description explains, "You probably already know that peta2 loves animals. But did you know that we also love boobies?"[36] The slogan refers to the use of nonhuman animals killed in the name of breast cancer research. All of the sexy vegetarian slogans are printed on women's T-shirts only: there are no sexy messages on men's T-shirts. The styles and sizing of the women's and men's shirts also lend to a sexy stylizing of the female versus the male body. The men's shirts, for example, come in one style, usually referred to as "unisex."[37] Distracting attention from advocacy for vegetarianism, the messages on the women's T-shirts advocate for the 3 percent of animals that are killed and tortured for fur and vivisection, while they promote sexiness in a manner that has the potential to provoke a feminist backlash. Through the slogans and T-shirts the agency of the woman wearing them is reduced to her corporeal appeal; her body (like those of the nonhuman animals) becomes a site for exploitation.

The sexy vegetarian message is also evident in the discourse and images of the two leading vegetarian magazines, *VegNews* and *Vegetarian Times*. Though the magazines are supposed to be about not eating meat, advertisements and articles are often about anything but vegetarianism. An ad for the Vegan Green canvas bag, for example, "celebrates the woman promoting a luxurious healthy lifestyle while insuring a sustainable future. From soul sisters to rock goddess, via pop queens and indie chicks, they can confidently wear it!" The copy is placed alongside the image of a very tall, long-legged, high-heeled, skimpy-bathing-suit-wearing blond model. An ad on the following page for "Stinky Hippie Body Wash" reminds us of the impetus for the sexy image: who wants to be the stinky hippie? Made possible by the Scrub Your Butt Soap Company, the ad copy proclaims, "Everybody Knows One!" The graphic of the female hippie is complete with hairy armpits that produce a presumably stinky odor. In an ad for TheSensualVegan.com, readers learn that their sex life can be vegan through the acquisition of vegan condoms, dildos, and personal lubricants. Again, these messages do not promote protecting the 97 percent of animals that are killed for meat consumption and focus instead on titillating rather than awakening a consciousness about animal rights.

Three definitive examples of the sexy vegetarian strategy are the PETA TV videos, "Veggie Love" (the banned 2009 Super Bowl Ad), "Tofu Wrestling," and the most recent, "Cruelty Doesn't Fly." According to PETA, in "Cruelty Doesn't Fly," Pamela Anderson "stars as a no-nonsense fashion cop who strips travelers of their fashion faux pas—animal skins! Pamela's fashion cop wardrobe, by top celebrity stylist Cannon, consists of knee-high boots, skimpy *Chips*-esque shorts, and a jeweled baton—and, of course, it's 100 percent cruelty-free."[38] Of course the advertisement is also 100 percent not about vegetarianism. Once again it merely serves to titillate, provoke, and distract.

PETA did begin to emphasize the vegetarian message in the television and YouTube commercial titled "Tofu Wrestling" during which *Playboy* model Kira Eggars (wearing a white thong) wrestles PETA's Kayla Rae Worden (in a blue bikini) in a pool of liquid tofu located on a busy urban street. The copy reads, "Their Battle? A fight for the lives of billions of animals killed for food each year." As the women roll around in the tofu, various facts are displayed, such as "Fact 2: Eating tofu is much sexier than eating the corpse of a dead cow."[39] At the end of the commercial the sexy wrestling is replaced with images of animals being slaughtered. The "Veggie Love" video was banned from airing during the 2009 Super Bowl game because it "depicts a level of sexuality exceeding [NBC] standards" including "rubbing pelvic region with pumpkin" and a woman "screwing herself with broccoli."[40] PETA's "Veggie Love" asserts vegetables are not only sexy, but that one can have sex with them. Set in an upscale residential home with female models clad akin to Victoria's Secret archetypes, the women in "Veggie Love" crawl across the floor to lick a pumpkin and rub asparagus across their bodies. The text reads, "Studies Show Vegetarians Have Better Sex. Go Veg." But the message does not appear to be having any effect. Given that the number of vegetarians in the United States has not grown and that the campaigns described above are the most visible of the animal rights messages, these commercials beg for rhetorical criticism and an explanation for why they are not changing attitudes about meat consumption.

While the sexy videos, slogans, and T-shirts may be effective in creating interest and media attention, they fail to create a persuasive argument to become vegetarian. Indeed, most of the messages are not even about vegetarianism, and in the case of "Tofu Wrestling" the tofu is irrelevant; the women could be wrestling in anything, and it would still be interpreted as sexy. The tofu does not add to or create the sexual appeal; in fact, if you did not know it was tofu it would be impossible to identify the substance in which they're wrestling. Moreover, does one want to eat something in which nearly naked people have been wrestling? The use of the tofu in the wrestling match further reifies tofu as "other" food. Perhaps it has moved from being "hippie food" to dirty food, but it is still far from mainstream.

As most people do not look like *Playboy* models and celebrities, these sexual images also create a lack of identification or connection for the viewer. Models present an unattainable body type, thus, associating them with tofu and eating a vegetarian diet suggests that these behaviors are also unattainable. According to Beth Eck, when women see female nudity the images are "objects to be studied, viewed, judged, and, above all, used as a comparison for the self."[41] Therefore, when women see *Playboy* models wrestling in tofu and think, "I'll never look like that," or "I hate my thighs[;] I have to get to the gym," it is the negative self-image that is associated with the protest; not the message of compassion for animals that PETA wishes to convey. When read this way, these images function to actually turn people away from the vegetarian lifestyle by making it appear as unattainable as the body and sexual images presented.

The "Cruelty Doesn't Fly" video is particularly damaging to the vegetarian message. Besides not being about meat consumption, in this commercial Anderson enjoys the gaze; taunting and provoking it, and appearing to understand its power. In the tradition of culture jamming, which is defined as "a variety of interesting communication strategies that play with the branded images and icons of consumer culture to make consumers aware of surrounding problems and diverse cultural experiences that warrant their attention," Anderson makes the most of her iconic status.[42] She moves and looks at the camera/viewer in seeming awareness that she has earned fame and fortune through her ability to attract the institutionalized male gaze and is now using her power to subvert it. She appears as no victim, but the heroine in control of what has become an international site for struggle about identity, security, and nationalism: the airport security checkpoint. "Security" in this context is reframed from "freedom from terrorist attacks" to "freeing animals from a life of suffering, cruelty, and exploitation." Yet the viewer never sees the animals being freed, only the outcome of their captivity—the animals' products. Visually this commercial reduces Anderson and animals into their parts, which may be read as an implied acceptance that this is the outcome of our use of animals *and* women. While reifying the male gaze and celebrating commerce, the advertisement actually contradicts the vegetarian message by maintaining the status quo.

Even the "Veggie Love" advertisement supports the status quo. One of the strategies used to reframe commonly held meanings in a culture is by showing the establishment and the status quo to be hypocritical. A frame in this sense is a collection of events, perceptions, understandings, and knowledges that work together to influence interpretation.[43] To suggest the establishment is hypocritical, as the rhetorical critic Robert L. Scott explains, social movements can employ "the use of language patterns commonly designated as obscene [which] helps intensify the charge that the dominant society is hypocritical."[44] Specifically, "nothing better reveals the fundamental corruptness of the dominant social values and the depth of the hypocrisy of the system than the use of the word 'fuck.'"[45] If we replace "language patterns" with "image patterns" and the suggestion of fucking rather than the word "fuck," the hypocrisy of the establishment becomes clear in the case of "Veggie Love." The entire video is about fucking from the images to the explicit copy, "Vegetarians have better sex." Thus this advertisement also fails to persuade viewers to "go veg."

"Veggie Love" is not any more sexually explicit or suggestive than a commercial for Victoria's Secret lingerie or the series of Burger King ads for the "Long Chicken" and the "BK Super 7 Incher." One poster for the Super 7 Incher reads, for example, "It'll BLOW your mind away" in large type followed by the description: "Fill your desire for something long, juicy and flame-grilled with the NEW BK SUPER SEVEN INCHER. Yearn for more after you taste the mind-blowing burger that comes with a single beef patty, topped with American cheese, crispy onions and the A.1. Thick & Hearty Steak Sauce." Cultural critic Tanner Stransky, in examining the ad, describes how a young woman with full, red lips that are wide open is, "about to go down on said Super Seven Incher."[46] It is no accident that this advertisement plays on the double meaning of "meat," the denotative meaning referring to animal flesh and the colloquial meaning referring to male genitalia.

Subway's "Five Dollar Footlong" commercial plays on this double meaning as well. Against the jingle "Five Dollar Footlong," various actors gesture "stop" and then hold their hands parallel, indicating a measurement of 12 inches. In one sequence, a Godzilla-esque monster lumbers through a city, frightening a Japanese woman, who shakes her head as if to say "no, it's too big." Next, Godzilla aggressively asserts the footlong hand gesture. The mixture of fear, paired with the double entendre of "meat" as food and male genitalia, suggests sexual violence is about to take place. Here, as feminist author Carol J. Adams asserts, "sexual violence and meat eating, which appear to be discrete forms of violence, find a point of intersection."[47] Just as the "meat" on the footlong Subway sandwich is about to be consumed, so is the Japanese woman in the commercial. Although sexually suggestive with overtones of sexual violence, this commercial was not deemed inappropriate by television network standards and has received considerable airtime.

When ads so similar in form and content are given such unequal opportunity for media penetration—unlike the PETA commercial, the Burger King and Subway advertisements were not banned—what is suggested is a set of hypocritical standards and values. By making outlandish videos that have no realistic chance of being aired on television, PETA exposes the hypocrisy of the establishment. As "[d]enouncing the hypocrisy is an obvious means of justifying a sense of unjust domination and of making common cause with others," whether intentionally or not, PETA distracts from the message and may cause viewers to think instead about how its message is treated compared to those similarly explicit, yet mainstream images that dominate the cultural landscape.[48] As Robert S. Cathcart argues, "Confrontational rhetoric shouts "Stop!" at the system, saying "You cannot go on assuming you are the true and correct order; you must see yourself as the evil thing you are."[49] Read this way, PETA either intentionally or accidentally elides the message of going vegetarian, and instead focuses the viewer's attention on the hypocritical culture in which we reside.

A second risk posed by these distractions is that viewers will not only fail to get the lesser message but also see PETA as offering yet another sexist portrayal of women.[50] In this case, PETA's rhetoric may be classified, according to Cathcart, as more managerial than confrontational. Managerial rhetoric is "designed to keep the existing system viable: they do not question underlying epistemology and group ethic."[51] Analyzed through a feminist lens, the women in the PETA videos and those wearing T-shirts with sexy slogans may be understood as objectified and commodified and thus detract from the message we might expect PETA to make. According to this reading, animal rights movements "produce a rhetoric that embraces the values of the system, accepts that the order has a code of control which must not be destroyed, while at the same time striving to gain acceptance of that which will perfect . . . the system."[52] When this occurs, the confrontational nature of the rhetoric gives way to the managerial, thus there appears to be consent and acceptance, rather than critique, of the system. PETA fails to change minds, because they are off-message when they titillate or challenge the media establishment through their campaign choices rather than staying focused on the goal of reducing cruelty to animals. Yet PETA succeeds in perpetuating PETA. As with all advocacy organizations, PETA faces the risk of extinction if they actually succeeded in their mission. Though less visible and less coherent, other animal rights organizations and groups also often distract attention away from the message of going vegetarian, while maintaining the status quo.

If nothing else, the sexy vegetarian campaign may aid the animal rights movement in solidifying, uniting, and motivating the already convinced. However, the campaigns fail to promulgate the messages, strategies, and tactics necessary to win additional social support for the animal rights agenda.[53] Offering what may be read as a sexist understanding of the videos, combined with the presentation of an unattainable body type, and by association, diet, the images and slogans fail to create identification with the movement. The videos and slogans confirm and reaffirm the values of current movement participants, as well as wider social norms about animal and women's bodies, but do little to motivate carnivores to become vegetarians.

VEGETARIANISM: A LIFESTYLE OR SOCIAL MOVEMENT?

PETA and the animal rights movement in general has hurt the cause of vegetarianism through poor messaging that distracts attention from the movement's purported goal. As a result, the entire movement is weakened, activism is discouraged, and what is left is fast becoming a marketing tool to a tiny segment of the population. In order to motivate Americans to reduce or eliminate the consumption of animal products, they must be confronted with questions of identity and lifestyle—what does a vegetarian life look like? How will my consumption patters reflect my political positions? Will the food I eat reflect my ethical beliefs? How do I explain this to my family and friends? Does my personal choice to eliminate animal products from my life mean I now must publicly advocate for animals? And who am I? I find, ultimately, that the promotion of lifestyle (as exemplified by the sexiness campaigns) over advocacy has diluted the vegetarian identity and political mission.

Author and food activist Sandor Katz reminds us of potentially the most persuasive of these questions: "vegetarianism is the original manifestation of food as activism." Yet, he complains, the current vegetarian movement is more akin to that of a social club than a political movement.[54] According to the North American Vegetarian Society, for example, World Vegetarian Day, "kicks off a month of parties, potluck, presentations, food tasting displays

. . . and lots of friendly discussions."[55] The movement has been reduced to discussion rather than activism and argumentation. A look at the two major U.S. vegetarian magazines, *VegNews* and *Vegetarian Times*, reveals this very lack of action. As Bob Torres, vegan author and activist, aptly puts it, *VegNews* is "veritable porn for this lifestyle."[56] As they self-describe on their website *VegNews* is the "premier magazine to focus on a vegetarian lifestyle" including lifestyle features such as "travel tales," "celebrity buzz," and the "hottest new vegetarian products."[57] While more culinarilly focused *Vegetarian Times* describes their purpose in similarly inactive terms:

> For over 30 years, *Vegetarian Times* has been at the forefront of the healthy living movement, providing delicious recipes, expert wellness information and environmentally sound lifestyle solutions to a wide variety of individuals. Our goal is to remain a trusted resource for our faithful readers and to reach out to the new generation of full-time vegetarians and flexitarians who find themselves increasingly drawn to the health-conscious, eco-friendly, "green" lifestyle we have always promoted.[58]

Incredibly, the editors of *Vegetarian Times* have failed to even mention meat or animals, falling back on the rhetoric of environmentalism instead. As explicitly stated, the purpose of both publications is to promote a lifestyle, rather than an activist agenda. Presumably, a lifestyle sells more products, thus generating advertising revenue, than a sociopolitical program. The message however is that being an eco-friendly vegetarian requires consuming new products (a primarily private act), and not publicly advocating for animals.

Thus, on the radically named website *GirlieGirl Army*, eco-vixen Chloe Jo Berman describes its purpose as anything but radical:

> GirlieGirl Army is your Glamazon Guide to Green Living; a call to arms for badass baby divas and head turning cougars, who want to save the planet from hacky sack and doom at the same time. Newbies, vegan vixens, the Mom next door, sexy emo boys, and anyone who wants to do their part without sacrificing their facials will heart our weekly newsletter and daily blog that give you tips on fashion, food, and fun—in the greenest way possible![59]

While there is some health information about a vegetarian diet on this website, most of the pages are devoted to cruelty-free fashion, makeup, and entertainment. Once again, commercial gratification of material desires of the (primarily female) body is employed as a pseudo strategy of political action while simultaneously weakening vegetarianism as an identity.

The label "vegetarian" has become diluted by commercial enterprises and poor messaging from organizations like PETA. This contributes to the lack of vegetarian food activism. Although 12 million adult Americans claim the label "vegetarian," the percentage of the population that follows an actual vegetarian diet is perhaps one third of the claimants.[60] Being a vegetarian has gone from a strict definition of not eating meat, fish, foul, or seafood to not eating *red* meat. And over time the term has become increasingly deprived of any political statement or specific action.[61] On one hand, the large number of claimants can be read optimistically because it illustrates that people want to live some form of the vegetarian lifestyle, and thus these claimants may become real vegetarians; yet, on the other hand, activists should be concerned that the term has lost any real meaning. If one doesn't know the meaning of "vegetarian," how can one foster vegetarian activism? The lack of meaning creates two significant problems for the movement: first, there is a lack of identification among vegetarians, and second, there are no longer clear boundaries about who is, and who is not.

Adding to the lack of vegetarian identity some business owners are purposely "deflecting attention away from a product's vegetarianness . . . to avoid the dreaded pitfall of 'veg-phobia.'"[62] Their rationale is that potential customers may be turned off from the label "vegetarian" or "vegan," assuming, for example, that a vegan cake will be less tasty than a dairy-filled one. Hiding the vegetarian or vegan nature of the product does little to advance the cause for mainstreaming vegetarian and vegan diets. Organic foods did not reach their current level of popularity by hiding their organic nature: the industry yelled it loud and proud on packages, fruits, and vegetables, and entire grocery store chains. One of the reasons that organic foods have done so well is that corporations have found them profitable. Vegetarianism, so far, has not been nearly as helpful to business' bottom lines. When PETA equates vegetarianism with sexist images of women, unsavory associations with tofu, and outlandish media spectacles, they fail to create a context appealing to business owners.

Calling for a "rhetoric revolution," Compassionate Cooks' founder Colleen Patrick-Goudreau wants us to "lay down our meat-dairy-egg-centric language and instead choose words that celebrate rather than belittle the plant-based foods of the world."[63] She argues that words such as "fake," "faux," "substitute," or "imitation" only serve to reinforce perceptions that vegetarian foods are "other," unappealing, and not real food. The food industry recognized this in 1973 when it succeeded in repealing the imitation rule. The rule, imposed by the 1938 Food, Drug and Cosmetic Act, said that an imitation food product had to be named such on the package. Pollan explains that, "slapping the word 'imitation' on a food product was the kiss of death—an admission of adulteration and inferiority."[64] Just as the food industry realized that "fake" and "imitation" food does not sell well, Patrick-Goudreau believes these labels do little for "mainstreaming the veg ethic" and instead reinforce the premier status of animal-based products as real food.[65]

Perhaps if PETA and other animal rights organizations spent more time redefining food, the number of vegetarians in the United States might grow. The basis for any movement has to be how it defines its terms in opposition to others. From here, rhetorical identification, strategies, tactics, and arguments follow.[66] Taking a lesson from feminist history, a similar pattern and concern has been raised about the term *feminism*. According to feminist scholar and activist bell hooks, a "central problem with feminist discourse has been our inability to either arrive at a consensus of opinion about what feminism is or accept definition(s) that could serve as points of unification. . . . Without agreed upon definition(s), we lack a sound foundation on which to construct theory or engage in overall meaningful praxis."[67] The power of unified definitions resides in the ability to name the struggle, foster community among activists, and shape campaign strategies. Just as an anything-goes definition of *feminism* fails to strengthen the women's movement, when "*flexitarians*" are considered vegetarians, it weakens the animal rights movement's ability to increase public support for the ideological position of ethical vegetarianism.

Similarly, the lack of meaning and political force behind twenty-first-century "vegetarianism" has resulted in what Kenneth Burke refers to as a lack of identification. As humans are "not motivated solely by principles of specialized activity . . . any specialized activity participates in a larger unit of action."[68] Identification, thus, "is a word for the anonymous activity's place in this wider context."[69] For a vegetarian, refraining from eating meat should not be *the* incentive; the activity should be motivated by a larger context (like animal rights). When the term vegetarianism loses meaning, it also loses its ability to create identification among supposedly similarly situated people for the very reason that they are not similarly situated. Thus, there is little shared sense of purpose or mission among raw foodists, vegans, vegetarians, lacto-ovo vegetarians, lacto-vegetarians, flexitarians, and so on.

Conversely, when a group is consubstantial, or in other words engages in identification, it develops a collective identity, the "shared definition of a group that derives from members' common interests, experiences, and solidarity."[70] The shared identification becomes the basis for shaping boundaries and actions for a social movement "so that collective self-transformation is itself a major strategy of political change."[71] Collective identity has three elements. First, "individuals see themselves as a part of a group when some shared characteristic becomes salient and is defined as important."[72] Second, the movement develops a consciousness or collective framework for understanding the self and relational and political networks. Finally, the concept of collective identity implies "direct opposition to the dominant order."[73] The combination of the three enables members to translate and form a bridge from personal identities to social and political realities. Keeping the identity centered on consumption, and lost in a maze of competing definitions, closes that bridge to a larger sociopolitical consciousness.

For the vegetarian movement a clearly agreed-upon and distinct definition of vegetarianism, its objects, and its objectives is crucial. Doing so would allow for greater participation so that individuals can see themselves as part of a larger group. Such solidarity would enable individuals and the larger movement to tackle meat-eating as a part of larger social, economic, political, and cultural contexts and establish clear boundaries and recognition of the opposition. Just as hooks explains that "defining feminism as a movement to end sexist oppression," (as opposed to a lifestyle choice) is "crucial for the development of theory because it is a starting point indicating the direction of exploration and analysis," so too is defining vegetarianism as a political movement to end exploitation of the nonhuman animals who are killed and the humans who must raise and slaughter them.[74] Confusing or substituting political action with purchasing cruelty-free products undermines the potential power of vegetarianism as a movement.

Moreover, keeping the vegetarian message in the closet as a strategy against "veg-phobia" does little to situate it as a mainstream consumer choice or as an issue of public policy debate. When PETA buries the message under primary arguments about sex and culture jamming, the message is positioned as something to be avoided, shunned, and shamed. In the context of the 'sexy vegetarian' campaign and Americans' puritanical attitudes about sex, the connotation again is that this is a bad, dirty practice with which one should not be associated. Practically, the decision to dilute the message from both a social movement and business perspective, which share the need to attract followers/customers, is odd. Given that both groups depend on large bases of support and are in competition with other movements and businesses, the choice to hide one's ideological or market niche is contradictory and counterproductive. The only reason for PETA to launch ineffective commercials, then, may be to maintain the support of the already-convinced. Corporations call this "brand loyalty." I call this bad activism.

In summary, the animal rights movement, as exemplified by PETA, is failing to increase the numbers of vegetarians in the United States. The public actions and videos, while successful in attracting attention and maintaining the support of brand loyalists, do little to foster identification among vegetarians or win over unconvinced viewers. This is illustrated by those commercials and magazines that emphasize vegetarianism as a lifestyle rather than a sociopolitical movement. The consequence of this lack of identification is a failure to capture an audience necessary to make change. To foster the consumer mainstreaming of vegetarian products, beliefs, and behavior, the movement, led inevitably by PETA, needs to create a climate and context wherein business owners and consumers do not experience "veg-phobia." Rather than orchestrating campaigns that isolate consumers or distract from the vegetarian message because these are sexist and reaffirm the status quo, the animal rights movement must create associations, definitions, and identifications that encourage audiences and consumers to think of themselves as members of an activist community.

Chapter Six

PETA and the Rhetoric of Nude Protest

Brett Lunceford

Public nudity as a form of protest has a long but rare history reaching back at least as far as Lady Godiva's storied ride.[1] Yet the amount of nudity in protest actions seems to have increased in recent years, and for some groups nudity itself has become the key focus. For example, Bare Witness, a group that spells out words such as "peace" and "no war" on the ground with their naked bodies, states that they are "using the power and beauty of our bodies to send out a message of peace."[2] World Naked Bike Ride claims to be the "world's largest naked protest against oil dependency and car culture in the history of humanity."[3] One woman in Greenwich Village protested the Iraq War by stripping naked to display "no war" and "stop the war," written on her body in red paint. She stated, "This is my only way to talk about my beliefs. It's a metaphor. When I am appearing naked, I have disarmed myself from any uniform because naked people, they never can make war."[4] In some cultures, public nudity is used as a shaming mechanism. In Nigeria, women "exposed their naked bodies, and most particularly their vaginas, to impose on oil company male dealers 'social death' through ostracization, which was widely believed to lead to actual demise."[5] In other words, these acts of public nudity were more than symbolic acts; rather, such acts can be seen as actual threats. These acts of public nudity are used as a last resort; community development scholars Terisa Turner and Leigh Brownhill note that in Africa "women who go naked implicitly state that they will get their demands met or die in the process of trying."[6] Whether functioning metaphorically or mystically, as in the case of the Nigerian women, the use of public nudity is a particularly interesting use of body rhetoric.

Some social movement organizations are incorporating nudity into their protest actions, and one organization that has made extensive use of this strategy is People for the Ethical Treatment of Animals (PETA). PETA has long been known for its provocative protest tactics, and some of these campaigns have resulted in backlashes. For example, its "Holocaust on Your Plate" campaign, in which PETA juxtaposed images from Nazi death camps with animal mistreatment or farming with captions such as "to animals, all people are Nazis," was denounced by the Jewish community and the Anti-Defamation League.[7] Their "I'd Rather go Naked than Wear Fur" campaign features nude—but strategically covered—models, musicians, and actresses. The latter campaign has caused controversy among feminists who question whether the pornographic undertones do more to harm women than to save animals.[8] Moreover, some scholars suggest that PETA's tactics may be counterproductive; legal scholar Maneesha Deckha argues that "attention to objectification is important not simply because it may harm women, but because it undermines the posthumanist project in general that PETA seeks to advance."[9] In spite of potential backlash, PETA has continued its relentless pursuit of media attention through titillating campaigns that are largely disseminated through the mass media, billboards, and advertisements.

PETA has incorporated nudity into its protest actions to the point where it seems to be an essential tactic in its repertoire of strategies. For example, it recently released a "State of the Union Undress" video that features a well-dressed young woman who engages in a striptease as she delivers her speech in front of an American flag. The speech is intercut with applause and footage from the congressional floor during an actual Presidential State of the Union address. In the speech she states, "We will use all legal means at our disposal in ways that will capture the public's imagination, spur debate about animal rights, and encourage people to set aside their busy schedules just for a moment to consider the staggering number of lives at stake. Often this will mean taking our clothes off."[10] As she continues to remove her clothing, she speaks about PETA's campaigns, such as those against KFC and furriers. She concludes her speech completely naked, stating, "In our tireless quest to save these animals from exploitation, we promise that we will work harder, we will shout louder, we will push further, and we will get nakeder than ever before."[11] The video then cuts to scenes of animal experimentation and factory farms.

It is clear that PETA has a strong affinity for using nudity in its protest activities and advertising. Although scholars have examined PETA's advertising campaigns, campaigns that involve activists performing staged public protest actions, such as PETA's "Running of the Nudes" during the running of the bulls in Pamplona, Spain or public displays of women chained or caged to protest the treatment of circus animals, have received little scholarly attention.[12] In these campaigns, PETA demonstrates its commitment to the promise to get "nakeder than ever before." This essay examines PETA's display of chained, shackled women and the Running of the Nudes to explore how public nudity functions rhetorically as a protest strategy. Although PETA's actions serve to attract media attention by providing media-friendly image events, my analysis suggests that these actions transcend mere shock value and spectacle. As critical theorist Guy Debord declares, "The spectacle is the acme of ideology."[13] Nude protest functions as a means for members of PETA to perform an ideology that equates humans and animals by providing a way for the protesters to become more animalistic by shedding their clothing and performing the animal role in the protest, e.g., playing the part of the bulls in the running of the bulls and the part of the caged animals in the circus. Moreover, these protests help to build cohesion and strengthen their collective identity by prescribing for PETA members the lengths to which they should go in defense of animal rights.

CHAINED WOMEN

One tactic that PETA uses to protest the treatment of animals is the public display of chained or caged women. These protests are often associated with the arrival of a circus. A *St. Louis Post-Dispatch* story describes one such street protest: "A few hours before the Ringling Bros. and Barnum & Bailey Circus opened a five-day run in St. Louis on Wednesday, a near-naked 18-year-old woman sat on a crowded downtown street corner, chains wrapped around her ankles, to protest what activists allege is the mistreatment of circus elephants. People stopped to stare and snap photos with cell phone cameras. It was 35 degrees in the sun, but a goose-bumped Amy Jannette said she'd sit there, 'For as long as I can.'"[14] But the final paragraphs of the article cast doubt on the efficacy of such a display, illustrating how revealing flesh can overshadow the message:

> On Wednesday, however, it was unclear how effective Jannette's protest was. Three men in dress shirts and ties walked by the near-naked woman and a large sign reading "Circus elephants: Shackled, lonely, beaten." Over lunch, they talked about what they had just seen. They wondered why she was out there.
> "You guys read the sign?" one of the men said.
> The other two just shook their heads.[15]

What must this tactic accomplish in order to be successful? After all, the news media covered the woman's protest and disseminated the message, even if those who were physically present ignored the message. Moreover, even if the message is ignored, these protest actions still seem to fulfill what rhetorician Richard Gregg refers to as the "ego function of the rhetoric of protest," in which "the primary appeal . . . is to the protestors themselves, who feel the need for psychological refurbishing and affirmation."[16] The woman can claim a moral victory as she demonstrates solidarity with the chained animals. She draws the attention of gawking onlookers with cell phone cameras and can reasonably believe that she is raising awareness of the plight of circus elephants. However, she asks nothing of the viewer. She functions not as argument but as statement and spectacle. Rhetorician J. Michael Hogan argues, "There is more to democratic persuasion—or at least there ought to be more—than making the news. Genuinely democratic discourse must not only attract media attention; it must empower citizens to act."[17] By adopting a strategy of spectacle, which, as Debord observes, "manifests itself as an enormous positivity, out of reach and beyond dispute," the protestor provides the concerned onlooker with no way to interact.[18]

But spectacle may be enough in today's media-saturated environment, where sound bites stand in for argument. Jannette's protest action is ideally suited to meet the constraints of sound-bite news. This is likely by design; members of PETA have repeatedly demonstrated their media savvy. One example of this can be found in a media event in which PETA co-founder and president Ingrid Newkirk and another member of PETA lay in make-shift coffins in the middle of Times Square. The *New York Times* noted that, "Ms. Newkirk, 56, was technically not nude, in the nude sense of the word. She wore white underpants, white stockings so thin you could see goose bumps, and white, flower-shaped pasties over her nipples, though not for the square inch of warmth they provided. A veteran activist, she later explained that the media would not use a picture 'if it has a nipple.'"[19] PETA seemingly understands what it must do to both attract and keep media coverage. It realizes the limits of the news media and is careful to keep media events within prescribed boundaries. Rhetorical scholar Peter Simonson notes that what makes PETA and other animal rights organizations distinct from the long tradition of concern for animal welfare is the media context in which current organizations exist.[20] Simonson further explains that PETA has been adept at inserting itself into popular culture, including music, fashion, and their own print outlets aimed at the true believers. He writes, "Entertainment cultures and their media include plenty of distortions, but they are also the symbolic worlds that many of us happily inhabit, as advertisers know too well. In claiming these worlds for their moral crusade, PETA is reminding us that democratic politics needs its popular pleasures."[21] In short, PETA creates a sustained, all-encompassing media presence that allows it to disseminate its message; integrating its political message with popular culture allows for the widest possible diffusion through the largest array of outlets.

PETA seems to recognize that protest can function as entertainment and spectacle. If part of that spectacle involves a bit of flesh and eye candy, so be it. Journalist John Elvin writes, "Most of the naked protestors say there's nothing suggestive or erotic in their behavior; they are just doing what comes naturally, or they are playing the part of dead bodies that result from war. A glance at PETA's calendar website provides assurance that animal-rights protestors are not so purist in their justifications."[22] PETA plays with the erotic charge that can come from seeing vulnerable, mostly naked women immobilized by chains or cages. As such, it protests the exploitation of animals through the exploitation of women. Rhetorician Edwin Black argues that rhetorical discourses imply an ideal auditor, for whom the discourse is designed, and this implied auditor can often be linked to a particular ideology.[23] Who then, is the ideal viewer of this spectacle? Two possibilities that stand out are those who would be aroused by such a scene and those who would be repulsed.

There can be no doubt that arousal is part of the spectacle; the spectacle could just as easily have been performed by a clothed protester. The choice to be partially disrobed is a conscious decision that adds little to a message such as: "Circus elephants: Shackled, lonely, beaten."[24] Concerning the fetishistic element of the caged woman, one allusion that cannot be lost on such a pop-culture literate organization as PETA is the connection to the "women in prison" movie genre.[25] But if arousal is the end result, does this actually help disseminate its message? With arousal as enticement, the ideal viewer would be drawn to the flesh, but as her/his eye lingered on the scene s/he would also take in the message. The viewer would then make the connection between caged women and caged animals. Yet, two of the men who witnessed Jannette's protest completely missed the point of the act, likely more interested in the display of her flesh than the symbolic act that was taking place. Perhaps one reason for this is the unpredictable quality of erotic emotions. Those who are aroused by the sight of a caged, vulnerable woman may be aroused by the fantasies invoked, yet these fantasies may range from a desire to save the woman from captivity (the preferred reading from the standpoint of PETA) to the more troubling desire to contain and control women through shackling, caging, and publicly humiliating them. Thus it is difficult to predict the likely response of an ideal viewer who requires arousal as incentive to observe the protest.

We can gain some insight into how nudity and sexual appeals work as persuasion by examining studies in advertising.[26] Advertising and marketing researchers Jessica Severn, George Belch, and Michael Belch found that "the use of sexual appeals . . . seemed to detract from the processing and retention of message arguments."[27] They found that brand recall was not affected, but recall of copy was hindered.[28] So it seems reasonable to concede that people may remember that the protester was involved with PETA, assuming that the logo is prominently displayed. However, in many of these actions, the woman holds a small paper with a slogan such as "Wild animals don't belong behind bars," with a small logo. Although in many cases the protesters are identified as PETA activists, in the case of Jannette's protest mentioned above, two of the three men that witnessed her protest did not even notice the sign and wondered what she was doing.[29] Therefore, even the brand can be overshadowed at times by the display of nudity. Moreover, marketing scholars Claire Sherman and Pascale Quester found that "adverts for products exhibiting greater congruence with nudity were more effective in creating positive attitudes and greater purchase intentions."[30] This may prove problematic for PETA, because animal rights and erotic displays are not generally connected in the mind of the general public in the same way as perfume and sexuality.

Viewer response to nudity may also depend on the viewer. Business scholars Jaideep Sengupta and Darren Dahl found that "consumers who have favorable affective reactions toward sexual stimuli—such as those who possess intrinsically positive attitudes toward sex per se—should evaluate sex-based ads positively in comparison to nonsexual ads, whereas the reverse should be observed for those with relatively unfavorable affective reactions toward sexual stimuli."[31] The gender of the viewer also plays a role in how such advertisements are viewed. Marketing scholar Michael LaTour found that "in terms of ad response, a nude model wins the popularity contest with men but not significantly more than women's feelings about a semi-nude model."[32] Perhaps part of this can be traced to how men and women view the display of female nudity. Sociologist Beth Eck states, "When women view the seductive pose of the female nude, they do not believe she is 'coming on to' them. They know she is there to arouse men."[33] Thus women may have a cynical view toward such displays and may see them as cheapening the message through sexual appeals to men. Eck's research suggests that, "for women, female nudes are objects to be studied, viewed, judged, and, above all, used as a comparison for the self."[34] As such, these displays are an invitation for women to consider their own appearances in comparison to the protester rather than an opportunity to reflect on the plight of animals. This may explain some of the consternation of women who decry the fact that the women that represent PETA are almost universally young, slim, and attractive.[35]

As evidenced by the advertising studies discussed above, PETA's nude campaigns are probably not effective in changing people's minds or even in getting audiences to engage in deliberations about PETA's messages. Yet PETA seems to buy into the conventional wisdom that "sex sells," despite the possibility that this strategy may backfire. Perhaps this type of ideal viewer represents PETA's view of the media and what gets their attention, as well as the attention of the general public, which at times seems fixated on sex. Thus, this ideal viewer requires spectacle—preferably of a sexual nature—to even pay attention to PETA.

The other ideal viewer of this scene is one who would be repulsed by such a display. Such repulsion would likely come out of pity rather than disgust. The sight of a helpless, vulnerable woman spurs a desire to protect and release her. This action elicits a powerful rhetorical connection between the vulnerability and imprisoned existence of the animals and that of the protester. The display of women in cages is a pitiful sight that invites the viewer to transfer this pity to the animals that are likewise caged. The ideal viewer would note the similar state of the caged or shackled protester to that of the circus animal and make the mental connection that just as humans should not be caged or shackled for our amusement, animals likewise should be free. However, the extremity of the sight may impede the viewer from making this connection. The nakedness of the protester presents a level of exposure that moves the audience to discomfort rather than sympathy; the level of pity that the scene stimulates becomes too much to bear. As such, the desire to protect and release the woman is given only to the protester and this desire overwhelms the ability of the audience to feel the same emotions for the animals that the protesters represent. As philosopher Joseph Libertson writes, "Nudity is a manifestation which is 'too manifest,' an appearance of that which should not have appeared—an impudency which shocks, and a vulnerability which inspires a pity that becomes desire."[36] Again, images of nudity fail to persuade.

But there is another audience here that is not external. Perhaps these actions are directed at a group other than the general population. Gregg notes that one aspect of the ego-function of rhetoric "has to do with *constituting* self-hood through expression; that is, with establishing, defining, and affirming one's self-hood as one engages in a rhetorical act."[37] Thus, by participating in these actions, protesters provide a model of what it means to be a member of PETA. They display a level of commitment that transcends that required in other social movement organizations. Debord argues that "the individual who in the service of the spectacle is placed in stardom's spotlight is in fact the opposite of an individual. . . . In entering the spectacle as a model to be identified with, he renounces all autonomy in order himself to identify with the general law of obedience to the course of things."[38] PETA members are invited to experience the suffering and humiliating existence of animals in a personal way. By disrobing and placing themselves on display, they demonstrate that they are willing to go through discomfort, both physical and psychological, to draw attention to the plight of animals.

This can be seen in slogans such as "we'd rather go naked than wear fur." It is not enough to simply believe it; a true believer must also demonstrate it by physically disrobing and participating in displays of public nudity. Although these displays may do little to alter the public mind, directed inwardly they define the level of commitment required of protesters and serve as a call to action for PETA members in general.

THE RUNNING OF THE NUDES

The running of the bulls takes place during the festival of San Fermín in Pamplona, Spain. This event was introduced to the English-speaking world largely through Ernest Hemingway's book *The Sun Also Rises*.[39] The bulls are run through the town on the way to the arena in which the bullfights will take place. Spanish scholar Timothy Mitchell writes, "The 'running of the bulls' in Pamplona is only the most famous example of what takes place in hundreds of folk festivals throughout both Castilles, León, La Mancha, Extremadura, Aragon, and Valencia, where communities ostensibly pay homage to their patron saints by stampeding and harassing bovids before slaughtering them and partaking of their flesh."[40] The running of the bulls is now firmly entrenched in popular culture as a display of bravery or drunken stupidity, depending on how the imagery is employed.

PETA draws attention to the opposition to bullfighting by staging a mock running of the bulls using nude activists. Participants in the "Running of the Nudes" wear the traditional red scarves of those who run with the bulls, fake bull-horns, and perhaps underwear (many are not actually nude, but some of the women are topless). Many carry placards that read, "stop the bloody bullfight" or "bullfighting" with the circle and slash motif. Some have slogans written on their bodies. The website for the Running of the Nudes describes the event this way: "Just two days before the first bull run, hundreds of activists—most wearing little more than a red scarf and plastic horns—ran through the streets of Pamplona for the annual 'Running of the Nudes.' Compassionate and fun-loving people from around the world met in Pamplona for the run to show the city that it doesn't need to torture animals for tourism."[41] And tourism is a serious consideration in this protest. Journalist Hilliard Lackey notes that the protest has an economic impact that enables authorities to overlook the illegal aspect of the action: "Authorities, however, are putting forth some semblance of a prohibition against nudity. Nevertheless, tourist dollars keep getting in the way. Tourism is the lifeblood of this area of Spain. The Running of the Nudes uprising—while illegal and uncouth—brings in a few more millions."[42]

Although the website includes bullfighting facts and a store to buy mer-chandise, the focus is on the sexiness of the runners. For example, there is a "Sexiest runner spotlight" and a page describing some of the "sexy runners" that participate. In fact, much of the site seems focused on the sexiness of the participants. On the page describing some of the participants, PETA makes the following appeal for joining the action: "How about slipping into some-thing more comfortable—like your birthday suit—and joining us for this fes-tive, cheeky event which is full of babes, not bulls? Speaking of babes, check out the profiles and pics of these hot-to-trot hotties you could be partying with in Pamplona!"[43] The profiles feature photographs and a short biogra-phy, complete with "hobbies," "turn-ons," and "turn-offs," that resemble a centerfold profile. Unlike the chained-women protest actions, the Running of the Nudes is a mixed-gender event. However, PETA's focus is still heav-ily slanted toward the women; of the 10 profiles listed, seven are female and three are male, all are attractive, and all but one are 29 or younger with the oldest being a 33-year-old woman.

In the videos of the action, there is a carnivalesque atmosphere.[44] There are banners and balloons and plenty of flesh. The participants seem to simply mosey down the street, in contrast to the frantic pace of the running of the bulls. The prurient interest is also present; one reporter states, "One observer might have the best advice so far: 'Forget the bulls, chase the nudes.' Surely, it is better to run behind just one Coppertone señorita than to run in front of a hundred enraged bulls."[45] In news reports, PETA reinforces the idea that the Running of the Nudes is meant to be a fun event. A PETA member recruit-ing participants in Covington, England, states, "Most people don't realise the bulls are running to the death in the other one. We've been recruiting people all month and our race is just a fun event."[46]

Protesters make a direct connection between their own nudity and the welfare of animals. One protester states, "I'm always proud to bare a little skin if it means helping animals keep theirs," echoing a common slogan from PETA.[47] However, others recognize that the message comes at personal expense. An 18-year-old woman, who describes herself as "shy and retir-ing," states, "I am taking part in this to attract attention about the cruelty to the bulls. If I stood with a placard which said this was cruel nobody would take much notice. If I have to take my clothes off to get the message across, then so be it."[48] This raises a significant question concerning the action's ef-fectiveness and the desired outcome. If passersby are unwilling to consider arguments concerning the cruelty of bullfights made by a clothed woman, are they any more apt to consider these arguments from a naked woman? What then is taking place and what kind of response is invited by such an act? The protest action seems geared to generate publicity and allows PETA access to the media through which it can explain why it is protesting the running of the bulls and the institution of bullfighting in general. In short, the action provides a platform that PETA may otherwise have lacked from which to disseminate their message.

PETA has seized on other opportunities to gain publicity by inviting government officials to participate in the Running of the Nudes. A short article in the *Columbus Dispatch* notes, "A biography of [Donald] Rumsfeld reveals that he once participated in the bull run. 'I invite you to tip the scales back a bit by coming to Spain to participate in the Running of the Nudes—also called the Human Race—an alternative to the cruel spectacle that occurs three days later,' PETA President Ingrid Newkirk wrote. No word on whether Rumsfeld plans to participate."[49] This provides an opportunity to gain some publicity while also providing the media with a lighthearted story, complete with amusing mental imagery.

In contrast to the chained-women protests, the Running of the Nudes succeeds in making its statement, partly by getting the attention of the media in a comical manner. Once PETA has the attention of the media, it is able to make short statements concerning its objections to bullfighting. The Running of the Nudes is much less confrontational than other PETA actions. Moreover, the participation of both women and men, as well as the large number of participants in the protest, removes some of the charges of simply exploiting women for PETA's cause. In a mass protest such as the Running of the Nudes, it is more about a moving mass of flesh than the display of a few choice specimens of female nudity as is seen in the chained-women displays.

The Running of the Nudes seems to function as a much more effective protest than the case of the caged women, at least in getting the general public to pay attention to the message, because the nudity does not overshadow the message itself. Perhaps this stems from the mode of participation. Rather than standing in symbolically for the circus animals that would be abused, the protesters in the Running of the Nudes stand in as humans in the place of humans. Observers are able to see the protest for what it is—raising a serious concern while still poking fun at humanity. In the Running of the Nudes the spectacle enhances the message, where in the case of the caged women the spectacle becomes the message.

THE RHETORICAL FORCE OF NUDE PROTEST

How best to get one's message into the public arena is a persistent concern in social movement protest. Sociologists Pamela Oliver and Daniel Myers note that "the link between public events and the public sphere is the mass media," and observe that "usually, a major goal of a public event is to attract the attention of the mass media, for only through the mass media can people communicate beyond their immediate social setting."[50] One effective way to do this is to stage what rhetorician Kevin DeLuca calls "image events": "In today's televisual public sphere corporations and states (in the persons/ bodies of politicians) stage spectacles (advertising and photo ops) certifying their status before the people/public *and* subaltern counterpublics participate through the performance of image events, employing the consequent publicity as a social medium through which to hold corporations and states accountable, help form public opinion, and constitute their own identities as subaltern counterpublics. Critique through spectacle, not critique versus spectacle."[51] In the case of PETA, it is clear that spectacle plays an important role in constituting identity and gaining access to the mass media. Of course, the more extreme the action, the more likely it is to wind up on the evening news or in the newspapers.

However, the question remains of whether the cost of nude protest actions outweigh the benefits of gaining the attention of the media and an otherwise apathetic public. This is especially problematic when considering the use of the female body in these actions. Although scholars such as Deckha and rhetorician Lesli Pace attempt to "identify moments of resistive agency" in some of PETA's campaigns such as the "I'd Rather Go Naked than Wear Fur" campaign, such arguments do not seem to hold up quite as well in the case of the caged women.[52] In her discussion of PETA's advertising, Deckha writes, "Through animalizing the bodies of consenting women (women as foxes), the ad attempts to make present the absent referent of those beings whose bodies are rendered completely abject and object in the constitution of human subjects."[53] In the case of the caged woman, the woman stands in for the absent animal, but fails to do so convincingly to the observer—she is still very much a naked, vulnerable, caged *woman*. This is problematic because, as Deckha observes, "Any campaign that relies on standard representations of women that associate them with and even reduce them to their bodies continues the very same logic of commodification and objectification that is used against animals."[54] She continues, "Reducing women to their bodies in a context of animality, whether by presenting them as sexualized 'bunnies' or 'foxes' or simply connecting their sexualized bodies to the idea of animals, solidifies the trajectory of thinghood. All the usual suspects of things, rather than persons, are still aligned: women, body, animals."[55]

Feminist critiques of PETA campaigns that employ the sexualized female body note these messages reinforce the objectification of women, a critique that holds true for the caged women. However, this is less evident in the case of the Running of the Nudes, which seems to take a more gender-neutral approach.

Perhaps one way that PETA can engage in erotically charged protest while avoiding the critique that they are merely objectifying women is to use both sexes in similar ways. Deckha notes that when PETA uses male nudity, it is comedic or nonsexualized, with the exception of black males and white males appearing with white women.[56] In the case of the Running of the Nudes, both sexes are used in ways that are simultaneously comedic and sexual, although as mentioned previously the emphasis remains tilted toward the sexual desirability of the female body.

On a practical level, PETA's strategy of nude protest seems to function well, if for different reasons, depending on the audience. The displays of chained women provide a powerful means of building a collective identity centered on the suffering and humiliation of animals. As a means of gaining access to the public consciousness, however, these actions seem too extreme and invite incredulous gawking rather than serious reflection on the issue at hand. Even if the mental image of the naked, chained woman remains (and it likely will), the reason for her bondage will likely be shortly forgotten, if the viewer ever even realized the cause. This raises questions concerning the efficacy of such extreme tactics. Research by persuasion and social influence scholars Joseph Scudder and Carol Bishop Mills examined the effects of shocking advocacy videos from PETA and found that it can raise the credibility of animal rights organizations and lower the credibility of animal processing plants.[57] Yet they are silent on whether this actually translated into a desire to pay more attention to where their meat comes from or whether they would stop eating meat. Changes in belief do not necessarily translate into changes in behavior; as social theorist Jacques Ellul observed, "there is not necessarily any continuity between conviction and action."[58]

The Running of the Nudes seems to function as a more effective means to gain access to the public consciousness. The core factor contributing to this is the playful tenor of the protest action. This event is less confrontational both physically (it takes place before the annual running of the bulls rather than during the event) and emotionally (there is no confusion of desire). The protesters state that this is meant to be a fun event and the images seem to reinforce this; the naked protesters seem to be having a good time. This stands in stark contrast to the tactics used in the displays of chained women next to a sign reading "Shackled, lonely, beaten." Thus, despite the even more dire occasion of bullfighting—the bulls *will* be killed; the circus at least has incentive to keep their animals alive—PETA is able to gain access to the media and make statements concerning the inhumanity of bullfighting without appearing self-righteous or strident.

In both of these actions PETA is able to disseminate a message mainly by getting the attention of the media. This is an indictment not only of the media but also of the general population. If observers are unwilling to listen to arguments concerning matters of public concern unless they are presented in the guise of spectacle, this does not bode well for the current state of the public sphere. As one observant protester states, "If I stood with a placard which said this was cruel nobody would take much notice. If I have to take my clothes off to get the message across, then so be it."[59] In their quest to gain access to the public sphere, members of PETA may see little alternative to participating in image events designed to shock or titillate the public. As such, ethical judgments must be tempered with rhetorician Franklyn Haiman's assertion that "perhaps the best one can do is to avoid the blithe assumption that the channels of rational communication are open to any and all who wish to use them."[60] If the only means of gaining access to the public sphere is through spectacle, one can hardly be blamed for employing image events as a means of disseminating one's message.

Extreme protests grow out of extreme ideologies. Research by political scientists M. Kent Jennings and Ellen Andersen suggests that "the strength of ideological orientations . . . proved to be a strong corollary of attitudes about disruption. Even in a group of activists with decidedly liberal leanings, the intensity of those leanings pushed in the direction of support for confrontation."[61] PETA evidently sees its cause as a literal matter between life and death. As such, it is not enough to simply believe in its cause; PETA is an organization that asks its members not only to do something but also to be something. To fully subscribe to PETA's ideology goes beyond opposition to animal cruelty; one must also become a vegetarian, eschew products made with animal products, oppose vivisection and animal experimentation, and oppose the use of animals in entertainment. Members of PETA share a common vision of what one should eat, wear, and believe. In this sense, eating and dressing are rhetorical acts that help define PETA's members. With this in mind, Jennings and Andersen's research suggests that PETA members would support extreme tactics of confrontation and protest.[62] As such, it comes as little surprise that they would engage in strategies such as nude protest, which is both taboo and confrontational.

Perhaps one reason for the power of this strategy lies in its resistance to co-optation; the strategy of nude protest will not likely be used by any opposition groups against them. Because of the strong taboo against public nudity in American culture, nudity is unlikely to be used by any but the most extreme, dedicated organizations. As such, social movement organizations that occupy more extreme ideological positions will likely maintain a relative monopoly on the tactic; it is unlikely to be used by those seeking to maintain the status quo. PETA can use this strategy as a badge that illustrates members' bravery as well as their progressiveness. This is similar to rhetorician Haig Bosmajian's assessment of the use of obscenity by the New Left in the 1960s: "The shouting of the obscenities may be the youths' vehicle for demonstrating their sexual, social, and political liberation. . . . The liberation may in the end be illusory, but for the moment the youthful demonstrators see it as real."[63] Because public nudity transgresses societal norms, PETA is able to define it is a brave act, rather than mere exhibitionism or perversion as acts of public nudity are done in the name of a greater good, despite oppositional claims that such tactics are degrading.

Public nudity is unsettling both because it is unexpected and because of the strong taboo associated with it. In some ways it functions much like the diatribe. Rhetorician Theodore Windt explains that "the diatribe is to rhetoric what satire is to literature. Each attempts to reduce conventional beliefs to the ridiculous, thereby making those who support orthodoxy seem contemptible, hypocritical, or stupid. Each seeks laughter, but not for its own sake. Rather, laughter serves as a cleansing force to purge pre-conceptions about ideas, to redeem ignored causes, to deflate pomposity, to challenge conventional assumptions, to confront the human consequences of ideas and policies."[64] Poking fun at a revered custom, such as the running of the bulls, allows PETA to draw attention to its cause while associating it with another, more well-known event. Adding the element of nudity to the protest invites the viewer to laugh at the ridiculous scene, yet in doing so, the viewer may see the ridiculous nature of the running of the bulls as well. Raising the level of discomfort through nudity is a powerful way to make an argument, because there is no way to argue with nudity; the observer is psychologically knocked off balance and assumes a defensive stance from the beginning. To witness such a spectacle is to giggle the uncomfortable laugh of one who sees that which should not be seen. Those who have seen or heard of the Running of the Nudes will associate it with the running of the bulls; the two will be forever linked in the public mind. This strategy of linking events can function as the first step in redefining the protested event, which is an important function for any social movement.

Part of the power in PETA's use of public nudity lies in the symbolism it evokes. In her discussion of Amerindians' use of animal parts, archeologist Chantal Conneller writes, "people take on the animal habitus in order to enter into a particular set of relationships with the world."[65] A similar impulse seems to be at work in the actions of PETA protestors. By removing their clothing, activists are symbolically becoming more animal-like. They have stripped away the civilizing garments of civilization and come closer to their "natural" state. By stripping off their clothing and chaining and caging themselves, they experience the world as naked, chained, caged animals experience it. DeLuca, in his discussion of Earth First! activists, writes, "Perched high in the Douglas fir, the protester sees the world from the tree's point of view and 'becomes' the tree. Rendered relatively immobile, his movements are limited to the swaying of the tree. The protester, like the tree, depends on nourishment to come to him. Finally, their fates are intertwined as the protester depends on the tree for support and shelter while the tree depends on the protester's presence to forestall the chainsaw."[66] In their discussion of becoming-animal, cultural theorists Gilles Deleuze and Félix Guattari write, "You do not become a barking molar dog, but by barking, if it is done with enough feeling, with enough necessity and composition, you emit a molecular dog."[67] PETA activists do not simply portray animals; they symbolically *become* animals.

Such symbolic acts of becoming animalistic constitute a powerful rhetorical strategy, albeit mostly self-directed. By complicating the performance of "humanity," PETA activists transgress expected modes of behavior and draw attention to themselves. This seems to be an end in itself in PETA's constant quest for media exposure. But this strategy also functions as a way to distinguish PETA activists from the rest of "humanity." Becoming animalistic enables them to demonstrate solidarity with their nonhuman allies and helps the protesters constitute themselves though the rhetorical act. Rhetorician Maurice Charland notes that, "ideology is material because subjects enact their ideology and reconstitute their material world in its image."[68] Through nude protest PETA enacts an ideology that considers animals to be equal to humans by becoming more animalistic, thus reinforcing beliefs iconically. In this mode of being, PETA is better able to speak on behalf of those who have no voice.[69]

PETA's acts of nude protest, then, fulfill two rhetorical functions. First, these help to galvanize the movement by providing its members opportunities to prove their devotion to the cause by stripping naked and displaying themselves in public. As members break this taboo they become symbolically more animalistic, which provides them with a different kind of viewpoint from which to protest on behalf of animal rights. It is easier to sympathize with animals when you have become more animalistic, if only for a short time. Second, the protests act as image events that draw media attention to their cause. PETA seems to come from the school of thought that any publicity is good publicity. Once PETA has the attention of the media, it is able to disseminate its message more effectively. Nudity is the loss leader that draws the media consumer into the marketplace of PETA's ideas.

Body rhetoric can be a potent force in social movement rhetoric. Seventeenth-century philosopher Baruch Spinoza stated, "No one knows in what way and by what means mind can move body," but I argue that it is equally difficult to know how the display of the body can move the mind.[70] Deleuze observes, "A body affects other bodies, or is affected by other bodies."[71] The only thing for certain is that the display of the body will affect others physiologically and emotionally; the precise nature of that effect is, however, uncertain.[72] We respond to the body because it is often used in a symbolic manner. Cultural theorist and critic Kenneth Burke reminds us, for example, that humans "by nature respond to symbols," and that persuasion can also be directed toward the self, as well as others.[73] By mobilizing the bodies of PETA activists and encouraging them to become more animalistic through display of their naked bodies, PETA orchestrates an act to which viewers cannot help but respond while simultaneously directing persuasion toward the activists themselves as they perform—and reinforce their belief in—their ideology.

Although nude protest is becoming more common, it will likely remain the province of only the most liberal and extreme groups. However, it may be these groups that most need such protest strategies. PETA's message of veganism and animal rights is incompatible with the status quo of American and British society. In order to reach the public, it must find a way to package its message in a manner that causes the general public to listen. PETA has learned well the power of spectacle in our media-saturated society, recognizing that naked protesters will always draw both a curious crowd and an interested media that thrives on the reporting of image events. So long as we all keep looking at the spectacle, PETA will have great incentive to supply us with something to look at.

Chapter Seven

Biting Back at the Empire

The Anti–Greyhound Racing Movement's Decolonizing Rhetoric as a Countermand to the Dog-Racing Industry

Jason Edward Black

On November 8, 2008, the voters of Massachusetts passed Question 3—alternatively known as the Greyhound Protection Act—which effectively ended the statewide practice of greyhound racing and pari-mutuel gambling related to the racing industry. The Act's declaration of purpose indicated that "the citizens of Massachusetts find that commercial dog racing is cruel and inhumane" and that it should therefore be "prohibited in the commonwealth."[1] The campaign to end greyhound racing through the ballot initiative was led by a number of groups—from mainstream animal protectionists like the Humane Society of the United States, the Animal Rescue League of Boston, and the Massachusetts Society for the Prevention of Cruelty to Animals, to more activist-oriented animal rightists such as Massachusetts-based Grey2K USA and the national Greyhound Protection League. The effort was the culmination of some ten years of dissent and came in the wake of an earlier public rejection of a proposed ban in 2000. The Greyhound Protection Act failed in 2000 by less than 2 percent because of a SLAPP (or Strategic Lawsuit Against Public Participation) launched by Wonderland Dog Park. The dog "park" filed spurious lawsuits against Grey2K USA on the eve of the election to sway voters. The campaign was marred in the eleventh hour "by a host of legal issues, accusations of defamation, and finger pointing" and failed, not on these merits or legal ills, but because a wealthy corporation was able to "chill the free speech of the ordinary citizens" advocating for the ban.[2] The 2008 "victory for the greys" passed by a margin of 12 percent and represents a pivotal moment of reform, as it avenged the 2000 loss and, as Grey2K USA exalts, was the "first time in history that dog tracks have been closed down by citizen vote."[3]

Part of the successful rhetoric of the Greyhound Protection Act's proponents involved situating (albeit not overtly) the racing industry as a colonizing entity—one that exploits dogs for the capital that they potentially attain, and abuses dog bodies as cogs in the larger "machine" of the gambling "business."[4] These arguments had also been employed by the larger greyhound protection movement (GPM) for the wider purpose of abolishing the dog-racing industry in the United States. Though these anti-racing activists never come out and label the industry a "colonizing" threat, they do intimate in their discourse that dogs are commodified in such a way that places their labor conditions and psychological duress in a similarly oppressive milieu. Part of what the ensuing discussion in this piece alludes to is a need for the GPM to take a firmer decolonial stand. As a member of the GPM, I applaud every effort of the movement to abolish dog racing. However, I find it problematic that the GPM only covertly intimates at the connection between greyhound bodies and colonized bodies and between the dog-racing industry and larger material/symbolic colonial structures. A decolonizing rhetoric, I argue, will have a significant impact on debates about the use of dog and animal bodies for corporate profit.

Blending my own GPM activism with my role as a rhetorical critic, I take up cultural theorist Stuart Hall's charge to work from the agency of an organic scholar undertaking reflexive analysis. As he is fond of charging, "Unless we operate in this tension [writing and acting], we don't know what cultural studies can do, can't, can never do; but also what it has to do, what it alone has a privileged capacity to do."[5] In other words, putting our scholarship into action makes such critical work utile and defensible. Criticism as criticism is fine as a first deconstructive move; reconstruction, however, takes great effort. It is my duty here to work the decolonial critique into a movement of which I am part in order to make my criticism matter beyond the page, conference, and classroom.

As a start, the present essay addresses the ways in which the GPM challenges the colonial structure of the racing industry by revealing these dominant modes, whether intended or not. The academic/activist area of critical animal studies has begun to look at the mistreatment of animals through postcolonial lenses to emphasize the ways that human superiority is scripted over animals and animal symbols.[6] Working through this approach, I argue that the GPM (particularly, the Greyhound Protection League and Grey2K USA) crafts decolonizing rhetoric that countermands the racing industry's discourse of commodification. I contend that this type of decolonization is other-directed in as much as advocates do not see "themselves as oppressed and exploited," but rather work for the rights of "others" unlike themselves.[7] (In this case, of course, the "others" are greyhounds.) Especially spotlighted are the advocates' enactment of economic language and enemy constructions. The homologies of the GPM's rhetoric and decolonization are vital from a praxis perspective, as these connections might be marshaled by future greyhound activists, as well as other animal welfare and rights proponents, to challenge animal use, cruelty, and abuse. Communication scholar Kathryn Olson writes that, "a homology argument emphasizes formal resemblances across discourses *in spite of* their apparently disparate contents and situations."[8] Importantly, homological discourses may differ in both their substances and rhetorical situations but may also share a common exigence. In the case of postcolonialists and the GPM (as well as animal advocates generally) that shared exigence is the oppression of sensate beings.

The "prescriptive" argument, here, is to suggest that appeals to decolonization be made within endeavors to end animal exploitation. Specifically needed, however, is the GPM's insistence on analogies between human suffering and animal suffering to add to a decolonizing rhetoric that intentionally and unequivocally links the suffering under the contemptible moniker of "colonization."

To accomplish this, a discussion of colonization as a rhetoric of control and decolonization as a resistive strategy is first offered. Then, I present an analysis of recent discourse by the GPM through the decolonial perspective. These discourses arise in the forms of position papers, Web content, pamphlets, and fact sheets. Finally, implications about making the connection between animal advocacy (especially greyhound protection) and decolonization are offered in terms of the "next steps" that the tactic presents to animal ethics movements.

COLONIZATION AS A STRATEGY OF CONTROL; DECOLONIZATION AS A TACTIC OF CRITIQUE

Broadly, decolonization as a discursive strategy involves a resistive rhetoric through which subaltern groups appropriate dominant discourses and turn them around to expose the problems and duplicity of these discourses. Reading these strategies through such a framework is part of the larger postcolonial project in the humanities. Accordingly, rhetorician Raka Shome notes that the postcolonial condition attends to the tragedies of colonization by exposing the "imperialism of Western discourses."[9] Colonization, to borrow from rhetorical critics Derek Buescher and Kent Ono, begins when "colonizers appropriate land, conquer indigenous people, and found colonialist governments to oversee the efficient operation of property and labor. . . . [Then] [they] teach the colonized the language, logic and history of the colonizer."[10] Postcolonial studies examines the ways in which these hierarchical relationships functioned over time and continue to function through issues beyond labor and territory and to symbolic constructions and control of the subaltern (the contemporary instantiation is deemed neocolonialism). As Shome and social critic Radha Hegde indicate, this research is "concerned with phenomena and effects and affects of colonialism" through "not only . . . the framework of dominance but also from that of resistance."[11] Thus, postcolonialism does not focus solely on dominant powers, as this re/centers them as foundational to the detriment of considering the larger transactional relationship in which resistant forces are also important. Postcolonialism, then, reminds us of the perspective of the subaltern.

Of course, postcolonialists write about postcolonialism in terms of human beings locked into a colonial structure and in terms of their efforts to demystify dominance through decolonizing means. And, this colonization manifests in terms of the material and symbolic.[12] In terms of the material, a good deal of scholarship by postcolonial intellectuals like Hall, Gayatri Spivak, Homi Bhabha, and Edward Said emphasizes the ways in which the human body/subject (and cultural identities as imbrications of the body and social spaces) are impacted by exploitative labor, capitalist structures, conditioned living spaces, deprivation of benefits, subsistent needs, and information, rhetorics of oppression, and exposure to diseases and drugs.[13] Animal rights advocates also fight against a system that has exploited the labor and territory of "beings" (the bodies as a space), while concomitantly reinscribing this exploitation by justifying it through the language of "humane" conditions.[14] Comparisons between the factory farm and the Nazi concentration camp, the circus and the sideshow, and the fur ranch and the American Indian reservation appear commonly in animal ethics literature.[15]

Rationalizations of colonialism also involve the symbolic, as both a generative precursor to and extension of the material realm. The way that these symbolic structures function has been labeled neocolonization. Susan Silbey writes of neocolonization that "control of land or political organization . . . is less important than power over consciousness and consumption."[16] In other words, representations of the "other" by colonial forces come to entrap as much as ephemeral conditions. This is the core spirit of Said's arguments about orientalism—that the linguistic symbolicity and public imaginary of, in his case, the "Eastern other" comes to *mean* above all bodily characteristics for an imperial (Western) system. Of these representations, he contends that what critics find in them almost universally are "systems of discourse by which the 'world' is divided, administered, plundered, by which humanity is thrust into pigeonholes, by which 'we' are 'human' and 'they' are not."[17] Neocolonialism can be extended to animals as well, especially when we consider, for example, the ways that symbol use impacts collocations like pork/beef (pigs/cows), machines (racing dogs/horses), vessels (puppy mill mothers), and fur (minks/rabbits). Such separation deprives the animal subject, in

these cases, of consideration and agency. In fact, the symbolicity metonymically reduces the subject to object. Ultimately, this neocolonial conception
lends credence to the social construction of lived experience, especially as
found in exchanges between dominant forces and subaltern subjects.

In terms of neocolonialism, animal activists do not overtly claim to be victims of colonization (though one might argue that being trapped in a culture
that supports animal uses for food, clothing, cosmetics, entertainment, and
medical purposes—and then alienates those who refuse to comport with this
ideology—qualifies as being controlled through materialism and symbol use
[i.e., "crazy PETA nut-job"]). However, animal advocates' fight for welfare
and rights is widely considered vicarious. In movement studies, such stand-in
agents are labeled "other-directed." Movement scholar Charles Stewart defines the type of rhetoric ascribed to these advocates as appearing to "affirm
and enhance an already exalted self-esteem by celebrating and recognizing
the protestor's moral principles, commitment, compassion, and humanitarian-
ism"[18] If "human beingness" is a requirement of postcolonial work or argumentative agency, then animal rights advocates as "other-directed" could be
justified in using decolonizing rhetoric, as they are the agents with voice, at
least voice that a dominant public and/or Establishment can understand.

"BITING BACK": THE ANTI-RACING MOVEMENT'S DECOLONIZING COUNTERMAND

Animal rights advocates—represented in this study through the GPM—turn
their attention to animals as victims and, hence, forego their own experiences
as disaffected. They do, though, position themselves as emancipators. The
GPM's motivation is best articulated by the Greyhound Protection League,
which states its purpose as: "to bear witness to the tragic history of the racing
greyhound so that the world will never again be lulled into silence, ignorance
or indifference . . . [and to] break the silence and speak out nationally against
the atrocities inflicted upon racing greyhounds."[19] The GPM, as do other
animal rightists, simultaneously focus decolonial critiques on animal users in
"the name of animals."[20] In the service of this end, the GPM countermands
animal use by revealing and challenging the economic timbre of the racing
industry and by centering animal users as murderous oppressors.

Economic Language

Typically, decolonial challenges by agitators begin with the demystification
of colonization as tied up in economics—particularly the use of territory and

labor to further the dominant's mission. Animal advocates commonly allude to the exploitation of animals in terms of the bodily (territory), performativity (as labor), and utility (as commodity/product, i.e., meat, fur, etc.). In the case of GPM's decolonizing rhetoric, dog bodies are territory, and their labor is their performance on the tracks. Such a challenge demands that these advocates position colonial conditions in such a way to reveal the ways that suffering and selfishness result from its economic mission.[21] They need also to show the emancipating potential of the decolonial resistance. For rhetorical and social critics, there is a responsibility to address both of these functions; this is in line with critical rhetorician Raymie McKerrow's insistence on "critiques of domination and emancipation."[22] One way the GPM enacts its colonial challenge is by crafting economic language to confront the dog-racing industry. This is performed in two noteworthy manners: the use of economic metaphors and the engagement of certitude.

First, the GPM uses economic metaphors to explain the relationship between the dog-racing industry as just that, a business, and greyhounds as the products or sources of labor. The Greyhound Protection League works through this language. For instance, it argues, that "[g]reyhound racing is first and foremost, a business. Most greyhounds do not receive the best of care (it costs money!) and the cost of the greyhound is not always a major factor in determining how well the greyhound will be treated as soon as it is determined the dog is less competitive than originally thought."[23] Notable words such as "business" applied to tracks and terms like the "cost" of the upkeep of greyhounds speaks to this theme. The cost, in this case, is too high to warrant the proper treatment of the laborers. As the group also comments, the "pressure to generate gambling profits can lead to negligent care. Adoption groups frequently receive dogs in a general state of neglect."[24] The public revelation of this neglect speaks not just to the GPM's mission to break the silence, but to the decolonization of the industry by locating its existence in a culture of suffering. In the end, the group contends, "[N]o one wants to pay the upkeep, feed and care for all these losers any more than a business would want to continue to pay an unproductive employee. . . . In short, economics determine the dogs' expendability at each stage of its racing career. It is cheaper to get rid of a losing dog, rather than spend money to care for it, especially when there is always an over abundance of greyhounds waiting in the wings."[25] Stuck in this gambling machine are the greyhounds themselves—whose bodies bear the brunt of economic strain and need. As used bodies become unproductive, new "units" are introduced in a long stream of unending commodity-bodies.

Continuing this theme of economic metaphors, the greyhound laborers are often labeled as near-Marxist cogs by the movement. Again, this is a relatively common trope in the rhetoric of animal protection. This is done, perhaps, to demonstrate just how dastardly a fellow sentient being can be treated by the racing industry. Grey2K USA recently noted in a recruitment flyer that female brood dogs, "[l]ike thousands of greyhounds nationwide [they are] nameless victim[s]—exploited and then discarded by an industry that just doesn't care. . . . The products of greyhound farms . . ."[26] The descriptor of "product" serves to de/sentien-tize the greyhounds as objects that can be used and thrown away. In some cases, as in a Greyhound Protection League fact sheet, the racing industry is said to discuss greyhounds as less-than objects, the material "waste" of tracks. The group notes that the tracks consider them "expendable *by-products* of the racing system" justified by the "interests of state-budget deficits, gambling profits and free market enterprise [emphasis mine].[27] "By-products" are metonymically less important than the product—in this case, the winning that translates into money for the tracks. Ultimately, greyhounds become "short-term investments" that according to Grey2K USA are "expected to generate enough profit during that time to make up for the cost of their food and housing."[28] Just as in human colonization, the "onus of labor" is shifted to the "victim."[29] And, as with decolonizing critiques, such a condition is exposed by the resister—in this case, the surrogate GPM and its related groups who stand in for the victims.

A decolonial challenge also characteristically makes an emancipating move to confront the colonizing threat. The GPM does this by clinging to certitude and the expectation of success, the latter as a motivating rally-call. The GPM does not indicate that suffering will be allowed, or that the movement will stand by idly complaining about the treatment of greyhounds. Theirs is a rhetoric of certitude, a conviction to act under moral ordinance. By calling into question the racing industry as having "inherent problems no one can remedy," for instance, the movement shifts its emancipatory strategies to the inevitability of tracks shutting down. Continuing on, the group claims that "in any equation in which man [*sic*], animals and the expectation of money are thrown together, economic interest will always prevail . . . [t]his fundamental fact is what makes greyhound racing inhumane and unfixable."[30] Who better to decolonize the industry by materially helping shut its doors than activists *themselves*. In accordance with this tactic, Grey2K USA states that its "first priority is to prevent track owners from receiving tax breaks, slot machines and other forms of financial assistance . . . we are committed to wiping out this exploitation state by state, track by track."[31] This decolonizing tactic in human postcolonial campaigns involves using the economic structure as a way to get back at the system itself. For instance, this is what Hall claims to be a rupture through which the subaltern uses the "master's tools to dismantle the master's house."[32] I deem this move "Biting Back at the Empire" for any

campaign of the overall animal rights movement. According to film scholar
Olga Gershenson, such *détournement*, or turnaround, suggests that, "colonial
discourse fluctuates between mimicry and menace."[33] She continues that this
"mimicry is charged with the danger of mockery. It threatens to undermine
the prevailing norms and authorities, the normalized knowledges and disci-
plinary powers of the dominant discourse."[34] Fighting the system from the
inside with its own tools is vital for decolonial rhetorical strategies.

Part of GPM's economic certitude also comes in the form of evidence cited
that indicates how the racing industry is on the ropes, failing to turn a profit
and, thus, exposed to defeat. Grey2K USA reports that "[o]ver the past two
decades, commercial dog racing has experienced a catastrophic economic decline, and now represents less than 1 percent of all wagers made each year in
the United States."[35] Such a move suggests that dog racing may be failing due
to its inhumane actions. This argument is made by linking it to external factors, seemingly so as not to enact causality. Grey2K USA, for example, writes
that, "Competition from other forms of gambling, coupled with increased
awareness of the cruelty of dog racing, has had a significant negative impact
on racetrack revenues."[36] The certitude that comes with the tracks' decline
provides a flag issue of sorts that serves not only to decolonize an industry
that exploits animal bodies and labor but also to motivate GPM members. To
this point, noticeably present in a majority of GPM discourse is the citation
of the Greyhound Protection League's "An Industry in Decline" that is drawn
upon generally, and whose updates were marshaled in the recent Greyhound
Protection Act victory in Massachusetts.[37] This living document has been
augmented since its inception in the early 1990s, and has become an index, of
sorts, for the successes of the GPM—an empirical sign of its successes—that
contributes to certitude. Based on similar reports, Grey2K USA often noted
in its 2008 campaign to ban racing in Massachusetts that dog racing "is illegal in 34 states. Greyhound racing is a national disgrace. It is illegal in most
U.S. states and should be outlawed nationwide. Seven states have banned dog
racing since 1993."[38] This certitude helps to decolonize the racing industry's
practices and simultaneously reveals its social ills and inhumane ideologies
as enemies of sentience.

Construction of the Enemy

The GPM's construction of the racing industry as an enemy—one despised
for its murderous tendencies and blood-thirst—is another decolonizing rhetorical tactic. The move to issue invective and the personalization of the
enemy is not new to anti-colonial social movement strategies.[39] It certainly
does not simply exist as an eleventh-hour or desperate "last resort" when all

else fails.[40] Rather, in the case of the GPM it confirms the movement's moral assurances in opposition to the racing industry, and also becomes a way to publicly unmask the industry for its practices.

One way that the GPM constitutes the colonizer is through the reporting of conditions of the "laborers." Peppered throughout the Greyhound Protection League's and Grey2K USA's discourses are accounts of animal abuse.[41] These abuses are continually associated with dog tracks' actions. A typical account is used by the Greyhound Protection League detailing the rescue efforts of Donna Lakin, President of Second Chance for Greyhounds in Michigan. Though dated, Lakin's graphic depiction is one of the most representative of abuse narratives:

> In early May our group took in six dogs from a 20-dog haul, rescued from the Sanford-Orlando Kennel Club, which was closing for the season. I had been warned that some of the dogs were in 'rough shape' but I was not prepared for what we saw when they arrived.
>
> Almost all of the dogs had deep, open pressure sores on their rumps, far worse than the usual crate baldness. All of them were heavily infested with fleas, ticks and internal parasites. One female had an infected gash on her neck; her tail was completely missing leaving her rectum exposed. Another female's back left foot had 'dropped toes,' usually the result of torn ligaments and/or broken bones. One male had a respiratory infection and a 105-degree fever. Another male had a staph infection; his entire body was covered with large pus-filled blisters.[42]

Lakin's narrative is a part of a larger commentary from the Greyhound Protection League regarding tracks. In the commentary, Lakin's story is expanded to suggest how tracks not only mistreat but also kill greyhounds in heinous ways. The website notes that "hundreds of cases" of death by means such as being "shot, starved, electrocuted and sold for research" have befallen "used up" greyhounds. The group further contends that "[i]ndustry insiders report that this is only the tip of the iceberg," insinuating that there may be far more cases of greyhound deaths than either the racing industry or the mainstream media report to the general public.[43] The strategy of constructing the enemy as "murderous" resonates throughout human decolonization discourse, from slave narratives and Native removal memorials to revolutionary rhetoric of former British subjects (including Americans) and accounts of contemporary genocide. The GPM, and animal rightists, rely on this tactic to build internal commitment and to expose the cruelties of animal use and abuse to the broader public. Such a "sentimental style" has been shown in rhetorical studies literature to foment a commitment to resist not just a disembodied systemic problem, but also the individuals responsible for, and who comprise, the system that perpetuates the ills.[44]

The enemy in GPM's rhetoric is also glossed as capitalistic and greedy to a fault. If one way of decolonizing is working through economic metaphors and certitude, then surely related to that is the lumping of colonizers with the malfunctions of the economic structure. In Grey2K USA's recent battle for the racing ban, it came up against resistance from the two Massachusetts tracks, Wonderland Dog Park and Raynham-Taunton Dog Park. These tracks were described as seedy and politically corrupt. In summer 2008, Grey 2K USA mentioned in a pamphlet that: "Dog Racing is subsidized. Across the country, wealthy dog track owners continually beg for handouts from state government. By giving millions of dollars in campaign contributions and hiring expensive lobbyists, track owners have convinced politicians to give them subsidies, tax cuts, and the right to operate casino gambling at their facilities."[45] Such a description insinuates that track owners must work insidiously through the political system to retain its grip on the dog-racing industry. Implicated in this decolonial critique is a challenge to the overall U.S. economic system and the pari-mutuel gambling enterprise that allows dog racing to exist and operate through these backroom dealings. Moreover, both the track ownership and the U.S. economic system are depicted as participating in the murder of thousands of greyhounds each year.

Concomitantly, track ownership's economic and political greasiness shows the lengths they will go to support their "killing machine." And, the GPM rhetorically decolonizes the industry by revealing some the political corruption or, in the least, overtly questionable tactics of some of the racing business' leaders. In an oft-cited article by Grey2K USA during the Question 3 campaign in 2008, George Carney of Raynham-Taunton Dog Park is exposed as overzealous in his efforts to defend dog racing: "'I am going to spend a lot of money and I am going to beat it' . . . Carney said he is prepared to top, if necessary, the $2.5 million spent in 2000 by the state's two dog tracks to beat back the last referendum campaign."[46] The irony of his admission is that the money used to fight the 2008 Greyhound Protection Act came at the expense of greyhound bodies and labor that gave him the means to spend on the campaign. An even more unfortunate absurdity of Carney's spending is that he was actually expending funds from greyhound labor to murder more greyhounds. This absurdity is called out in Greyhound Protection League discourses, wherein the racing industry is said to "make money off them [greyhounds], kill them, then repeat the cycle."[47] In the end, here, the gluttony of the colonizers assists in their characterization as ludicrous, which makes their murder of thousands of dogs seem even more tragic and unwarranted.

Finally, the GPM's decolonial challenge moves toward an emancipationist effort to confront the colonizing perils of the racing industry. In comportment with the insistence of certitude and the expectation of success discussed above, the GPM invectively constitutes the industry as a near-defeated foe. The Greyhound Protection League comments that "[f]ate has brought us full circle. In twenty-first century America, it is the racing industry itself that is facing a death sentence for failure to deliver a winning performance in the economic arena. Changes in societal values, competition from other forms of gaming, media exposés and pressure from the humane community have all taken their toll."[48] This statement is a lucid example of the *détournement* or turnaround tactic involved in decolonizing rhetoric. This is the strategy that postcolonial scholars like Arnold Krupat discuss as a foremost component of decolonization: "to take possession of the 'master's' books is to obtain some important part of the master's power—which then, to be sure, may be turned to one's own purposes."[49] There is also a sense of the carnivalesque here, where the colonized becomes the "victor." In this instance, it is not the colonized greyhound body being killed for not performing, but the tracks themselves. This death knell tolls for the colonizer. The enemy is, thus, constituted as fallible in its pursuits of economic stability. Ostensibly, the racing industry's failure translates into the failure of a murderous system.

IMPLICATIONS FOR ANIMAL PROTECTION MOVEMENTS

This essay has tracked the way that the GPM (particularly the Greyhound Protection League and Grey2K USA) works through decolonizing rhetoric that countermands the racing industry's discourse of commodification. These advocates rely upon the tactics of enacting economic language and enemy constructions to embolden themselves against the dog-racing industry through exposing publicly the ills of dog racing as a colonial construct. The homologies of the GPM's decolonization are vital, as these links could feasibly be used by other animal activists in the service of eradicating inhumane animal uses and abuses. The potential of the GPM emboldening its activism with an overt colonial critique is what motivates my analysis—an insistence, a charge—that decolonization become a recognizable trope in the GPM, just as it has begun to be in the overall animal protection movement.

Though the economic language and constructions of the enemy that are a part of the GPM's rhetoric are powerful, and were potentially successful in the passage of the Greyhound Protection Act (again, however, I am not attributing causality), I want to argue that the GPM could take the decolonial challenge one step forward. Namely, the movement could visibly and openly evidence the ways that animal and human suffering are homologized in terms of their similar positioning in an overall colonial structure of property and labor. After all, as I have discussed elsewhere, "homology opens the door to examining rhetorical movements in a new way, thus suggesting that our hard and fast boundaries of social change are more blurred than rigid."[50] There is strength in aligning joint oppressions and pooling agitative tactics in order to resist larger dominant structures.

The linking of animal and human suffering is a common argument of animal rightists. In fact, in his activist literature Charles Patterson contends that animal exploitation became the template for human oppression. To this point, he writes that: "Not only did the domestication of animals provide the model and inspiration for human slavery and tyrannical government, but it laid the groundwork for western hierarchical thinking and European and American racial theories that called for the conquest and exploitation of the 'lower races,' while at the same time vilifying them as animals so as to encourage and justify their subjugation."[51] But, there still seems to be a relation made through sentience with the GPM, an ontological connection to beingness based on feeling and caring, and life and death. This is a good first move, but at the same time it elides social and political dynamics.

To follow up that ontological move, I wonder if positioning animal use in terms of colonization, and GPM and animal rights resistance in terms of decolonization, could add a sociopolitical dimension to animal welfare and rights protest. Making these connections might usher in a new paradigm in animal activism that equates humans and animals through sentience *and* shared experience as victims of ideological systems of control regarding property and labor. Surely, if colonized people, as rhetorician Haig Bosmajian notes, have been identified as "animalistic," then animals could be recognized as colonized.[52] Metaphors have vehicles and tenors, after all. Seemingly, all the pieces of this are present: animal bodies are used as property in the service of exploiting their labor. Animals are kept in cordoned-off areas, whether pens, cages, or houses. (This is reminiscent of barracks, reservations, ghettos, bases, factory towns, and workers' villages.) These animal oppressions are situated along a hierarchy of lesser-than-to-greater-than. And, of course, physical and psychological harm and death befall the colonized.[53]

There is also a neocolonialism at work for both human and animal colonial structures. Neocolonialism involves numerous components, but the notions of controlling symbol use and justifications for colonization are the most prominent. Just as postcolonialists have argued about the "otherizing" of Natives or colonial subjects contributing to exploitation, so too does otherizing as a mechanism impact human views of animals. Animal activist-scholars Lynda Birke and Luciana Parisi claim that humans must "recognize that the animal kinds with which we are most familiar are precisely those which we human beings have culturally and symbolically constructed as 'Other.'"[54] These animals are then powerless to impact their conditions. Symbolically, their cultural meaning "*is* as bodies, as flesh, as commodities. . . . They are not selves in the way we see ourselves."[55] Part of animal protectionist rhetoric—and, certainly, the GPM's discourse—is to fight the labels appended to animals that demarcate them as "other," which thus justifies for human cultures writ large their animal use for food, clothing, experimentation, and entertainment.

Ultimately, the above analysis might motivate the GPM to continue employing decolonizing rhetoric in their advocacy campaigns, as it moves into other states such as Florida and Arizona to abolish the dog-racing industry. I am not suggesting that movement organizations are cognizant that they are using decolonization as a strategy—such a claim is my own as a rhetorical critic and greyhound advocate for the past ten years. But, given that the GPM's emphasis on reform through economic language and constructions of the enemy (both key postcolonial moves) have yielded some success, especially as measured by the passage of Question 3 and the closure of some eight tracks in three years, perhaps a "next step" taken could be to spotlight the colonial and decolonial connections between humans and animals. The rationale for my argument here is that it is more difficult for a larger public to deny the ills of colonialism given context and history. Perhaps glossed in this frame, the dog-racing industry might appear similarly oppressive. Such a strategy is dangerous, especially considering how PETA's "Holocaust on Your Plate" campaign drew major criticism from human rights advocates in addition to animal welfarists and rightists who called the homologizing of the European Holocaust with factory farming "outrageous, offensive and taking chutzpah to new heights."[56] But, in the face of thousands of greyhounds being murdered each year for a mere one percent of the nation's gambling industry (not that a higher percentage would justify racing), more has to be done to continue the fight. As Grey2K USA exalted in its victory press release in November 2008, "dog racing still exists in ten other states and we are committed to ending dog racing nationwide."[57] The campaign to end greyhound racing seems poised to "Bite Back at the Empire" colony by colony.

Part Three

CRITIQUES OF ANIMAL MANAGEMENT RHETORIC

Chapter Eight

The Biomedical Research Industry and the End of Scientific Revolutions

Greg Goodale

During a lecture, William James mused upon what he called the classic stages of a theory's career. James taught: "First, you know, a new theory is attacked as absurd; then it is admitted to be true, but obvious and insignificant; finally it is so important that its adversaries claim that they themselves invented it."[1] A century after James' lecture, the Biomedical Research Industry (BRI) (the sector of the economy that produces drugs, vaccines, prosthetics, and other medical interventions) has turned the first and second stages of a theory's career—attacking a theory as absurd or admitting that it is obvious but insignificant—into a bulwark against the third and potentially revolutionary stage of James' analysis. Such a revolution would threaten funding, divert attention from established researchers, diminish the power of entrenched organizations, and upend tracks of upward mobility within the industry. As a skeptic, I know that power and money always threaten the "truth," but I am still surprised at the scope of the BRI's efforts to impede challenges to orthodoxy.

Though there are a few examples of potentially revolutionary biomedical theories that have been condemned and suppressed by the BRI that the public knows about, I focus here on one practice that has been widely questioned by the public and a growing body of scientists and philosophers, yet remains sacrosanct in biomedical research sanctuaries: vivisection. The BRI continues to champion the usefulness of this practice even though modern vivisection does not accurately predict human outcomes because of the complexities of genetics and molecular biology, a problem that sometimes produces fatal results in human consumers. Carcinogen tests in rodents, for example, produce false negative results almost two-thirds of the time, potentially exposing humans to grave risk. Animal studies to determine whether a drug or substance would cause human birth defects are correct only 50 percent of the time. Hundreds of treatments for stroke, cancer, and HIV/AIDS that were tested on and found effective in nonhuman animals (NHA) have not been helpful for humans. Of the 150 stroke drugs that produced positive results in NHA, for instance, none have been effective in humans. And safety testing on NHA for Vioxx, TGN1412, and other drugs failed to predict the deaths of tens of thousands of people.[2] Reliance on vivisection leads to human harms either directly via false safety tests or indirectly because of the waste of limited resources and time. And this cost reflects another significant cost: the suffering and death of the millions of NHA upon whom strokes are induced, who are exposed to radiation so that they will get cancer, and into whom HIV is injected, to mention just a few of the uses to which these test subjects are put. A revolution in the biomedical research paradigm is long overdue.

In this essay, I argue that the BRI, with its researchers, lobbyists, bureaucrats, technicians, and salespeople, employs a variety of communication strategies to attack or diminish new theories—in particular that of replacing vivisection—thus preventing scientific revolutions. In terms set forth by John Waite Bowers and Donovan Ochs in 1971, BRI professionals employ control, suppression, avoidance, deflection, denial of means, harassment, and counter-persuasion—strategies that I examine below—to avert challenges to the governing paradigm.[3] These strategies are often invisible though they occasionally appear in the texts of professional medical journals and public relations materials. The most common strategies for maintaining the status quo, like rejection letters, personal ridicule, and harassment rarely enter into the published record. What does get published with regularity is the rhetoric of orthodoxy. As critical scholars, we know that we cannot treat the statements, essays, and press releases of spokespersons for institutions as if these were true. Rather, we know these pronouncements are constructed to be persuasive.[4] Thus, after examining the context and motives of the BRI, I analyze defensive communication practices, first in the pages of scholarly works and next in the efforts of public relations professionals.

The result of these manipulations is unwarranted limits on knowledge, the restricted development of new techniques for curing disease, and the suffering and death of millions of NHA. Employing philosopher of science Thomas Kuhn's theory of scientific revolutions, I argue that the BRI impedes progress by protecting a key premise of its governing paradigm: that vivisection is necessary to biomedical research. Kuhn discovered that as anomalies (in the form of mistakes, poor results, and unexplained phenomena for example) accumulate, researchers are forced to rethink the premises that produced the anomalies. These premises are then replaced by new theories that better account for the results, thus eliminating anomalies.[5] Most famously, Galileo's heliocentric system replaced a geocentric system that could not account for the retrograde motion of Venus, sunspots, and other anomalies, and in turn was replaced by an astronomy that recognized even the sun is not at the center of the universe. But as Galileo discovered, scientific revolutions do not come easy.[6] Kuhn reflected Galileo's and James' lesson when he wrote, "In science . . . novelty emerges only with difficulty, manifested by resistance, against a background provided by expectation. Initially, only the anticipated and usual are experienced even under circumstances where anomaly is latter to be observed. Further acquaintance, however, does result in awareness of something wrong or does relate the effect to something that has gone wrong before."[7] Though he anticipated resistance to change, Kuhn could not have predicted the BRI's efforts to reiterate the anticipated and suppress further acquaintance with things gone wrong.

As the sociologist of science Bruno Latour argues, science is an infinitely human practice that is more rhetorical than philosophical. Latour explained the rhetoric of science-writing: *"By itself a given sentence is neither a fact nor a fiction; it is made so by others, later on. You make it more of a fact if you insert it as a closed, obvious, firm and packaged premise leading to some other less closed, less obvious, less firm and less united consequence."*[8] That vivisection is necessary for the development of human medicines is a premise that Latour would call a black box; it is an unexamined assumption that researchers assert as a closed, obvious, firm, and packaged premise that they *believe* (rather than know) will lead to medical discoveries.[9] This essay begins, then, by describing anomalies that should cause scientists to question one governing paradigm of biomedical research. Given the magnitude of the anomalies produced by researchers, I ask, why have scientists not questioned false premises that put humans at risk and cause NHA to needlessly suffer? This question propels us into a discussion of the BRI itself and its motivations. Once I have illustrated that the BRI's goals are not always scientific, I shift to a discussion of two communicative strategies the BRI employs to protect the status quo. I first argue that the BRI controls most of the pertinent information sources in a manner that hides its own shortcomings and prevents insurgent voices from being heard. Second, the BRI employs public relations professionals to justify animal experiments and attack and intimidate those few competing scholars who are able to publish. These efforts contradict the very purpose of science, endanger human life, and disturb modern ethics.

THE ACCUMULATION OF ANOMALIES

There has been an accumulation of significant anomalies in scientific practice and public opinion that should have led by now to a revolution. One such anomaly is that animal experiments have become increasingly unreliable predictors of human outcomes in the age of microbiological research. Currently, government agencies like the U.S. Food and Drug Administration (FDA) mandate that all new drugs first be tested on NHA before these proceed to human clinical trials. Part of the motive for this rule is that it "covers the asses" (to use an expression popular in Washington, D.C.) of bureaucrats and elected officials who fear retribution from voters disturbed by the side effects of medical interventions. Requiring all drugs to be tested on animals permits bureaucrats and elected officials to tell the public that they did everything they were supposed to have done as a defense against later complaints of adverse reactions. However, of the drugs that prove effective and safe in animal tests, the overwhelming majority are found ineffective and/or unsafe during human tests. According to the FDA itself, 92 percent of drugs that pass the animal testing phase fail to make it to the market, a figure that climbs to a 95 percent failure rate for "major scientific discoveries with therapeutic potential."[10] Furthermore, of the small percentage of drugs that make it to market, up to half must be recalled or relabeled because they produce serious adverse effects (like death) that were not predicted by the NHA experiments.[11] Vivisection fails to predict human reactions more than 95 percent of the time, an anomaly that should leave scientists scratching their heads.

Though the public is largely unaware of this extraordinary failure rate, it is nevertheless wary of vivisection as evidenced by an increasing aversion to such tests. And while defenders of vivisection once argued that animals do not feel pain, the public has long known otherwise, a common sense recently buttressed by scientific studies that repeatedly illustrate animals suffer physical and emotional pain. Not surprisingly, recent polls reveal that 89–90 percent of the British people think animal testing should only be used as a last resort.[12] Even those who perform the animal experiments know: 97 percent acknowledge that the NHA they subject to experiments experience pain.[13] While the BRI rejects this anomaly as a problem of ethics rather than as a scientific failing, the extraordinary failure rate of animal experiments and public opposition to vivisection are intricately connected through the commonsense notion that if causing harm produces a negligible benefit, researchers should not cause harm. Public opinion surveys illustrate, if not a conscious awareness, a suspicion that the benefits of vivisection do not outweigh its costs. This too is an anomaly; though they may not be able to put their finger on it, the public suspects that biomedical research is unethical. Perhaps this suspicion is based in reality.[14]

Public suspicion of biomedical research practices creates an additional problem for the governing scientific paradigm. Medical ethicists José Luiz Telles de Almeida and Fermin Roland Schramm have argued that medical science faces "paradigmatic instability" as a result of shifting approaches to ethics.[15] Though Kuhn focused on science rather than ethics, at the level of human practice the two concepts are inextricably related. Scientists do not practice their craft in an ethical vacuum, as Albert Einstein recognized after atomic bombs were dropped on Hiroshima and Nagasaki.[16] The biomedical research paradigm, in particular, is caught in a web of ethics that often becomes headline news: stem cells debated; CIA human-testing experiments uncovered; euthanasia protested. . . . Biomedical research is supposed to be about the improvement of *life*. Because it is about life, it is not only a scientific endeavor, but an ethical endeavor as well.[17] Hence the orthodox paradigm of biomedical research should become unstable as a result of shifting trends in society's beliefs about ethical medicine. This shift is also a result of broader shifts in attitudes about what separates humankind from NHA, a shift that has put the BRI in an illogical bind.

Researchers have long justified animal experiments by arguing that human and NHA physiologies are so similar that results of testing on one group will be the same or very similar to the other group. Yet defenders of vivisection simultaneously and contradictorily argue animals are so different from humans that causing them pain is ethical. This claim is the tail end of a series of failed arguments for distinction: Humans are the only animal capable of speech? Wrong. Humans are the only conscious animal? Wrong. Humans are the only animal that suffers? Wrong, and on and on.[18] This arbitrary exercise has gotten so silly that some defenders of the paradigm have resorted to the distinction that humans are the only animal that makes tools that make tools.[19] These distinctions, which have been employed to support the BRI's governing paradigm, illustrate how the defense of vivisection is based on non-scientific assumptions intended to buttress a failing premise: that NHA are not like humans and thus can be used in any manner humans please.

In addition to arbitrary distinctions offered between humans and NHA, vivisection is defended by arguments based on centuries-old evidence. It is true that significant discoveries like the circulation of blood and the importance of air to survival were predicated on seventeenth-century animal experiments.[20] But this history is now used to defend vivisection at the molecular biological level, the level at which medical research is practiced today. Indeed, the practice of vivisection is so entrenched that it has never been subject to the same monitoring, testing, and proofs that new methods must undergo before gaining widespread acceptance in medical research. The black box premise was recently celebrated with the presentation of the Nobel Prize in medicine, the BRI's most prestigious honor, for the creation of genetic knockout mice (mice that are genetically manipulated to suppress or express specific traits), even though no tangible medical benefits have been derived from this "advance." The prize illustrates vivisectors' assumptions about the value of animal research and provides a fallacious argument from authority in favor of vivisection: If the Nobel Committee says it is valuable, it must be.[21] As a team of public health researchers led by Pandora Pound argued, "Clinicians and the public often consider it axiomatic that animal research has contributed to the treatment of human disease, yet little evidence is available to support this view." Pound and her assistants further noted that, "anecdotal evidence or unsupported claims are often used as justification—for example, statements that the need for animal research is 'self evident' or that 'Animal experimentation is a valuable research method which has proved itself over time.'"[22] When the BRI and the Nobel Committee reiterate the "self evidence" of vivisection, the public and many researchers may be misled into believing it.

While the authority of long-dead natural philosophers like William Harvey (the seventeenth-century discoverer of the circulation of blood) might still be authoritative for questions about universal biological processes, today's medical researchers pose questions at the molecular and genetic levels, where interspecies and even inter-individual differences are significant. Every doctor who has taken an anatomy class knows that, while there are norms, each cadaver has its share of deviations. This problem of genetic and biological difference is magnified when attempts are made to extrapolate NHA physiology to human physiology.[23] When researchers studying diabetes, for example, recently questioned a long-held assumption that humans and mice produced insulin the same way, they found that the two insulin-producing systems are incomparable and in doing so advanced the search for a cure by refocusing efforts on the human system.[24]

Experiments on NHA produce results that do not reliably predict human reactions because of differences in physiology, metabolism, distribution, absorption, excretion, genetic makeup, genetic expression, protein activity, and protein-to-protein interaction that occur among species, among different strains within a species, and even among individuals. These differences, in turn, increase costs, endanger researchers (animal bites, emotional pain, attacks by animal activists), and distort results.[25] I recognize there are similarities across all species, however, it is the differences that render extrapolation from NHA to humans tenuous at best. Thus, while there are occasional successes in animal experimentation, there are far more failures. So why does vivisection continue?

WHAT DRIVES THE BIOMEDICAL RESEARCH INDUSTRY?

Given the massive research budgets of thousands of government bureaucracies, educational institutions, research corporations, and non-profit organizations, and given the immense profits from the sale of drugs, vaccines, and medical devices, it is no wonder the BRI pours billions of dollars into public relations even as the public grows increasingly suspicious about the ethics of vivisection. For institutions affiliated with the BRI, the status quo is critical to the bottom line. Not surprisingly, then, in 2006 the pharmaceutical industry spent $19 billion on marketing and promotions, and another $5.3 billion on advertising in the United States alone, and this was not simply for product sales. As P*h*RMA (one of the industry's lobbying groups) explains, advertising is also intended to "educate" the public about the BRI. In other words, P*h*RMA sees advertising as an extension of public relations efforts designed to protect the status quo.[26] Those multibillion-dollar figures are only part of the funds spent on public relations experts, lobbyists, industry trade groups, international campaigns, educational institutions, and affiliated industry groups and professional organizations. The BRI also provides substantial funds for patient-affiliated grassroots organizations and dummy front groups whose policy-making decisions are bent to the financial interests of the drug companies.[27] As a former lobbyist for health-related associations, I experienced bending to the will of the BRI to further my advocacy work for people with disabilities.[28] Thanks to the efforts of public relations professionals in a wide range of local, national, and international bureaucracies, and thanks to the press operations of politicians and cause-oriented celebrities who promote the BRI, an intricate web of connections between the BRI, government, and media has emerged to protect the governing paradigm. When actor-activist Michael J. Fox lobbies Congress to support Parkinson's research and when anchorwoman Katie Couric promotes research to cure cancer, for example, they also promote the BRI.[29]

Even in the face of this nexus between political power and celebrity, Marcia Angell, former editor in chief of the *New England Journal of Medicine*, discovered the public has become skeptical of BRI claims. She writes that, "It is mainly because of this resistance that drug companies are now blanketing us with public relations messages. And the magic words, repeated over and over like an incantation, are *research*, *innovation*, and *American*. Research. Innovation. American. It makes a great story. But while the rhetoric is stirring, it has very little to do with reality. . . . Research and development (R&D) is a relatively small part of the budgets of the big drug companies—dwarfed by their vast expenditures on marketing and administration."[30] The purpose of that spending is threefold: First, the BRI is ultimately geared toward the sales of products. Second, the BRI (including university biomedical centers, nonprofit research hospitals, and so on) must seek and protect corporate, government, and non-profit research funding streams. The combined proceeds of sales and research funding are quickly making the BRI a trillion-dollar industry.[31] Lastly, in order to accomplish the first two goals, the BRI must guard its reputation in the global market of public opinion. It is only through protecting its image that the funding streams will continue to grow and to profit stakeholders in the variety of corporations, institutions, and bureaucracies that support vivisection.

The public relations efforts of the BRI come with a heavy price. The public relations machine distorts information to protect the status quo, and the industry's web of relationships makes scientific progress almost impossible, because the BRI controls most of the sources of information that could encourage change. That control has been granted to the BRI because of the breadth and complexity of medical research.[32] Given the profits and power of the BRI and the difficulty that individuals face in evaluating thousands of complex claims of truth, the BRI's public relations machine has manipulated the public into relying on "experts" who promote the paradigm. These experts are not unbiased truth-seekers who open-mindedly participate in the scientific process. As doctor and professor of medicine John Ioannidis found, "for many current scientific fields, claimed research findings may often be simply accurate measures of the prevailing bias."[33] Explaining how defenders of vivisection believe their own dogma about the efficacy of NHA research, James Gluck (MD) and Steven Kubacki (PhD in psychology) discovered "ample evidence in the published literature about the dark side of research to chasten even the most committed researcher."[34] Many animal researchers ignore ethical lapses, failed experiments, and false results. The pro-vivisection bias that appears in reports of animal testing rests largely on the assumption that the work performed is morally good, a disposition that can lead at least to the unconscious neglect of data and other less-than-ideal scientific practices. Here is the resistance to change that Kuhn described. When the resistance is magnified by the BRI's public relations machine, the "truth" and the "good" of orthodox biomedical research becomes very difficult to challenge, and scientific revolution becomes impossible. Examining exactly how the BRI controls information will help to illustrate and undermine the dogmatic adherence to a paradigm that should have failed long ago.

CONTROLLING INFORMATION

When the biomedical research community was recently shocked at the failure of a highly touted new drug that was expected to reduce the effects of stroke, I was not surprised. Because of numerous failures and the acknowledgment of poor animal testing methodologies, NXY-059 was tested on NHA using gold-standard protocols. These protocols included more consistent use of blinding, randomization, standardization, and other laboratory methodologies. The BRI was convinced that these improved protocols would lead to better data and prevent the failure of this promising new drug. After successfully testing the drug on NHA, researchers were certain that the same positive results would ensue for humans. Instead, during the human-testing phase, placebos tested almost as well as NXY-059. After this latest debacle, the BRI ironically claimed that the failure was only the result of poor protocols. In her eulogy for NXY-059, Andrea Gawrylewski, former associate editor of the BRI mouthpiece *The Scientist*, lamented that animal research models are still not methodologically rigorous enough.[35] Rather than accepting the anomaly of a >95 percent failure rate, the BRI controlled the damage and deployed a strategy of deflection to pin the blame for NXY-059's failure on methods and data collection.

Similarly, researchers have ascribed their field's Proteus Phenomenon (the more research, the less certain the findings) to non-standardized methodologies and poor data keeping.[36] Yet the least complicated explanation, and according to Occam's razor the most likely cause of vivisection's repeated failures, is that humans and NHA cannot be reliably compared at the molecular biological level. Much like the seventeenth-century "scientists" who tried to save the geocentric universe with preposterously complicated explanations of galactic anomalies, biomedical researchers today are focused on the problem of uniform reporting requirements and standardized methodologies when they would help science to progress by simply acknowledging that humans and NHA are different.[37]

Regardless of how rigorously data is collected and protocols are imposed, errors will continue to be commonplace because of interspecies differences in physiology; the more humans delve into the intricacies of biology, the further away from universal truths we get. This is a failure of Platonic science and an illustration of why ethics (not to mention rhetoric) are important measures of the success or failure of scientific paradigms. One team of medical researchers led by Peter Greaves was forced to admit, "despite the experience-driven evolution of practical methods through the use of new analytical techniques, better laboratory animals and improved study design and data management, the actual data to support current practice remains limited."[38] In other words, try as they might to improve study design, data collection, and even the genetics of lab animals like knockout mice, defenders of vivisection have been unable to prove that animal research is effective. Their *faith* in the paradigm has gotten in the way of their ability to logically appraise the black box premise for what it is: a failure. Rather than asking, "is animal research necessary to find cures for human diseases," defenders of vivisection assume the answer is "yes" and thus they interpret data in a way that reiterates the "truth" of the efficacy of vivisection. While the BRI may blame failed animal experiments on poor data and methods, the BRI should be blamed for spinning results every which way except for the obvious direction: that the experiments failed because NHA are not human.

The BRI's ideological shell game was recently exposed when two paradigms came into conflict over a proposal by vivisectors that doctors refrain from using a common anesthetic on children because of a risk of brain injury found in NHA experiments. Neonatal and pediatric practitioners claimed, however, that the results of anesthetic research done on animals did not equate to results in human babies and thus continued to employ methods that have been in use for decades and have shown no appreciable side effects. Even so, after rejecting the vivisectors' recommendation with a list of non-equivalences between the test subjects' and childrens' brains, one pediatric researcher paid homage to the importance of vivisection, a testament to the power of orthodoxy and the ability of the BRI to ensure fealty to the governing paradigm.[39] A more obvious conclusion would have been that human and NHA brains are not equivalent, so doctors should not rely on vivisection to inform pediatric anesthesiology. Moreover, the doctors should have concluded that researchers should stop experimenting on NHA because the results cannot be applied to humans. Even though two biomedical practices came into conflict here, the episode illustrates how the BRI controls information in a manner that hides flaws and perpetuates orthodoxy. Doctors on both sides were expected to reaffirm the paradigm of vivisection.

Just as the Catholic Church defended the Ptolemaic system by decrying Galileo's argument for a heliocentric universe, the BRI defends its orthodoxy by mandating loyalty and attacking those who are disloyal.[40] Defenders of vivisection reproduce ad infinitum their ideology in medical journals and the popular press, and condemn those few who challenge their assumptions. As Latour noted, "the power of rhetoric lies in making the dissenter feel lonely."[41] Rhetorical critic Dale Sullivan lists a variety of practices intended to make opponents feel lonely including crying anarchy, setting impossible standards, co-optation, repetition, and forum control. He then describes four distinct types of forum control: peer review, the denial of public forums, public correction when opponents speak, and published ridicule. The journal review process, for example, often forces authors to conform to orthodoxy. Essays that fail to conform are usually rejected.[42] Editors do not justify the rejection of oppositional manuscripts because of the reality that these threaten the paradigm, but instead for reasons that logically fail on their face. For example, this essay originated as a partnership between the named author and a specialist in the neurological sciences who has submitted manuscripts to medical journals illustrating high failure rates for developing effective treatments because of the BRI's reliance on vivisection. The manuscripts were rejected because, as reviewers complained, the author's work was "nihilistic" and "ideological," reminding us of James' first stage of a new theory: the theory is attacked as absurd.[43] Reviewers also objected that too many similar articles have already been published, a reminder of James' second stage: that the theory is known and irrelevant. In reality, medical journals have published few articles that challenge the efficacy of animal research, particularly in the field of neurology, where the most harmful vivisection practices occur (both in terms of failed experiments and the pain caused to NHA). In the massive corpus of biomedical research publications, studies that describe the failures of the governing paradigm account for a tiny fraction of published scholarship. Furthermore, even as reviewers exaggerate the number of articles that draw attention to failures, they fail to recall that scientific research requires the replication of studies, and thus repeated articles on similar subjects. These reviewers do not share the same complaint, for example, about the many articles that repeat previous animal experiments. The level of control exerted by the BRI is exemplified, as the reader has probably already figured out, by the proposed second author's need to remove him/herself from authorship of this essay because a critique of the BRI's vivisection practices would have threatened his/her career prospects in the neurosciences.[44]

The flood of papers supporting vivisection is one, tautological, method of controlling the forum: vivisection retains its necessity because its use is affirmed by the huge number of articles supporting vivisection. Yet many of the published reports of vivisection are inaccurate. According to Ioannidis and public health research teams led by Pablo Parel and Pound, vivisection often produces false positive results.[45] While most researchers do not consciously work to achieve false positives, rhetorical critic Alan Gross has recognized that science writing "is not a window on reality, but the vehicle of an ideology that systematically misdescribes experimental and observational events."[46] Or, for the social change scholar Herbert Simons, in writing about pharmaceutical research reports, "reporters of every kind not only *do not* 'tell it like it is,' but *cannot*. Moreover, even if they *could*, they would be under considerable institutional pressure *not to*."[47] The false positives that researchers produce, in turn, produce a helpful side effect—publication—which the BRI employs to justify the governing paradigm.[48] Medical journals prefer to publish "breakthroughs" rather than the results of failed experiments, and it is usually only years after a false positive is published before the reality of a flawed study becomes apparent. Moreover, some of these studies are buried by the regulatory agencies that are supposed to oversee the drugs. One such study, warning that a new antipsychotic drug named Seroquel caused significant weight gain, diabetes, and hyperglycemia, was suppressed by the

FDA, permitting the drug's manufacturer to reap tens of billions of dollars in earnings—and this for a drug that has proven no better than older antipsychotic drugs.[49] These negative discoveries are usually overlooked in medical journals, are not trumpeted by the BRI's public relations machine, and are only mentioned in the mainstream press if they result in serious side effects to humans or harm the economic prospects of the pharmaceutical company that was expected to profit from the research.[50] Regardless of the ultimate results of the false positives, the published articles become permanent "proof" of the efficacy of vivisection for the sole reason that these studies were published. This feedback cycle then reinforces the decision-making of funding sources to continue to support animal experiments and the *faith* that researchers have in vivisection.

Against the tens of thousands of published articles promoting animal research, stand only a handful of articles pointing out the problems of vivisection. This lacuna is not for lack of trying or evidence, but rather because of the difficulty of publishing results contrary to the prevailing orthodoxy. In an essay about gender dimorphism, rhetorical critic Celeste Condit described the barriers and attacks that opponents of governing biomedical paradigms face. Revealing James' first and second stages, Condit was attacked for writing a letter to the editor of *Science* as "ideological" and "emotional" on the one hand and yet also adding nothing to the subject of brain-sex research. And so her letter was not published.[51] On the rare occasion when a challenging essay is published, the author and editor may be subjected to other kinds of attacks. Simon Festing, Executive Director of the Research Defence Society (RDS), a British Public Relations and lobby group that receives funding from the BRI, is responsible for one recent instance of bullying. Festing publicly called for the journal *Biogenic Amines* to retract a paper by Dr. Jarrod Bailey that noted the failures of animal experimentation. Festing claimed that this *peer-reviewed* essay was "extreme anti-vivisection propaganda" that was only published because one of the journal's editors was biased (never mind the thousands of journal editors who are biased in favor of vivisection). Festing also contacted Bailey's superiors with a warning that Bailey's activities were contrary to the interests of his institution, a university where medical research is performed.[52]

In a blatant example of the repression of dissent, bioethicist David Benatar was prevented from publishing an essay challenging the orthodoxy about vivisection. Expecting that Benatar approved of the ethics of primate vivisection, medical editors had sought his contribution to a volume about NHA experimentation. But Benatar wrote that ethics have shifted since the nineteenth century and argued that researchers now find themselves in the awkward position of having to accept one of three difficult positions: that the intentional infliction of pain is cruel; that modern ethics should be rejected; or that it is possible to adopt a middle path that justifies their own work while claiming to minimize the pain they cause.[53] Benatar described this dilemma: "The first choice would threaten their livelihood or professional development; the second, their sense of themselves as scientists of integrity. The upshot is that the third option is psychologically easiest, especially given the human capacity for self-deception. The problem, however, is that selective ethics is bad ethics for just the same reason that selective science is bad science."[54] After being solicited, then rejected for this essay, Benatar replied to the editors with a letter noting that: "they wanted to be able to *say* that the volume included attention to the ethical issues, but in fact they wanted the ethical discussion only if it reached the conclusion that primate experimentation is morally acceptable." In response, the editors claimed that Benatar's ethics were "one-sided," a reaction that can be charitably described as ironic.[55]

Competing theories, whether ultimately proven correct or not, are the lifeblood of scientific progress. Yet these are being silenced by the BRI rather than published. As Latour understood, what counts when marshaling evidence of proof in science is not truth but rather which side can produce the greatest number of supportive publications.[56] The BRI controls what is published by chilling debate and threatening opponents into silence, by refusing to publish theories opposed to orthodoxy, and by promoting the orthodox paradigm through the publication of false positives that carry assumptions about the necessity of vivisection. Animal researchers find reassurance in these journals, believing their work validated by the overwhelming number of supporting articles. That is not science the way that thinkers from Galileo to Thomas Kuhn envisioned science. Beyond the devastating implications for science, the suppression of free speech has the potential to endanger the entire public sphere. Not surprisingly, industry groups that exploit animals in other ways, such as the greyhound racing industry, have adopted similar strategies to protect financial interests.[57]

PUBLIC RELATIONS

Even as industry groups attempt to silence the protests of their opponents, they pour extraordinary resources into dominating the media with public relations messages friendly to their interests. Public relations experts employed by the BRI have manipulated communication practices about vivisection through a wide variety of methods and targets. One practice of the BRI lies in the use of certain words and the rejection of other terms. The terms "vivisection" and "animal testing," for example, illustrate the rhetorical power of the BRI to manipulate the English language. During the nineteenth century, the term vivisection (from the Latin "to cut the living") was commonly employed to describe NHA experimentation. Its usefulness lies in its descriptive accuracy. However, the term acquired a cruel connotation, particularly after publication of Lewis Carroll's essay "Some Popular Fallacies About Vivisection" in 1875.[58] During the twentieth century, the BRI discouraged scientific and popular use of the term in favor of "animal testing," a deceptive phrase that suggests Carroll's fictitious animals are taking a quiz somewhere down Alice's rabbit hole.

The naming practices of the BRI's public relations organizations are particularly indicative of this kind of manipulation and illustrate the rabbit hole's depth. As professor emeritus of medical cell biology Michael Balls writes in *ATLA* (*Alternatives to Laboratory Animals*): "Who could doubt the objectives of Animal Aid, the British Union for the Abolition of Vivisection (BUAV), the European Coalition to End Animal Experiments (ECEAE), the Fund for the Replacement of Animals in Medical Experiments (FRAME), the Humane Research Trust (HRT), the National Anti Vivisection Society (NAVS), People for the Ethical Treatment of Animals (PETA), the Royal Society for the Prevention of Cruelty to Animals (RSPCA), or the Universities Federation for Animal Welfare."[59] By contrast, those advocacy organizations whose focus is on continuing vivisection are more broadly named Americans for Medical Progress (AMP), Speaking of Research, Coalition for Medical Progress, Medical Research Council, Research Defence Society (RDS), the European Biomedical Research Association, and the European Biomedical Research Coalition (notably, the last three of these share the same address which would explain the "coalition"). Thus, while AMP sounds so broad that it encompasses all Americans and all those who favor medical progress, the mission according to its own website is extremely narrow: "Americans for Medical Progress protects society's investment in research by nurturing public understanding of and support for the humane, necessary and valuable use of animals in medicine."[60] Similarly, the organization called Speaking of Research only speaks about one kind of research, according to its promotional materials: "Speaking of Research (SR) is a campus-oriented group that seeks to provide university students and faculty with accurate information and resources about the importance of animal research in medical science."[61] Rather than inform the public about their missions by calling themselves something like "Association for Animal Testing," or "Students for Vivisection," or "Coalition for Animal Research in Medicine," these organizations hide behind positive and ethically acceptable, if deceptive, names.

Alice's rabbit hole of deception, manipulation, and sleight-of-hand is epitomized by a 2008 children's coloring book produced by the North Carolina

Association for Biomedical Research (NCABR) and promoted by the U.S. National Institutes for Health (NIH—a government institution that provides approximately $30 billion every year for medical research). The cozy relationship between a public relations group (NCABR) and the grant-making institution for which it often advocates (the NIH) illustrates the nexus between money and power that the BRI has created. And the coloring book illustrates just how devious the BRI's public relations efforts can be. The book can be purchased by schools or can be downloaded for free through the NIH's website for children.[62] Through the coloring book, children are taught that researchers develop cures for dogs and humans by testing medicine on mice that are sick, and in doing so help to cure the mice as well. A veterinarian explains the research process to two children with a sick dog named Lucky: "A long time ago, a research scientist found the medicine I gave Lucky. I'll tell you how. She did research in a **lab**. A lab is a place where scientists work, and it is short for **laboratory**. She had mice in her lab. They lived in nice, clean cages. They were fed good food. But they were sick with the same disease Lucky had."[63] At the end of the coloring book, the children are so impressed with the veterinarian's story that one child decides to become a veterinarian himself, while his sister tells the vet: "I love animals too, Dr. Smith. But I want to be a research scientist. Then I can help animals and people!"[64] Of course it is more than convenient that the veterinarian neglects to mention that the mice are sick because the research scientist made them so, and further that mice died because other medicines and dosages failed. Similarly, the nice, clean cages sound almost domestic, as if the mice might be running in a wheel in a cage by the children's beds. Imagine the disappointment the girl will face when she learns that she must harm and cut these mice open to do research.

Indeed, the coloring book manipulates the children's love for animals by relying on the seventeenth-century justification for animal research: that animals and humans are physically very similar. After all, the medicine that cured the mice also cured Lucky and, if the need arose, would cure the children too. The veterinarian explains: "The mice in the lab, puppies like Lucky and children like you are all animals. Our bodies might look different, but we really are very much alike under our skin."[65] Ignoring the >95 percent failure rate for tests that had achieved positive results in NHA but not in humans, this coloring-book spokesperson for vivisection encourages the children to love "animal research" as a substitute for loving animals. If we are not bothered by the omissions and redefinitions because these maneuvers are standard to all public relations efforts, we should at least be incensed that the targeted audience here is children, young people without the critical skills to challenge blatant propaganda.

In confronting the haze of BRI public relations, I am reminded of Alice's encounter with Humpty Dumpty: "'I don't know what you mean by glory' Alice said. Humpty Dumpty smiled contemptuously. 'Of course you don't— till I tell you.'"[66] The public has, until recently, played Alice to the BRI's Humpty Dumpty. The redefinition of words, images, and concepts is at the heart of the BRI's public relations effort. Simon Festing, Director of the RDS and his assistant Robin Wilkinson, for example, practice spin-by-redefinition in their essay "The Ethics of Animal Research: Talking Point on the Use of Animals in Scientific Research."[67] The London-based RDS describes its purpose as representing "UK biomedical researchers in the public debate about the use of animals in biomedical research."[68] In short, Festing and Wilkinson are paid to practice rhetoric in defense of the orthodox biomedical research paradigm.

In the first sentence of their essay Festing and Wilkinson define animal research as "good" by equating it with the word "vital" (even though many NHA must die) while setting the BRI against opponents who are demonized as "extremists," an accusation that appears in the public relations materials of other, pro-vivisection groups.[69] Expanding into hyperbole and cataplexis (the language of threat), the authors caution against the "enormous and severe consequences" of a monolithic "animal rights" position—never mind the complexities of the variety of animal ethics movements and that some opponents are simply concerned about the harm vivisection does to humans. The public relations professionals deftly return to these themes in the essay's last paragraph when they conclude by warning of the "severe consequences for public health and biomedical research" that would be caused if animal rights extremists were permitted to stop current practices.[70] Though a transparent argument for those critical of public relations in general or of vivisection in particular, this epideictic, ideology-reinforcing, and team-building exercise shores up support within the BRI by posing the vitality of animal research against irrational enemies. Notably, the introductory and concluding paragraphs of this essay illustrate once again James' first stage in the history of a theory: claiming that the competing hypothesis is absurd. Festing and Wilkinson also model James' second stage (the opposing theory is accepted as obvious but unimportant) when they recognize the ethicality of laws and regulations that already restrict vivisection.

Festing and Wilkinson assume that vivisection works and refuse to accept the arguments of scientists who point out the waste of resources and the harmful consequences to humans, or ethicists who describe public suspicions about the use of NHA in experimentation. Furthermore, the public relations professionals never bother to demonstrate that animal research is integral to medical progress. Rather, they found their entire argument on an enthymeme:

because their audience has been trained by history and by public relations (like the children's coloring book) to believe that animal experimentation is necessary. All the authors do is repeat the mantra that animal experimentation is vital. Sadly, this is a difficult burden for opponents to overcome, as it requires the audience to be critical.[71] Remarkably, however, audiences have become skeptical of the BRI's claims.[72] Too many false positives, too many harmful effects, and too many anomalies are contributing to increasing support for non-animal experiments. Humpty Dumpty may be cracking.

CONCLUSION

Festing and Wilkinson are effective advocates for vivisection; that is their job. They are not paid to advance science, but rather to defend the BRI. And, though we may salute them as effective, we must criticize them for preserving a paradigm that is so flawed it produces what should be intolerable anomalies. Those repeated failures, both of scientific result and of public ethics, ought to be enough to cause a scientific revolution. We cannot trust the BRI's spokespeople to be neutral on the question of vivisection even though good scientific practice demands the position of neutrality.

Given that animal experiments fail to predict human outcomes more than 95 percent of the time; given that modern ethics have little tolerance for the intentional infliction of pain with minimal public benefit; and given that reliance on vivisection leads to human harms directly and indirectly, it is past time to question the black box assumption that experimenting on NHA is necessary for curing human disease and promoting human health. I recognize that the questioning will not come from those who uncritically follow BRI orthodoxy, but must instead come from scientists who are willing to acknowledge anomalies and question premises. Thus, nonscientists must defend the opponents of orthodoxy from intimidation and retaliation. Indeed, we must celebrate these scientists as modern Galileos. It is to them that we must entrust the work that philosophers of science from Galileo to Thomas Kuhn demanded; the work that has produced extraordinary advances in our understanding of the universe and of ourselves.

As rhetorical critics, we have the tools to examine the communication practices of the BRI and the media that illuminate the unethical and unscientific efforts of public relations professionals, journal editors, lawyers, lobbyists and others who defend a dead orthodoxy against which anomalies have been piling up for decades. The public has a responsibility to employ what critical thinking skills it has or may acquire to see through the haze of control and dominance that the BRI has sought to exercise over discourses about vivisection. As a starting point, I am convinced that we must abandon the Alice-in-Wonderland euphemisms "animal testing," "animal experimentation," and "animal research" in favor of the more descriptively accurate term that Lewis Carroll employed: vivisection. Perhaps, then we can begin to break through the first and second stages of a scientific theory and achieve James' promised result: adversaries will claim that they had opposed vivisection all along. In doing so, we will begin to build our critical literacy regarding animal ethics in a manner that reveals the machinations of biomedical orthodoxy while responding to ideology with logical reasoning and ethics that are not informed by self-interest.

Chapter Nine

Protection from
"Animal Rights Lunatics"

The Center for Consumer Freedom and Animal Rights Rhetoric

Wendy Atkins-Sayre

The animal rights movement and People for the Ethical Treatment of Animals (PETA) in particular have long been known for their attention-grabbing tactics. Although street protest is still one of PETA's staples, the "fight in the streets" has shifted to a fight in newspapers, on television, and online. PETA has used shocking publicity to gain the platform that is needed to attract an audience to its message: "animals are not ours to eat, wear, experiment on, or use for entertainment."[1] With an understanding of this use of the media, the Center for Consumer Freedom (CCF), a self-described "consumer rights group" primarily funded by food and beverage industries, has used similar strategies to undermine PETA's messages by questioning the group's credibility.[2] Describing the "animal cult movement," CCF argues, "The modern animal rights movement is not what it seems. Today's activists have perverted once-sensible animal welfare goals by putting animals ahead of human beings and employing a 'by any means necessary' philosophy to achieve their goals of 'total animal liberation.'"[3] The animal rights movement, and PETA as a representative, it argues, poses a threat to society and is a "terrible scam. The world deserves to know the truth."[4] That truth, of course, coincides with the corporate interests of the food and beverage industry.

The animal rights movement emerged fulsomely in the United States with the creation of PETA in 1980. Although animal rights were discussed prior to this moment, PETA was the first organized group to put the issue on the larger American political radar. Since then, PETA has succeeded in bringing attention to animal rights messages and, consequently, has become the lightning rod for groups opposed to the overall movement.[5] Going beyond the mission of many animal welfare organizations, the group argues that animals "should have the right to equal consideration of their interests."[6] Although PETA alone cannot receive credit for changes in beliefs about animal rights, there are indicators that support for animal rights is on the rise.[7] As reporter Larry Copeland writes, "The growing influence of animal rights activists increasingly is affecting daily life, touching everything from the foods Americans eat to what they study in law school, where they buy their puppies and even whether they should enjoy a horse-drawn carriage ride in New York's Central Park."[8] Given the success of the movement, and PETA's provocative campaigns, it is not surprising that it would be the target of anti–animal rights groups.

Perhaps no organization has so vehemently and methodically attacked PETA as CCF. Established in 1995, CCF defines itself as "a nonprofit coalition of restaurants, food companies, and consumers working together to promote personal responsibility and protect consumer choices."[9] CCF originally formed with close ties to the tobacco and food industry giant Phillip Morris (owner of Kraft and General Foods), which served as an early major contributor.[10] In the initial pitch for funds from Phillip Morris, Richard Berman (a public relations company owner and founder of CCF) explained that the group would "unite the restaurant and hospitality industries in a campaign to defend their consumers and marketing programs against attacks from anti-smoking, anti-drinking, anti-meat, etc. activists."[11] The group is hesitant to release information about its corporate contributors, arguing that it does not want its clients targeted by activists, but admits that roughly one hundred companies contribute to its coffers.[12] The Center for Media and Democracy, a Washington-based watchdog group, claims that some of its largest contributors include Coca Cola, Wendy's, and Tyson Foods.[13] In 2005, CCF reported over $3.8 million dollars in expenditures, with Berman's public relations firm billing over $1.6 million of that sum.[14]

The grassroots side of CCF is even less accessible. Although the organization claims to represent consumers and the website and advertisements solicit support, membership information is conspicuously missing. This predominant dependence on corporate backing without clear public support makes CCF appear to be an "Astroturf" organization—corporate interests simulating grassroots to make the organization appear to have broad support—rather than a grassroots movement.[15] Nevertheless, CCF rhetoric crafts grassroots language, claiming to struggle against a "growing cabal of activists" including "animal-rights misanthropes" who "claim to know 'what's best for you.'"[16] CCF offers to fight for consumer choice and to protect consumers from the radicals.

The group attacks a wide range of grassroots and professional organizations and governmental agencies, including Public Citizen, the American Medical Association, and the Centers for Disease Control and Prevention. Its primary targets, however, are the Center for Science in the Public Interest, an organization focused on nutrition and food safety, and PETA.[17] One of CCF's websites attacks PETA (the subtitle of the page is "The truth about PETA and other animal-rights extremists" and the group's name appears all over the page), describing the danger of the organization and "other animal-rights extremists": "Today's activists want to force you to eat nothing but beans and greens; and wear nothing but cotton, rayon, and rubber. They want to ban hunting, fishing, zoos, rodeos, and circuses. Some want to permanently end Kosher slaughter. They even want to outlaw the use of animals in the search for cures for AIDS, Parkinson's Disease [*sic*], and cancer. And a growing number take the law into their own hands, crossing the line from peaceful protest to violent crime."[18] This attack provides an introduction to the variety of arguments that CCF marshals against PETA. The Astroturf group frequently resorts to slippery-slope and false-dichotomy fallacies in exploring the future of animal rights effects, arguing that animal rights groups pose a threat to individuals and emphasizing PETA's ties to violent acts. In doing so, CCF situates itself as presenting the "truth" and protecting consumers from animal rights "radicals."

Examining a selection of CCF advertisements, this chapter analyzes the textual and visual components of the messages.[19] A rhetorical analysis of the advertisements shows the emergence of one primary theme centered on the idea of the threat that PETA, and animal rights groups more broadly, pose to consumers. According to this theme, the animal rights message threatens personal freedom, family, and natural order. That message is a key CCF tactic to undermine PETA's credibility and is developed through rhetorical strategies such as slippery-slope fallacies, false dichotomy, and enthymemes that are deployed to make the case that PETA acts as a terrorist organization. Using rhetorical critics Kevin DeLuca and Jennifer Peeples' concept of the public screen, I argue that although PETA is able to gain an audience for its message through spectacle, CCF uses a similar tactic to undermine PETA's message.[20] Though the public screen provides a useful tool for social movements looking to disseminate a message, I contend that the medium privileges conservative over radical messages, because the animal rights messages require the audience to make significant changes in their beliefs. This case study, therefore, provides an opportunity to examine the limitations of the public screen, particularly the notion that messages of change as articulated through image events face difficulty because they unfold as fragmented arguments that require a great deal of assemblage on the part of publics. In a contest of images in particular, the more conservative position gains preeminence as the most viable option. This is so because publics do not have to pull together and reconcile the status quo within their belief systems, as they do with messages of change expressed through image events. In order to develop this argument, I first explain the idea of the public screen and its use by animal ethics and corporate interest groups. I then analyze CCF advertisements, drawing conclusions about the usefulness of the public screen concept to social movement rhetoric.

THE PUBLIC SCREEN

In their discussion about the changing nature of public deliberation, DeLuca and Peeples argue that Jürgen Habermas' idea of the traditional public sphere is limited in its ability to explain the ways that individuals form opinions.[21] As Habermas explains it, the public sphere is the "sphere of private people coming together as a public; these people soon claimed the public sphere as a locus of power against the public authorities themselves. While this was first applied to the realm of politics in the eighteenth and nineteenth centuries, the public sphere now enables "the people" to engage in debates over the general rules governing relations in the mostly privatized but publicly relevant sphere of commodity exchange and social labor."[22] DeLuca and Peeples, however, argue that Habermas imagines a flawed idea of public deliberation, one based on a "privileging of dialogue and fetishization of a procedural rationality."[23] Instead, they argue that in this fast-paced, hyper-mediated world, it is dissemination, not dialogue that largely guides our deliberation. Dissemination of the message takes place through the public screen—"television, computer, and the front page of newspapers."[24] The authors extend this concept of public screen to include advertising and public relations campaigns, explaining that "on today's public screen corporations and states stage spectacles (advertising and photo ops) certifying their status before the people/public *and* activists participate through the performance of image events, employing the consequent publicity as a social medium for forming public opinion and holding corporations and states accountable. Critique through spectacle, not critique versus spectacle."[25] Although it may seem, prima facie, that advertisements are often solely designed to catch the audience's attention, there may be critical arguments put forth within and/or because of the message.

Given this change in the way we deliberate, images on the public screen have become an important part of this process. Consequently, DeLuca and Peeples argue that as critics, we must take spectacle, or "image events," seriously. DeLuca and rhetorician John Delicath, in examining the tactics of radical environmental groups, further define image events as "staged acts of protest designed for media dissemination."[26] Although these media events are capable of creating a message, image events are limited in the rhetorical work that they can do. Delicath and DeLuca point out that image events "are an effective tool for addressing the problem of the 'distracted and disinterested' audience." Because they "communicate fragments of argument in the form of highly charged visuals they are possibly quite effective in shaping public discourse and affecting public debate."[27] The important language here is "fragments." Although audiences are confronted with arguments in the form of image events, they must complete the argument, reconciling their own beliefs with the argument put forth by the images. Thus, as Delicath and DeLuca conclude, image events "shift the responsibility for argument construction to the audience. Image events do not produce immediate persuasion."[28] That shift means that the rhetor loses control over the interpretation of the message. This is not unlike any message that works enthymemetically, but because image events often operate based on "risky" messages—in other words, actions that may be highly questionable to some—that loss of control in the interpretation of the message threatens to completely unravel the original argument.

Furthermore, reconciling the argument fragments that emerge from image events with our own beliefs leads to a confrontation with the status quo. In order for individuals to be swayed by radical messages, they must abandon their previously held beliefs. Thus, image events produced by the animal rights movement often threaten our belief systems by forcefully questioning current beliefs and placing alternative ideologies in our line of sight. The rhetorical "payoff" for this tactic is sometimes rewarding because individuals may, in fact, be persuaded by the oppositional power of the argument fragments. However, the forcefulness of the image event may also be risky, because it can be perceived as a threat to individual belief systems and thus to the individuals themselves.

Regardless of the risk associated with image events, the use of the public screen has become an important part of public deliberation. This form of argumentation is not only used widely today, but also has historical roots. As rhetorical scholar Davi Johnson points out, Martin Luther King, Jr. successfully used the civil rights protests in Birmingham to bring images of racial injustice to a wide audience, using "the power of images to stage public dramas that made racial conflict visible."[29] These images act as lightning rods, stirring controversy and potentially stimulating discussion.

It is this tactic—the use of the image events—that prevails in many of PETA's campaigns. No longer able to draw sufficient attention to the movement message from street protest, letter-writing campaigns, and boycotts alone, PETA relies heavily on confrontational advertisements and media stunts, adding to the "images, hypermediacy, spectacular publicity, cacophony, distraction, and dissent" that is the public screen.[30] The group is, perhaps, best known for its anti-fur campaigns featuring naked celebrities. As rhetorician Lesli Pace points out, PETA received significant media attention with these anti-fur advertisements, but there were mixed reactions over the use of women's bodies to send an animal rights message.[31] The media splash that accompanies these types of ads and the controversy that they often spur provide additional access to the public screen.

There are numerous examples of PETA using these tactics. In making the argument for a vegan lifestyle, for example, the group created a set of wall-sized posters comparing the slaughter of cows for food to the Holocaust. Although the posters appeared on a number of occasions, it was the media splash in response to the campaign that brought more attention to the group and its message.[32] Similarly, PETA's fashion show protests in opposition to the wearing of fur, their shockingly counterintuitive advertisement campaigns (like the "Got Beer?" campaign in opposition to milk consumption), and public denouncements of "ill-informed" celebrities, such as actress Jennifer Lopez and *Vogue* editor Anna Wintour, have also attracted a great deal of media consideration.[33] Writing about PETA's "Barnum-like genius for attracting attention," *New Yorker* columnist Michael Specter explains that PETA is happy to receive the coverage—both good and bad: "PETA's publicity formula—eighty percent outrage, ten percent each of celebrity and truth—ensures that everything it does offends someone."[34] Whether offending people, making them laugh, or motivating them to question their actions, PETA's campaigns are generally successful at bringing attention to the animal rights message—for better or worse.

Not to be outdone by PETA's tactics, however, CCF has been vigilant in attacking PETA's messages with similar campaigns. Using a strategy of détournement or what rhetorical critic Christine Harold describes as a "pranking" rhetoric—"playfully and provocatively folding existing cultural forms in on themselves"—CCF turns PETA's tactics against them.[35] Spending hundreds of thousands of dollars on full-page newspaper advertisements, television commercials, and billboards, the group has also managed to make its way to the public screen.[36] For example, when CCF accuses PETA of using an alleged front organization (the Physicians Committee for Responsible Medicine) to denounce particular foods, calling them "phony physicians," media outlets are able to talk about the "food fights" between the two groups, thus giving both free publicity that reaches a far wider audience than the original messages.[37] In breaking a story about PETA employees disposing of euthanized animals, CCF directed people to a specialized website, petakills-animals.com. Placing a billboard in the center of Times Square in New York with only this website listed, the group grabbed the attention of the *New York Times* and other media outlets.[38] CCF is able to create a space for its own message by attacking the ideology of other well-known groups. After all, a "food fight" or "billboard war" makes for an attention-grabbing news story. Moreover, this pranking strategy allows CCF messages to pull from the cultural cachet that PETA creates through its own style of image events.

The difficulty with the use of the public screen, of course, is that rhetors lose a certain amount of control over how their messages will be interpreted. With both organizations, there is a double usage of the public screen. Both, for example, craft paid advertisements that are intended to be controversial and, thus, may stimulate discussion about the issue. The paid advertisements, however, lead to free access to the public screen because the controversy created by the ads draws media attention. While the paid advertisements offer more control over the message, "free media" is dependent on the media's interpretation of the message. Rhetorical critic Julie Shutten points out that although the public screen has been discussed as an alternative framework for understanding social movement rhetoric, "acknowledging the increasing relevance of the public screen does not in itself answer the question of whether media visibility helps or hinders movements."[39] As Shutten argues, the public screen creates an image of an argument (and of the movement itself, in this case), but that image might not match up with reality. Of course, as Shutten and DeLuca and Peeples point out, gaining access to the public screen and, therefore, further disseminating the message can often be beneficial regardless of the outcome.[40] The "screen wars"—that is, the use of image events by dueling entities that allows both access to the public screen and dissemination of competing messages on that screen—that have occurred between CCF and PETA provide an opportunity to explore the limitations of the public screen. In the end, although the public screen may provide a platform for social movements, it also acts as a double-edged sword in some instances. In the case of PETA and CCF, the anti–animal rights forces use the rhetorical tactics of PETA to undermine its message.

POSING A THREAT TO CONSUMERS

Offering a number of slick print advertisements, commercials, and websites, CCF's anti–animal rights publicity varies in tone from angry to humorous to matter of fact. There is a heavy reliance on the use of images of children and mothers in the advertisements and those images of family are often juxtaposed with the violent images of animal rights groups (although viewers are encouraged to read the actions as specifically those of PETA) and the words of PETA. Animals are portrayed in the advertisements, but are placed in a domesticated position, thus strengthening the division between human and animal. Read together, the advertisements send an overwhelming message that the animal rights group is threatening. The threat comes in a number of forms: threats to personal freedoms, to family, and to assumptions about the place of animals in the so-called natural hierarchy. Moreover, CCF seems to indicate that PETA's overall message acts as a threat to individual belief systems.

Before exploring the strategies used by CCF, it must be noted that there is a glaring omission from the group's message. As an organization composed of restaurant and food industry corporations that are purportedly devoted to protecting consumer choices, one might assume that CCF would, for example, question PETA's push for a vegetarian lifestyle. In fact, most of the attacks on PETA are labeled a response to "food radicals" because it would be hypocritical to attack the choice to go vegetarian. When reading the advertisements, CCF rarely refutes PETA's claims to a healthier lifestyle, a more ethical existence, a more humane treatment of animals, and so forth. Instead of directly attacking PETA's claims, the central theme of CCF's message is the threat that PETA poses to individuals and their families, in addition to the attacks on the credibility of the organization. Perhaps the image event as a tactic obscures the veracity of PETA's claims, thus leaving the organization's credibility as the central target of CCF's attack. In the end, although the strength of the CCF's argument is questionable, the scare tactics and ad hominem attacks are easier arguments to make and are also more conducive to the public screen in that a fight between organizations makes for a more intriguing news story than a discussion about ideology.

The first strategy used by CCF emphasizes a concern for personal freedom and is developed in the form of a slippery-slope fallacy. Given that CCF claims to be devoted to protecting consumer freedom, this message falls neatly in line with its mission. In a print advertisement, the words of the "food police" are boldly printed in the center of the page: "You are too stupid . . . to make your own food choices." Arguing that, "they're going too far," the group puts forth a mantra: "It's your food. It's your drink. It's your freedom."[41] A similar radio advertisement alludes to more sinister animal rights action. The advertisement mentions no specific groups, but pokes fun at the way the "food police" offer scientific studies to support their messages. An announcer runs through a string of conclusions from "the latest studies." Although the tone is satirical, the issues that the message addresses hint at a larger concern. Going against all the "latest studies," if you do eat meat, the group argues sardonically, you should be "forced to wade through red-faced picketers wielding pointed wooden sticks with signs that read 'Eat Tofu or Die' on the way to your classic cheeseburger and fries."[42] The image of the stick-wielding vegetarians and animal rights activists, indicates an attack on individual freedom, not an invitation to consider an alternative diet. The language in the ads—especially the emphasis on the "food police"—also indicates the potential for a police state. That is, the ads indicate that today we are experiencing pressures to watch what we eat and drink, but tomorrow we may see strict regulations of our intake.

A CCF television advertisement targeting "food police" provides a more visual representation of this loss of freedom. Opening the ad, a narrator assesses the state of things: "Everywhere you turn, somebody's telling us what we can't eat." The ad then runs through a series of images—a nondescript hand grabbing an ice cream cone away from a child, smashing a piece of cheesecake, wrenching a beer out of a man's hand in a bar, and yanking a hot dog from a man about to take a bite. It ends with this appeal: "Find out who's driving the food police at consumerfreedom.com."[43] The music (a lighthearted, jazzy tune), along with the playful Louis Armstrong–like narrator's voice and the extreme situations envisioned in the ad pose two entities against each other. On one side is the common person, enjoying personal freedoms with food and drink. The other side, represented only by violent gestures, infringes on those freedoms. Thus, the "food police" have already begun a more intrusive campaign against "food choice," according to CCF.

The loss of freedom is a theme that plays out easily on the public screen. While PETA (and other organizations interested in changing eating behaviors) argues that individuals should consider the rights of animals when making choices about food, CCF claims that this consideration represents a loss of choice. Not only do CCF's ads represent the "food radicals" or "food police" as being irrational and overbearing, they also compare the rights of humans to the rights of animals. Given the assumption of a "natural" hierarchy that puts humans at the top, CCF is able to appeal to the widespread belief that the rights of humans supersede the rights of animals.[44] When comparing the two entities—"food police" (implicitly including PETA) and CCF—on the public screen, CCF makes even small concessions seem like a dangerous slippage of freedom.

A second rhetorical strategy used by CCF is that of false dichotomy. In this case, the group poses animal rights against the rights of humans, indicating that support for animal rights is a threat to humans. While PETA's advertisements push viewers to question the distinction between human and animal, CCF advertisements pose the two in separate frames and ask the viewer to make a rational decision. In two similar advertisements, CCF shows an image of a boy in a hospital gown weakly smiling at the camera. On the opposite side of the page is a picture of a rat. "Lab Rats or Sick Kids?" reads one version of the ad.[45] The other version uses PETA's words to make the distinction clear. PETA founder Ingrid Newkirk is quoted above the images as saying, "Even if animal research resulted in a cure for AIDS, we'd be against it."[46]

There is a clear dichotomy at work in these ads. First, the images pose rats against sick children and encourage viewers to place animals and humans back into the "proper" hierarchy. The second dichotomy poses the seemingly unreasonable words of PETA's president against the reasonable message that CCF poses. That is, although CCF advertisements often directly attack PETA's radical notions of animal rights, they also use imagery and PETA's quotations to undermine PETA's message and provide an alternative to that message. When apposing the two entities, the implication is that one "wins" and one "loses," leaving no nuance in the debate. Thus, viewers are asked to choose between support of animal rights and support of children. The threat of animal rights activists targeting children and hindering medical advances is intended to trigger fear.

The forced dichotomy that is a part of CCF's message also hinges on an understanding of PETA's disruption of the "natural" order. The assumed hierarchy of culture over nature means that humans are privileged over animals.[47] PETA attempts to disrupt that hierarchy in many of its advertising campaigns that anthropomorphize animals, attempt to create empathy for abused animals, and visually blur the lines between human and animal through manipulated images.[48] CCF, on the other hand, confirms the "natural order" of humans being at the top of the hierarchy. The words in the advertisements confirm this belief because they call PETA's attempts to alter the hierarchy "crazy," "nuts," "radical," and "ridiculous." One advertisement featuring a series of women questioning animal rights "lunatics," for example, points out the conflict between the "animal rights movement's" (they don't directly mention PETA here) view of the hierarchy and the "normal" hierarchy: "The animal rights movement would rather stop medical research using mice and rats than cure breast cancer," one mother states. Another jumps in and declares, "They're crazy."[49] As we have seen, in other advertisements CCF images add to this message by setting children and animals against each other, emphasizing the differences between human and animal.

The clearest example of this juxtaposition is in the advertisement posing an image of a lab rat opposite a child in a hospital bed. In two other advertisements, animals (presumably the pets of the featured children) are placed within the frame. These animals, however, display no human-like characteristics as they might in advertisements created by PETA. In these ads, they are merely acting in the role of "pet," that is a domesticated animal kept as a companion. In the role of pet, animals may receive rights to be free of abuse, but their rights do not supersede the rights of the "owners." This is a description of the animal-human relationship with which CCF is comfortable. It also allows the group to display an alternative love for animals. More importantly for the rhetorical goal, it is a message with which the audience is likely to easily agree. It is, after all, difficult to disrupt hierarchies (like the human-nonhuman animal divide) and the more comfortable message is that which reinforces already existing beliefs. Thus, when CCF confirms the "natural order," and claims that animal rights groups pose a threat to this order, they also encourage the viewer to choose between humans and animals. On the public screen, this false dichotomy not only places animal rights opposite human rights but also counterposes CCF's general message with PETA's message. Consequently, audience members are not only encouraged to agree with the "natural" order but also to more closely identify with CCF and its message.

A third strategy used by CCF is the conflation of PETA with all animal rights groups and the enthymematic argument that animal rights groups pose a terroristic threat to others. One of the first notable characteristics of the advertisements is the heavy reliance on images of children (in print) and mothers (in the television advertisements). One print ad, featuring a freckled red-haired girl hugging a stuffed animal, asks, "What is PETA teaching your child?" Commenting on a flyer produced by PETA and featured in the lower corner of the ad, the group informs parents that PETA "often bypasses parents to spread destructive and violent propaganda to kids about food and fur."[50] The child appears to be vulnerable—smiling and looking into the camera while hugging her stuffed rabbit—while PETA attacks with vicious words and images. The featured PETA literature—what CCF informs the viewer is a "PETA booklet distributed to grade schoolers"—features a cartoon image of a demented-looking woman wielding a knife and plunging it into an unseen animal, all in the form of a graphic novel. The title reads: "Your Mommy Kills Animals." Two other print advertisements feature images of young girls with their pets. In one, a blond girl smiles at the camera while cuddling her cat.[51] In another, the girl is crouched in the background watching her puppy bound toward the camera.[52] Next to both of these images are the shocking words of Newkirk ("I openly hope that it comes here" [speaking of the hoof and mouth epidemic]) and PETA spokesperson Bruce Friedrich ("It would be great if all the fast-food outlets, slaughterhouses, these laboratories and the banks who fund them exploded tomorrow"). The stark contrast between the winsome images of the children and PETA's words and images creates a clear dichotomy between comfortable images and words that cause concern. PETA's threatening words create a feeling of an imminent threat through the rhetorical trope of antithesis. Hoping for disease and violence, PETA appears as the rabid terrorist, while the children and their pets (the very symbols of innocence) are their potential victims. CCF argues that if consumers do not come together and fight against the animal rights "lunatics," your family will be at risk.

In addition to the use of children in the advertisements, CCF also depends on "concerned mothers" to express their fears about PETA. One television ad features a close-up shot of a mother who claims, "I'm concerned about a radical group called PETA."[53] She continues: "They take animal rights to extremes." She later explains that she is teaching her "kids to love and respect animals," but rejects the larger, threatening message spread by PETA. The ad reflects an intimate and emotional tone with the mother casually confessing her fears as if talking with a friend. Viewers are invited to share their concerns and to band together to fight against animal rights radicals. While the mother discusses her fears and concerns for her children, words flash up on the screen: "PETA . . . extremists . . . PETA supports arson." The dichotomy between the concerned mother and the "radical group" sets up the threat that the group poses to this family, which stands as a synecdoche of all families. In opposition to family, the use of words like "extremists" and "arson" pose PETA as a terrorist organization intent on destroying families, children, and mothers.

Another television advertisement shows a series of women, some of whom identify themselves as mothers, asking questions ("Am I an animal abuser because I give my kids milk?") and explaining the "crazy" stances of the animal rights movement (animal rights groups would: "make us all vegetarians," "put farmers out of business," "rather stop medical research using mice and rats than cure breast cancer").[54] Flashing back and forth from one worried person to another, the tone is one of frantic concern. One woman ends the commercial emphatically proclaiming, "They ought to mind their own business."[55] In this case, it is not just concern that surfaces, but anger over the attempts of the animal rights activists to encroach on their families lives. The music and images in this ad set a tone that is different than the casual, intimate tone that occurs in the previously mentioned commercial. The soundtrack and visuals that accompany this ad are edgy, with an electric guitar playing in the background and words and images jumping quickly across the frame. Both ads indicate that PETA (and other animal rights groups) acts as a terrorist organization in posing a threat to families.

The image of PETA terrorizing society is even more explicit in one television advertisement that opens with an image of a smiling girl cuddling with her cat. Panning from a screen displaying the name "People for the Ethical Treatment of Animals" and with sinister music playing in the background, the camera then zooms into her photo. Simultaneously, the audio switches over to the words of Friedrich: "Of course, we're going to be, as a movement, blowing stuff up and smashing windows."[56] As Friedrich's words run in the background, footage of a burning building, protestors smashing a car window with a large metal barrier, and agitators rushing forward toward law enforcement officials flash across the screen. The ad ends with a black screen and asks, "PETA: As warm and cuddly as you thought?" It is noteworthy, as in other advertisements, that the message juxtaposes the innocent child with the threatening words and images. The quotations and the images portray PETA as a terrorist organization. The images in the video are not necessarily PETA activists, yet because the advertisement opens by naming PETA and then flows into Friedrich's words, these are all associated with the organization. As with the threat to freedom, a message crafted through a suggested threat to family or youth is likely to produce a strong emotional response. Viewers, of course, are able to assess the validity of the message and/or may already be supportive of the animal rights message, but the threat of violence has the potential to cause some concern among viewers.

In the end, it is this message of a threat—to personal freedom, natural order, family, and safety—that foments a powerful argument against PETA's animal rights rhetoric. Turning around PETA's words and employing its own powerful visual imagery, CCF contends that consumers should not only reject the animal rights position but also actively work against the threat of animal rights messages. By constantly apposing animal rights messages with the "normalized" images of children with their pets, mothers acting out of concern, and children being harmed by threats to medical advances, CCF invites a comparison of the two positions as a false dilemma. The threat also extends to individual beliefs. PETA's messages ask viewers to change their belief systems and then their actions. CCF makes that "threat" to individual beliefs a central part of their message. Given the threat that viewers may already believe the animal rights movement poses, CCF's use of the public screen to encourage viewers to reject radical notions of animal-human relationships provides an additional argument against supporting the animal rights movement. It is this use of the public screen to which I now turn.

SCREEN WARS

In an idealized version of Habermas' public sphere, competing parties would have a rational discussion about the reasons to support or denounce a vegetarian lifestyle. In this vein, charges launched against animal rights groups might be addressed based on facts. As DeLuca and Peeples argue, however, that idealized public sphere does not exist and should be called into question because "it holds static notions of the public arena, appropriate political activity, and democratic citizenship, thus ignoring current social and technological conditions."[57] Instead, deliberations happen on the public screen, allowing image events to act as "visual philosophical-rhetorical fragments, mind bombs that expand the universe of thinkable thoughts."[58] There are certainly benefits to this medium as social movements, once denied a platform, are given an opportunity to disseminate their messages. The loss of control of the message that occurs within this medium—especially with "free" media—makes the public screen a double-edged sword, however. Of course, the platform for the message is welcome, but particular groups will find this platform makes their messages more persuasive than the arguments of others.

The radical message is more difficult to construct from the image fragments, because it typically requires a major shift in perspective for it to be persuasive. The public screen allows for fast-paced messages to be spread to large audiences. There are advantages to this medium. Because radical groups are able to use "mind bombs," or messages that disrupt ways of thinking, they create a space for a completely new perspective.[59] But the public screen message must work enthymematically because of the limitations to the time/space that is given to each message. As Delicath and DeLuca explain, "how image events impact public argumentation depends largely on how the audience encounters, assembles, and utilizes the fragments."[60] It is this argumentative work that must happen within each individual that becomes problematic for radical groups.

A more conservative, mainstream message has an advantage over radical arguments, because it allows individuals to maintain their current beliefs. Therefore, individuals are more likely to know how to complete the message and feel more comfortable with the reconstructed argument. As DeLuca and Peeples argue, the public screen offers a quick glimpse at a social movement message, a chance to disseminate but not fully participate in dialogue.[61] Delicath and DeLuca note that image events "provide fodder for argumentation and a source for generating argument," but these argument fragments are not fully formed.[62] With this mediated form of dissemination, there are expectations that viewers will be able to identify with the message or, at the very least, will be able to complete the argument. As argumentation theorists Chaim Perelman and Lucie Olbrechts-Tyteca explain, an argument must begin with the audience's position in mind.[63] Conservative movements are, by definition, "satisfied with the existing order" and "suspicious of change," thus they reify the audience's position. "Radical" movements are "dissatisfied with the existing order" and committed to change.[64] If conservative movements have the status quo on their side (and, thus, many of the audience members are more familiar with/supportive of that stance), then it is natural that conservative movements have an advantage when advancing arguments enthymematically. That is not to say, of course, that radical movements cannot be successful, but the obstacles at play are worth considering. Cultural critic Jo Littler points out that image events are likely to be employed by corporations in today's media-heavy climate, and those conservative uses of image events can "quash or neutralize the potential effects of radical image events."[65] Littler investigates the co-opting of image events—détournement or pranking—by corporations and calls for more research into the implications of these practices. It is the conservative versus "radical" examples shown in CCF and PETA's image events that answers this call. Given the competing messages, the conservative position is privileged.

Supporting the animal rights ideology is, for many people, difficult because it means changing personal behavior (purchasing animal-friendly products, changing food choices), questioning scientific research, and always thinking about the effects of our purchases and behaviors on the well-being of animals. The argument for the status quo—placing human well-being above animals—is easier because it maintains current behavior. If image events act as "mind bombs," as DeLuca and Peeples contend, we might carry out that imagery.[66] An exploded bomb leaves chaos in its midst, scattering bits of material across a wide path. Individuals then begin the tedious and painful work of gathering the detritus and attempting to reassemble some sense of order. There is no denying that the bomb gathers attention, sends a message, and forces a reaction, but the extreme event leaves the area in complete disarray. Lastly, when people reconstruct, they tend to rebuild on exactly the same old lots and with much of the same old material, gradually putting back together the area much like it had been before. Likewise, "mind bombs" draw immediate attention to the message and force individuals to reorder their beliefs, but the extreme nature of the message is risky. Individuals may choose to completely reassemble their beliefs, incorporating the new ideas put forth by the message. However, most viewers likely choose to explain the image event as threats to their belief system and embrace their prior beliefs as comforting. Given competing messages—neither of which is fully developed on the public screen—audiences are drawn again to the status quo.

Thus, although the public screen affords some rhetorical advantages to radical groups hoping to spread its messages, there are also drawbacks. Such is the case with PETA and their animal rights message. PETA has depended heavily on the use of the public screen. Being a well-funded consumer rights group run by a public relations firm, however, the CCF understands PETA's tactics. Discovering the weaknesses in PETA's message, most importantly the fact that PETA seeks to redefine animal-human relations, CCF has responded with similar strategies. As Peter Kerr, a counselor for PETA, explains: "They are an industry hack. . . . By Richard Berman's own admission, their job is to shoot the messenger. They know they can't win on substance, so they have to attack the messenger."[67] PETA has attempted to downplay the importance of the attacks. However, the group has also created a counter website (www .consumerdeception.com) centered on attacking CCF's credibility, indicating that PETA sees CCF as enough of a threat that it warrants a response.[68] Thus, the battle continues between the more radical animal rights message and the more conservative message disseminated by CCF.

In analyzing larger campaigns, it is impossible to fully understand the effect of the message and such a question is beyond the scope of this study. It is, however, important to note the competing messages and the medium from which they emerge. PETA's and CCF's conflicting messages present a unique example of "screen wars." That is, both groups primarily use the public screen to spread their messages. CCF has taken advantage of this medium in attacking PETA not on the issues, as such, but on their reputation. The public screen provides a particularly effective platform for this type of message. Given the instantaneous nature of public screen "debates," audiences are quickly and briefly distracted by emotionally charged advertisements. The "real" debate of the issues (assuming that can happen at all) is lost in the speed of the public screen. However, like DeLuca and Peeples, I choose not to fall victim to "despair and nostalgia" over the loss of the public sphere.[69] There is certainly room for reasoned consumption of the messages. Nevertheless, it is wise to further consider the consequences of social movements relying too heavily on a public screen presence.

If, for example, it is true that we have primarily become a distracted society, one that is more likely to participate in public deliberation through sound bites and image events, then it becomes important for social movement organizations to find a variety of ways to communicate in this environment. The public screen provides one alternative, but the limitations of the medium may be particularly problematic for radical groups countering a strong status quo. Because image events work in argumentative fragments, it is difficult for audiences to construct compelling arguments without falling back on their assumptions. Placed within a multitude of rhetorical strategies, as with the animal rights movement, image events may be particularly powerful in driving home the message and acting not only to support an argument, but to develop the argument. Taken out of context, however, image events potentially require too much intellectual work on the part of the audience in reconciling the argument fragments with their own beliefs. Thus, dependence on image events may mean that audiences will choose to maintain their current beliefs, falling to the more conservative side of the discussion. Finding alternative ways to "speak" to the distracted audience, then, should be a concern of any social movement organization. As critics, we should be compelled to not only continue to understand the strengths and limitations of the public screen, but to identify rhetorical strategies that best speak to the audiences that we encounter today.

Chapter Ten

Whale Wars and the Public Screen

Mediating Animal Ethics in Violent Times

Richard D. Besel and Renee S. Besel

"We're out here off the coast of Antarctica, and behind me is the *Nisshan Maru*, which is the largest whale killing machine on the planet," begins *Steve Irwin* captain Paul Watson. Kicking off the first-ever episode of *Whale Wars*, Animal Planet's new hit reality show/melodrama, the crew of the *Steve Irwin* launches an attack on the largest ship in the Japanese whaling fleet. The *Nisshan Maru* fights back, and within minutes, a Sea Shepherd deckhand is yelling, "The Captain's been shot!" The scene of a magnificent, blue Antarctic Ocean dissolves to black as three words ("Three Months Earlier") pull the viewers into a flashback that spans the rest of the season.[1]

The television series *Whale Wars* was born when cable network Animal Planet agreed to send a camera crew onto the *Steve Irwin* for the Sea Shepherd Conservation Society's 2007–2008 Antarctic Whale Defense Campaign. During the seven episodes in Season One, the history of the campaign is gradually revealed. Watson began the Sea Shepherd Conservation Society (SSCS) in 1977, believing that Greenpeace, which he co-founded, and international laws were insufficient to protect marine life. Whaling continued unabated and Greenpeace did not favor the direct confrontation tactics Watson believed were needed. Using direct intervention and lessons learned from Sun Tzu's *The Art of War*, SSCS strives to reach its mission of ending "the destruction of habitat and slaughter of wildlife in the world's oceans in order to conserve and protect ecosystems and species."[2] The organization recruits young, passionate animal rights activists who are willing to put their lives on the line to defend ocean mammals. And if they can pull a few carefully crafted stunts to gain media attention at the same time, or what rhetorical critic Kevin DeLuca calls "image events," well, so much the better for the cause.[3]

With a pirate flag hoisted high and equipped with little more than cameras and stink bombs, the crew of the *Steve Irwin* tries to balance their convictions

163

and their personal lives, all while carefully portraying a pirate image in front of anxious armchair adventurers. According to Watson, "This is why we present the pirate image, it's all theatrics. Kids love the pirate image."[4] Apparently, children are not the only ones. The first season of *Whale Wars* proved to be a success for Animal Planet. Nielsen ratings report that *Whale Wars* attracted over a million television viewers. By its second airing, the show had also set a five-year record for Animal Planet's virtual telecasts.[5] However, the show has not been without its controversies, as some critics have called the Sea Shepherds' tactics extreme.[6] Fortunately, network executives learned years ago that "extreme" actions tend to keep viewers coming back for more. Hoping to mimic the success of shows like Discovery Channel's *Deadliest Catch,* Animal Planet's President and General Manager, Marjorie Kaplan, "has been re-branding Animal Planet with compelling, reality-style entertainment."[7] The decision appears to be paying off in terms of ratings.

Although the public's response to the show is one measure of success, perhaps the most important measure is the effectiveness of the SSCS's direct interventions. The campaign, which is rooted in ethical convictions, is also considered a success because it has helped to halve the number of whales killed by Japanese hunters.[8] Indeed, the mere act of observing the whaling has accomplished a great deal in curtailing the killing. Journalist Christopher Bantick argues that when the shepherds are there, the whalers stop hunting; when the activists leave to refuel, the slaughter continues.[9] The moral spotlight of the shepherds is not helping the public to see actions hidden by darkness, but hunting hidden by distance.

Despite the success of both Animal Planet's television series and the SS-CS's campaign, we argue *Whale Wars* relies on an implicit anthropocentrism that ultimately limits the effectiveness of its animal rights rhetoric. Rather than drawing attention to the shepherds' ethical position regarding whales or the possibility of valuing whales as living creatures, viewers are invited to bear witness to human conflict. In other words, a concern for animal ethics is secondary to the human conflict captured by the reality programming. This is not to say the shepherds are at fault. Instead, our reading complicates readily accepted reality programming as a vehicle for the communication of ethical norms. As animal rights rhetoric is absorbed into the nearly endless matrix of cable broadcasting and capitalistic spectacle, attracting viewers for ratings trumps changing behavior toward animals. To analyze the Sea Shepherd's campaign as portrayed in *Whale Wars*, we will first examine the role of image events and their relationship to public sphere theory. Following this, we will explore the historical context for the Sea Shepherd's campaign. Next, we will engage in a close reading of season one before, finally, drawing conclusions about the ethics of image events in the animal rights movement.

SPHERES, SCREENS, AND IMAGE EVENTS

A public's understanding of animal ethics is not only informed by personal interactions with animals and the natural world but also shaped by a variety of discursive encounters that take place within a media-saturated culture. The importance of media culture for today's society should not be underestimated. According to philosopher and media critic Douglas Kellner, a "media culture has emerged in which images, sounds, and spectacles help produce the fabric of everyday life, dominating leisure time, shaping political views and social behavior, and providing the materials out of which people forge their very identities."[10] Although few scholars would likely disagree with Kellner's assessment of media culture's contemporary pervasiveness, they are divided about whether to celebrate or mourn this relatively recent development.

For many scholars, a heavily mediated culture is one in which its members have lost their ability to rationally and critically engage one another on matters of common concern. In other words, media-saturated cultures do not possess what Jürgen Habermas has conceptualized as a healthy "public sphere;" that area of our social lives where we can deliberate about society's most important issues.[11] In the Habermasian view of the public sphere, it is assumed that people have open access to it, that social inequalities are bracketed for the sake of the common good, that rationality is privileged, and that participants have consensus as their objective. Turning to television, rhetorical scholars like David Zarefsky have argued that a media-saturated culture is one that cannot have an active and healthy public sphere: "Thanks largely to television, people have been transformed into passive consumers of messages and images, rather than participants in a dialogue."[12] Similarly, Christopher Lasch believes engaging in public argument is now a "lost art."[13] To borrow a phrase from Neal Postman, many believe we are "amusing ourselves to death."[14]

While the Habermasian public sphere certainly offers a normative point of comparison for society, it has also been heavily criticized. Feminist scholar and critical theorist Nancy Fraser, for example, has argued Habermas' view of the public sphere is not yet capable of "theorizing the limits of actually existing democracy."[15] A central element of Fraser's argument is that we do not actually bracket differences between people and that some marginalized groups have found it necessary to form "subaltern counterpublics."[16] Sociologist Michael Schudson criticizes Habermas on historical grounds.[17] Was the public sphere of the French salon or the colonial American town hall meeting really worth using as a normative model for contemporary democracy? More recently, scholars have noted an aversion of the visual in public sphere theory. Rhetorical critics Cara Finnegan and Jiyeon Kang have accused Habermas and other public sphere theorists of iconoclasm.[18] Our purpose here is not to revisit every argument leveled against the Habermasian public sphere, nor do we wish to offer a defense of it. Instead, we wish to address recent trends in the latter critique developed against the Habermasian public sphere as a theoretical point of departure for our analysis. In other words, what role does the visual play in a society where public opinion formation and political culture is heavily influenced by mass mediated messages?

In his studies on environmental activists, DeLuca has argued subaltern counterpublics often use "image events" to draw attention to their cause. Echoing the view of Greenpeace member Robert Hunter, DeLuca argues these image events are "mind bombs" that rattle public consciousness and shape public opinion in ways face-to-face methods could not.[19] Image events, for John Delicath and DeLuca, are "staged acts of protest designed for media dissemination."[20] Rhetorical critic Davi Johnson, a student of DeLuca's, offers a more specific summary:

> An "image event" is a type of rhetorical address that is ocular, rather than verbal. Image events are often orchestrated by social movements, and they are defined as deliberately staged spectacles designed to attract the attention of the mass media and disseminate persuasive images to a wide audience.[21]

Although the idea of an "image event" provides scholars with a much-needed tool to analyze the rhetoric of a mediated society, it does not fit neatly into the iconoclastic notions of the public sphere. As Delicath and DeLuca note, "Within the conventional usage of Habermas' liberal public sphere, however, image events do not register. That is, they neither count nor make sense within the rules, the formal procedures, of such a public sphere."[22] Yet, for Jennifer Peeples and DeLuca, in a society where "TV places a premium on images over words, emotions over rationality, speed over reflection, distraction over deliberation, slogans over arguments, the glance over the gaze, appearance over truth, the present over the past," understanding the role of the image event in contemporary discourse has never been more vital.[23]

Realizing the image event could not cleanly fit into the traditional understanding of the public sphere, DeLuca and Peeples have suggested the idea of the "public screen" is needed to supplement scholarly understanding of the public sphere.[24] As our culture has become increasingly saturated with the signs of the spectacular and technology further connects us to one another, the manner in which we participate in democratic culture has changed. For DeLuca and Peeples, a concept like the "public screen" is desperately needed in our technologically developing world; it is a concept that "takes technology seriously." They argue scholars "cannot simply adopt the term 'public sphere' and all it entails, a term indebted to orality and print, for the current screen age."[25] As our socio-technical culture changes, our theoretical understanding of it should as well.

Ultimately, DeLuca and others have argued scholars need to change the way they see image events. Image events are not explicitly included in the Habermasian public sphere, yet, they are not irrelevant in a world filled with public screens. For DeLuca and Delicath, "Theories of rhetoric and argument that would too readily dismiss image events as debased forms of more authentic, reasoned debate fail to understand the need to explore social problem construction and opinion formation in terms of the way people actually gather and process information."[26] Image events have fundamentally changed the way subaltern counterpublics may voice their opinions for and to a larger public. In turn, critics now have a new way to "critique through spectacle, not critique versus spectacle."[27]

According to DeLuca, his coauthors, and students, image events should be viewed with a sense of optimism. Image events provide inventional spaces for subaltern counterpublics and give voice to those who would not otherwise be allowed to participate in the public sphere. According to Delicath and DeLuca:

> Image events create opportunities for generative argument as they are sources of confrontational and creative claims-making and refutation. They may spark the imagination, inspire argumentation and debate, and promote innovative argumentative practices. Environmental image events create opportunities for generative argument by increasing the visibility of environmental issues, subverting the privilege of dominant environmental discourses, and expanding the range of thinkable thoughts with regards to environmental matters. To the extent that they challenge taken-for-granted assumptions and disrupt the existing grid of intelligibility, environmental image events are uniquely capable of animating public argument and rearticulating the rhetorical boundaries of environmental knowledge.[28]

However, despite their optimistic assessment, the notion of an image event is not without its critics.

Although image events are filled with the potential to disrupt dominant power structures operating within the public sphere through the use of public screens, some scholars have questioned the rhetorical effectiveness of image events. Image events, in addition to forcing subaltern issues into the public sphere, have the potential to polarize parties involved in disputes. Following the work of environmental communication scholars Michael Spangler and David Knapp, performance studies critic Jonathan Gray has argued, "Image events often work counter to traditional concepts of effective rhetorical discourse, bringing outrage and backlash down on the heads of the activists and their cause."[29] Image events are not designed to disseminate mediated messages of unity or consensus; they are designed to challenge dominant public practices by breaking from normative tactics of protest.

Most of the initial work on image events and the public screen has used environmental movements as primary topics.[30] However, there is little reason to suspect that these concepts could not be used to analyze animal rights rhetoric. Some scholars have already done so: Lesli Pace and C. Richard King each use the concept of the image event to analyze PETA's anti-fur rhetoric, Hunter Stephenson uses the concept in relation to seal hunting protest, and Brett Lunceford employs the image event to understand nude protests for PETA in this volume.[31] This essay likewise uses the image event and the public screen as central theoretical elements in the following analysis. However, one important distinction must be noted. Although Watson has long been known for using image events, *Whale Wars* is in the unique position of being a reality show designed to observe activists as they are creating image events. One might even say the show is a kind of metacommunication, a mediated image event about making image events. Although the first appropriation of an image event on *Whale Wars* is to garner media attention, we must remember that the reality programming does not necessarily do the same thing in the second appropriation. Thus, the text itself may contain contradictions and tensions worthy of analysis. However, before we turn to our analysis of the television series, a brief exploration of whaling's history is in order.

WHALING'S HISTORICAL CONTEXT

Sustenance whaling has existed for millennia. The enormous mammals provided an abundant source of food, as well as blubber and bone for a variety of early peoples. Evidence discovered by a team of University of Alaska researchers and their Russian colleagues revealed that the indigenous peoples of Un'en'en on Russia's Chukchi Peninsula were hunting whales as many as 3,000 years ago.[32] Because the Native peoples hunted the creatures for their own survival, and not for commercial distribution, sustenance hunting had a negligible impact on whale populations. The Industrial Revolution changed this, however, and by the 1840s and 1850s, commercial whaling was booming. Every part of a whale was in demand. The blubber produced enormous amounts of oil and the baleen (or "whalebone") in the mouths of certain whales could be warmed, shaped and cooled to give form to hoopskirts and corsets.[33] Whale byproducts were also used in makeup, perfume, cold cream, hairbrushes, fishing rods, umbrellas, pet food, fertilizer, lamp fuel, paint, varnish and even ice cream.[34] But when oil was discovered in Pennsylvania in 1859, the commercial whaling industry suffered a severe setback, as whale oil was no longer the only resource—or even the cheapest resource—for lighting homes and businesses. However, baleen was still in high demand, and as its value more than quintupled between 1870 and

1904, whalers once again hit the oceans in record numbers in search of making "big money quickly." As Eric Jay Dolin, author of *Leviathan: The History of Whaling in America*, wrote, "Whaling voyages were now being dubbed whalebone cruises, and with a large bowhead capable of providing upward of 3,000 pounds of baleen, the profits for a really successful cruise were simply astounding."[35] The end result was that between 1904 and 1978, 1.4 million whales were killed in the Antarctic alone.[36]

Sensing the potential devastation of such dramatic hunts, twelve nations created the International Whaling Commission (IWC) in 1946 under the International Convention for the Regulation of Whaling. From the time it came into force in 1948, the main purpose of the Convention and Commission was to "provide for the proper conservation of whale stocks and thus make possible the orderly development of the whaling industry." Its main duty was to review and revise the parameters laid out for international whaling, which protected certain species, identified whale sanctuaries, limited numbers and size of whales that may be killed, set seasons and areas for whaling, and prohibited the capture of suckling calves and their mothers. The IWC also prepared and released catch reports and other statistical and biological records as well as coordinated and funded whale research.[37]

Despite the IWC's focus on regulating the whaling industry, many species of whales were on the brink of extinction, and the IWC knew it needed to take action. The IWC began to seriously discuss banning all commercial whaling until populations rebounded and a detailed resource management plan could be enacted. In 1982, they succeeded. To the dismay of pro-whaling members of the organization, the five-year ban on commercial whaling took effect in 1986 and has been repeatedly renewed. It remains in effect today, though exceptions do exist for aboriginal sustenance hunting and scientific research.[38]

The controversy around modern-day whaling resides within the IWC's exceptions. Who is considered aboriginal? What is considered sustenance hunting? What qualifies as scientific research? How are the exceptions and limits enforced? While the IWC reviews proposals for sustenance hunting and grants permission to the aboriginals seeking to maintain their traditional way of life, member nations interested in conducting scientific research merely submit a proposal to the IWC and then make the final decision for themselves. According to the IWC, "Whilst member nations must submit proposals for review, in accordance with the Convention, it is the member nation that ultimately decides whether or not to issue a [scientific] permit, and this right overrides any other Commission regulations including the moratorium and sanctuaries. Article VIII also requires that the animals be utilised [*sic*] once the scientific data have been collected."[39] Of all the categories of whaling, scientific permit whaling takes the greatest number of whale lives annually. During the 2007 whaling season, 951 whales were killed under scientific permits, and all but 39 of those were taken by Japan.[40] Japanese whalers argue that, "scientific whaling is necessary to understand whales' biology and monitor their population dynamics with a view to eventually resuming commercial whaling."[41] However, critics argue that Japan's scientific permits are merely a thin veil covering their real purpose: getting around the moratorium on commercial hunting. The "research" ships are the same harpooning vessels previously used for commercial purposes.[42] And as the final Season One episode of *Whale Wars* reveals, one of the six vessels in the Japanese whaling fleet is the *Nisshan Maru*, which is dedicated to the immediate processing of the hunted whales while at sea.[43] No time is lost as whale products are immediately unloaded for commercial distribution once the ships return home. In November 2007, the Japanese whaling fleet began its annual hunt, and whaling activists were not far behind.

IMAGE EVENTS AND A WILLINGNESS TO DIE

Whale Wars makes it abundantly clear that Watson and the shepherds are motivated by one overriding concern: saving whales. This goal of fighting for a group of other beings different from themselves is characteristic of organizations that are part of what Charles J. Stewart calls an "other-directed social movement."[44] Both Stewart and Jason Edward Black have argued that the animal rights movement is an exemplar of this kind of movement.[45] That the SSCS is an other-directed social movement organization becomes clear in the first few episodes of the season. In episode one, "Needle in a Haystack," Watson makes the position of the SSCS apparent: "You don't beg criminals to stop doing what they are doing. You intervene and physically and aggressively shut them down." The narrator even notes in a voiceover that Watson "is a man who will die for the whales and he expects his crew to do the same." Not to be outdone by Watson, the officers of the *Steve Irwin* are likewise framed in a way that features their devout concern for the whales. Kim McCoy, executive director of the SSCS, claimed in the same episode: "You see that whale and there's a connection and you just feel a sense of obligation to do something." Second Mate Peter Hammarstedt even commented on how far he was willing to go for the whales: "I didn't join Sea Shepherd until I could say with 100 percent conviction that I was willing to risk my life to save a whale." Watson and the *Steve Irwin* officers are framed as being among the few people in the world who would die for their beliefs.[46]

In addition to verbally showcasing the motives of Watson and his officers, *Whale Wars* visually illustrates their perspective. Aside from verbal claims,

Whale Wars features short segments of the whales in their natural environments. In episode one, for example, crew members are given a "reminder" of why they are there; footage of whales breaking the ocean's surface show the viewers what is at stake in this nontraditional war. The whales are only dwarfed by the gigantic icebergs floating nearby, sublime in their frozen beauty. But not all of the visuals are so pleasant. Throughout the episodes viewers are also shown graphic images of whales being harpooned, gutted, and processed. These images of blood, bone, and intestines let the viewers see what it is the SSCS is fighting against. By the time the shepherds encounter the Japanese whaling fleet for the staging of their first image event, viewers have seen what it is that motivates Watson and his officers.

In episodes two and three, "Nothing's Ideal" and "International Incidents R Us," the sea shepherds finally have the opportunity to stage their first image event. After finding the *Yushin Maru 2*, a Japanese harpoon ship, Watson reveals his plan during a crew meeting: two members of the *Steve Irwin* are to board the harpoon vessel. Betting the Japanese will take the crew members into custody and not allow them to leave when they request to do so, Watson tells the crew they will create an international incident by accusing the Japanese of kidnapping. Although the crew is hesitant at first, two members finally step forward. Cook Benjamin Potts and Engineer Giles Lane agree to board the whaling ship. With a helicopter circling above to take pictures and crew members hurling stink bombs onto the deck of the *Yushin Maru 2*, Potts and Lane successfully board by using a small inflatable Delta boat, and as expected, are taken into custody. Immediately following confirmation of their boarding, Watson and the sea shepherds begin to notify the press, sending out video and photos of the incident.[47] Their first image event appears to be a success in terms of press coverage with Watson spending over 36 hours on the satellite phone being interviewed. The media-savvy Watson is well aware of the orchestration he is directing: "We live in a media culture, so it's very important, images are very important. The camera is probably the most important weapon we have."[48] However, as with any orchestration and as the title of episode two indicates, nothing is ideal. As we shall see, the members of this other-directed social movement garner more attention than the whales for whom the movement is fighting.

ANTHROPOCENTRISM AND
PERFORMATIVE CONTRADICTIONS

Despite the appearance of being a show that attempts to draw in viewers because of its "save-the-whales" message, virtually every episode features dramatic human relationships as a means of keeping audience members focused on the screens. In other words, *Whale Wars* uses the audience's concern for other human beings as a primary motivator to keep watching. Animal Planet explained the goal of *Whale Wars* in more detail: "The series attempts to capture the intensity of the group, their personal motivations, their mistakes and mishaps, their internal conflicts and their encounters with whaling vessels in the seas of Antarctica."[49] Because television requires scripting and editing, staging and direction, there is the potential for an animal rights reality TV show to create a great chasm between the featured organization's cause (protection and preservation of whales) and the objective of the broadcast network producing the series (ratings and profit). Notice that Animal Planet never mentions stopping the killing of whales as an underlying goal, nor do they take an ethical side concerning the IWC's policies. The show, at times, even begins to take on the dramatic elements of an animal rights soap opera.

In episode one, the animal rights activists no longer appear as stereotypical fanatics hell-bent on saving whales. As audience members see the novice associates of the crew face seasickness and logistical tasks associated with being a deckhand, viewers are invited to identify with the activists as human beings. There are a number of dramatic moments in episode one where the focus of the show is clearly on the crew and the human relationships they have with one another: Potts damages the blades of the helicopter, possibly compromising one of the crew's most valuable reconnaissance tools against the Japanese fleet; when a boat fails to launch and members of the crew are put into harm's way, senior crew member Peter Brown is blamed. As Shannon Mann quipped, "He's [Brown] a little bit crazy."[50] Audiences even get to witness snapshots of the conflict between the SSCS and Greenpeace. Although the Greenpeace members believe Watson's tactics are counter-productive, they nonetheless collaborate with the SSCS for a brief stint.

The kidnapping incident in episodes two and three also features the human relationships of the crew members. When Watson first explained his plan to the crew, the reality programming captured the tension and disagreement between the veteran crew members and the new recruits. For Watson, "There's always risks involved. And if you aren't willing to take those risks then I wouldn't think that you would be on the vessel." Boarding the Japanese whaling ship was just another routine image event waiting to be staged. New medical officer Scott Bell had a different view of the plan: "It's a foolish idea. It's a dangerous idea. You've got to think about the personal safety of the people who would volunteer and I don't think that's being taken into account by Sea Shepherd at all. In my opinion they'd be just a couple of sacrificial lambs." Communications officer Wilfred Verkleij concurred: "If you board somebody else's ship, you're a pirate. You're invading somebody else's country. I don't think it's a smart idea." Despite the objections of many crew members, the

SSCS proceeded as planned. Fortunately, the image event worked, the volunteers (Potts and Lane) were eventually returned, and the SSCS garnered a great deal of media attention.[51] While the image event could be deemed a success, the success of the reality coverage should be viewed with a sense of skepticism. Professional producers are editing and framing the shot footage in such a way that the whales are no longer the primary concern. Are viewers tuning in to watch some of these members who are a "little bit crazy?" Are viewers tuning in to cheer for their animal rights heroes, a dramatic conflict between the good humans (sea shepherds) and the evil humans (the Japanese whalers)? Are viewers tuning in to watch the crew encounter growing pains as the shepherds lash out at one another? We can probably answer yes to all of these questions, but we also have to ask whether or not whales even matter for these answers. One can imagine the same reality framing at work in any extreme context. The human interest element is what is featured by a very capable cable company. Are any of the viewers invited to watch because the attention is on the whales? Is the show even trying to emphasize the plight of the whales, or is the human drama what counts? The later episodes allow us to better answer these questions.

In episode four, "We Are Hooligans," audience members are exposed to a cat-and-mouse game as the *Steve Irwin* is being followed by a spy ship, the *Fukuoshi Maru*. The shepherds realize they are being followed so the Japanese whaling vessels will always know their location. Unable to locate the Japanese whalers, the shepherds first have to lose the *Fukuoshi Maru*. Hiding behind an iceberg, the sea shepherds eventually charge at the trailing vessel, scaring them off. Apparently the *Fukuoshi Maru* did not wish to engage the SSCS directly. Allowed to return to their main task, the *Steve Irwin* begins to pursue the *Blue Oriental*, the main fueling vessel of the Japanese fleet. However, the shepherds' attempts to lose the *Fukuoshi Maru* proved to be futile as they once again discover the spy ship close behind. Planning a second attack on the spy ship, the shepherds damage the crane used for lowering the Delta boats into the water, the first of their many mechanical problems.[52] Again, it is the shepherds who are the agents in the editing and framing. Getting caught up in the cat-and-mouse game almost makes you forget why they are there to begin with.

In episode five, "Doors Slamming and Things Breaking," the shepherds not only have to address their broken crane, but they lose one of their motors as well. Deciding it is better to repair and regroup in port rather than attempt to challenge the Japanese fleet with severely compromised equipment, the *Steve Irwin* crew decides to dock in Melbourne, Australia. On the way, Brown passes down an order for the crew to refrain from "partying" until they reach port. A number of crew members disobey the order. Audience members get to see the activists drinking and, eventually, hung over. The next morning the captain declares the ship a dry ship. Hammarstedt, in a crew meeting, tells the crew members that if they have a problem with how the ship has been run, porting in Melbourne is now their opportunity to leave. Once again, the tensions between the crew members are featured. While in port, the SSCS is forced to replace a number of crew members. Some of the more notable losses include now demoted communications officer Wilfred, medical officer Scott Bell, and McCoy. Although the *Steve Irwin* loses many of their hands, the SSCS finds replacements with ease. As Brown put it, "Most of these people are one-timers anyway."[53] While McCoy is not one of the "one-timers," her reason for leaving is prominently featured in episode five. Receiving word from the SSCS office, Hammarstedt relays a message to Kim over the loudspeaker. Alex, a member of the SSCS who works in the main office and is Kim's significant other, has asked Kim to marry him. She happily accepts. The emphasis of this episode is slanted in favor of seeing how the crew lives and how their relationships with other humans flourish or fall apart. Even as the *Steve Irwin* slowly sailed into Melbourne, the episode focused on the possible legal consequences for Potts and Lane (no action was taken against them), the hero's welcome the crew received from the public, and the family members who welcomed the crew home.[54] Once again, *Whale Wars* was turned into a human interest story.

Although human relationships are emphasized in episode five, episode six, "Ladies First," also draws attention to this. With new crew members Tod Emko (communications officer) and David Page (medical officer) and financial help from musical groups such as the Red Hot Chili Peppers, the crew set sail once again. Unlike their last image event, Watson this time suggests sending over four of the crew's female members to serve an arrest warrant, believing "they're [the Japanese] not gonna know how to deal with it." Dissent soon emerges. Even Potts, now the only member of the crew who has experience boarding another vessel from a Delta boat, objects to the idea. As before, the SSCS locates the *Yushin Maru 2* and decides to go through with its plan. A slow launch with an inexperienced crew, lack of communication between the main vessel and the small boats, and losing the target, produces high tensions and high drama. During the course of the failed image event, audience members discover cook Amber Paarman and Hammarstedt are partners. The audience also discovers that female volunteer Shannon Mann is seriously hurt with a pelvis injury incurred during the mission. As if these trials were not enough for the *Whale Wars'* heroes, the episode ends with a power outage as the ship is left to navigate its way past icebergs in the dark.[55]

The final episode in season one, "Boiling Point," picks up where episode six leaves off. The crew manages to restore power. The next morning, the crew finds the main ship of the Japanese whaling fleet, the *Nisshan Maru*. For the SSCS, this is a significant encounter. The flagship of the whaling fleet is the factory vessel that processes and packages the harpooned whales while at sea. For Watson, the *Nisshan Maru* is "the most evil ship on the planet." And for deckhand Laurens de Groot, "That ship stands for everything I hate."[56] Without the factory ship, the entire whaling fleet would be out of commission. With Jolly Roger raised high and stink bombs in hands, the *Steve Irwin* launched its attack. Unlike the strategy used with the *Yushin Maru 2*, the SSCS decided to pursue the larger whaling ship with the *Steve Irwin* itself. After one successful pass, the *Nisshan Maru* began to flee with the *Steve Irwin* giving chase. After three days of pursuit, the season builds to its final dramatic conflict. The SSCS makes a second successful pass. On their third and final pass, the sea shepherds launch their remaining bombs, despite warnings from the Japanese that they will launch tear gas and flash grenades in response. After what appears to be a successful final pass, it is revealed to the audience that Watson believes he has been shot. Although we never see any footage of gunfire, audiences see Watson open his jacket to reveal a bulletproof vest with a bullet hole. To this day, the Japanese fleet denies ever firing on the *Steve Irwin*. Audiences are never provided with a definitive answer as to whether or not Watson was staging another image event. Once again, it is the human interest element of the episodes, an assault on one human life, that gains the focus of the episode, not the killing of whales.[57]

CONCLUSION

While both the television series and the SSCS campaign were successful by certain standards, *Whale Wars* relies on an implicit anthropocentrism that ultimately limits the effectiveness of its animal rights rhetoric. The strength of the show is that it softens the image of the animal rights activists, often portraying their actions as passionate and reasonable, rather than extreme. However, to do this, the show focuses on the actors rather than the animals. By villainizing the whale hunters and humanizing the activists, a drama-filled stage is set where the whales are relegated to the role of supporting cast. Although viewers are indirectly persuaded they should care about saving whales because of the whales' inherent worth, the stronger message emerging from *Whale Wars* is that we should care about whales because the people we have grown to care about care about whales. In other words, we should care about whales only to the degree that they influence human lives. Even some members of the SSCS have allowed this worldview to make its way into their discourse, despite their convictions to the contrary. As Johnny Vasic, film producer and SSCS fundraiser, notes, "We are in a war of sorts, a war to save humanity through saving the diversity of our ecosystems."[58] This anthropocentric view may increase the viewership of *Whale Wars*, draw attention to image events, and even increase the popularity of the Sea Shepherds, but we are still skeptical about whether it will sway the opinions of viewers who are not committed to whale preservation.

As animal rights activists search for ways to garner more public support in an increasingly mediated world, it seems likely that we can expect an increased reliance on image events. While such a tactic is surely beneficial in some respects, mixing image events with another popular form—the reality television show—is likely to meet with severe limitations. Reality TV is designed to allow viewers to feel as though they are experiencing the action firsthand. However, during the controversial SSCS campaign, Animal Planet repeatedly stressed "it isn't endorsing Watson's campaign, simply documenting it."[59] By appropriating the SSCS rhetoric, Animal Planet effectively engages in what Jo Littler calls the corporate "neutralization" of the image event.[60] The SSCS, an "other-directed social movement" organization, appears to have saving whales as its primary concern. Animal Planet, however, is not an "other-directed" corporation. We are not contending that Animal Planet should not be airing a reality TV program about animal rights. However, we are deeply concerned that an animal rights organization's cause is being used by corporate interests to boost ratings and turn a profit and that the important animal ethics message is taking a distant second place to trite human conflicts.

To be fair, we realize that criticism without suggestions for future construction can appear condemning. It is with a spirit of engagement that we offer a few tentative suggestions, incomplete as they may be. Perhaps Animal Planet could create an equally captivating and financially successful series by humanizing the whales, much like they did with the animals in the popular program *Meerkat Manor*. Of course, we realize this has an anthropocentric problem of its own, but it is an anthropocentric bias that is, perhaps, a degree better than what is being produced in *Whale Wars* now. But this problem could be modified with another alternative suggestion. Perhaps Animal Planet should consider editing the show to feature the whales as agents as often as they feature the humans. Additional footage of whales, which are social, family-oriented creatures, living and dying could have allowed viewers to care for the mammals rather than the activists. However, this raises the question of whether or not Animal Planet would then lose viewers who were watching for the human interest element. This may be the case in the short run, but we believe that as more messages about the inherent worth of animals become increasingly mainstream, viewers will slowly start to reward the network with ratings. Given this observation, social movement activists are in a precarious position because they have to face the rhetorical problem of convincing networks that exist in an instant-ratings culture that long-term ratings are what they should care about. This is a difficult rhetorical constraint to overcome, mostly because access to the activists' message is dependant on the ratings to keep the show afloat. Ultimately, this case study illustrates the difficulties faced by a social change organization as it encountered its image events falling subject to the mangle of modern capitalistic practice.

Season two began airing in June 2009, and the camera crews have returned. Unfortunately, it seems the network has no plans of changing the program's format or of taking a position in the whaling debate. And why should they? The first season of *Whale Wars* was a commercial success, despite its lack of advocacy. Watson and his deckhands are once again navigating the treacherous and icy waters of the Antarctic in pursuit of animal justice, and we can rest assured that no human motivation, mistake, or mishap will go uncaptured.

Part Four

A CRITIQUE OF ANIMAL ETHICS AND ANIMAL MANAGEMENT RHETORIC

Chapter Eleven

Feral Horses

Logos, Pathos and the Definition of Christian Dominion

Jane Bloodworth Rowe and Sabrina Marsh

Debates over animal ethics engaged in by animal rights advocates and conservation groups reveal important tensions, especially with regard to the definition of animal "rights." Conflicts continue over the viability of animal rights with advocates such as People for the Ethical Treatment of Animals (PETA) arguing for animals' "inherent worth" apart from "their usefulness to humans" while government bureaucracies charged with conservation, like the federal Bureau of Land Management, pursue habitat protection for the sake of science, education, and recreation.[1] What appears striking about ongoing animal ethics discourse generated by both advocates and conservationists is its reflection of Christian traditions. Animal ethics remains a debate that is rooted in ancient Christian rhetoric articulated through the lens of modern rhetorics of science.

One current debate over animal rights and the proper relationship between human and nonhuman animals exemplifies the influence of Christian rhetoric on animal ethics discourse. The Corolla Wild Horse Fund (CWHF), a non-profit group formed in 1989 to protect the feral horses who roam the beaches of northeastern North Carolina and southeastern Virginia, is an animal rights advocacy group that, although it does not identify itself as Christian, exemplifies the influence of Christian rhetoric on animal ethics debates. The CWHF advocates for wild horses descended from Spanish mustangs brought to North America in the sixteenth century. Members are opposed to the conservationist policies of the U.S. Fish and Wildlife Service (USFWS) and the North Carolina Department of Environment and Natural Resources (NCDENR), which operates the North Carolina Estuarine Research Reserve. Officials from these government organizations seek to limit the wild horse population to 60, arguing that they are destructive to local wildlife habitats and the natural terrain. However, the CWHF offers the counterargument that this limit threatens to harm the horses' genetic health and thus has proposed an increase in population size to 110.[2] The CWHF also maintains that the wild horses possess intrinsic rights, including the right to coexist and share the land with humans. USFWS and NCDENR, however, focus their efforts on controlling or even eradicating species considered undesirable. Interestingly, both perspectives reflect Christian biblical teachings that remain foundational to their respective understandings of the human/nonhuman relationship. These two stakeholders reflect engagement with a centuries-old conflict over interpretations of human "dominion" with regard to nature as reflected in Genesis: "Then God said, 'Let us make humankind in our image, according to our likeness; and let them have dominion over the fish of the sea, and over the birds of the air, and over the cattle, and over all the wild animals of the earth, and over every creeping thing that creeps upon the earth.'"[3] The government agencies seemingly adhere to interpretations of that passage advanced by St. Thomas Aquinas and Francis Bacon that deny nonhuman animal rights and assert nature as created solely for human use and domination.[4] The CWHF, on the other hand, articulates an alternate interpretation of human "dominion" expressed by Christian theologians such as St. Francis of Assisi and Andrew Linzey, a contemporary Christian animal rights activist. This view interprets the word "dominion" as a charge to treat animals with compassion and respect.[5]

The study of these organizations' mutual grounding in Christian rhetorics signals important connections among religion, science, and public policy; connections of interest to rhetorical scholarship. Thomas Lessl, for instance, examines such connections in his argument linking modern natural science with Christian theology from the Middle Ages and Renaissance.[6] Lessl contends that the rhetoric of science is grounded in Christian *mythos* and indicates that there is a close relationship between science and religion. This relationship is exemplified in the philosophy of Bacon, who maintained that humans, through scientific experimentation, could acquire the knowledge necessary to assert their God-given right to exercise full control over nature.[7] In addition, Elizabeth Walker Mechling and Jay Mechling conclude that scientific discourse holds the capacity to "conflate scientific and religious ideas" and articulate "a moral rhetoric" that transcends scientific conclusions to make argumentative claims based in "moral assumptions and principles."[8] Similarly, James McDaniel argues that Christian rhetorics remain fundamental to public policy. McDaniel's analysis shows the importance of "re/dis/figure[ing]" public debate at its points of intersection with religion, acknowledging the impact of religious theology on public discourse while at the same time remaining skeptical of the "perils" that such influences pose.[9] Intersections between Christian theology and activist/conservationist animal ethics discourse, as in the example of the CWHF and USFWS/NCDENR, exemplify the linking of Christian rhetorics to the rhetoric of science and the consequent development of public policy.

This essay seeks to demonstrate, through homological analysis, how the CWHF and USFWS/NCDENR establish similar argumentative groundings in Christian theology. Thus, we discover homological patterns of interest shared by conflicting stakeholders in environmental and animal ethics debates. Homology, rhetorician Jason Edward Black explains, connotes similarity between ideas and "reveals commonalities" held between seemingly divergent groups.[10] We analyze theological and philosophical writings and their intersection with the rhetoric of the CWHF and USFWS/NCDENR to show that the two groups reflect similar notions of human "dominion" over nonhuman animals. The CWHF and USFWS/NCDENR both embrace the notion of "natural" human dominance, envision the human/nonhuman relationship as corrupted by human contact (this corruption originating with the fall and corruption of the physical world as narrated in the Christian tradition), and envision humans as "saviors" that will restore ideal human and natural conditions. These are the similarities.

Yet the groups diverge in their characterizations of the proper *exercise* of human "dominion." The CWHF understands the human/nonhuman relationship as one of shepherd/protector with humans taking responsibility for the care of the less powerful and the creation of a universe in which humans and nonhuman animals live together peacefully and share natural resources. This concept is very much in line with traditions extending from St. Francis' ministry to nonhuman animals. USFWS and NCDENR, on the other hand, see their relationship to nonhumans as one of control and manipulation, as they attempt to create a "Garden of Eden" to be used for human consumption. This view remains tied to St. Thomas and to Baconian science with its notions of human domination as part of the natural order. These divergent interpretations of shared Christian traditions lead animal rights activists to articulate the desire to protect wild horses and government managers to advocate on behalf of the park's environment, rather than individual animals.

Despite the differences of perspective, homological analysis indicates an opening for convergence between the two stakeholders in this debate and the possibility for new public policy that reinterprets Christian tradition with regard to animal ethics. Homological analysis of this case illustrates Black's claim that homology may "allow patterns to be re/discovered across varying movements" while also suggesting ways for activists to pursue critiques of public policy. As Black argues, "change must be acquired through filtering new ideologies through old ideologies."[11] Examination of divergent viewpoints presented by animal rights activists and conservationists in the case of

Corolla's wild horses presents an opportunity for discovering new ways to bridge ideological conflicts with regard to the ethical treatment of animals.

This study will begin by reviewing the current status of the debate between the CWHF and USFWS/NCDENR with regard to treatment of wild horse populations. We will then analyze the rhetoric of the government managers and that of its activist counterparts, including examination of advocacy materials, correspondence, and position statements of the stakeholders, as well as telephone interviews and e-mail correspondence with Karen McAlpin, Executive Director of the CWHF, and Mike Hoff, manager of the federally directed Mackay Island National Wildlife Refuge. Study of these groups' discourse reveals homology with regard to Christian rhetorics as underlying divergent positions in the modern animal ethics debate. We conclude by discussing the implications of the bridge that homological analysis provides between these groups, and in particular the possibility for new public policy that furthers animal rights.

HISTORICAL BACKGROUND

The feral horses, descendants of the mustangs brought to this country in the sixteenth century, have roamed the Atlantic beaches of northeastern North Carolina and southeastern Virginia for centuries. During the early 1990s, USFWS officials removed the horses, which were considered an invasive species, from Back Bay National Wildlife Refuge in Virginia Beach. Because the horses had tremendous public support among local residents in Corolla, a beachfront community in Currituck County, plans were made to confine them in a 12,000-acre fenced sanctuary on Corolla Beach, south of the Virginia/ North Carolina line. The purpose of this sanctuary was to prevent the horses from straying northward into Virginia as well as to prevent them from straying onto coastal highways, where several had been struck by cars. Even so, the horses continue to be threatened by traffic, development, and tourism. The Corolla Wild Horse Fund, a 501(c)(3) non-profit, was formed in 1989 by "a group of concerned citizens" to manage the horses, provide veterinarian care, and educate the public.[12] Advocates for the horses were successful in having laws passed that prohibit harassing, feeding, or coming within 50 feet of the horses, but there are continuing concerns about tourists approaching or harassing these animals and vehicle traffic on the beach.

The number of horses has produced the current conflict between the concerned citizens of the CWHF and officials at the Mackay Island National Wildlife Refuge, who operate Currituck National Wildlife Refuge as a satellite facility, as well as officials at the North Carolina Department of Environment and Natural Resources, which operates the North Carolina Estuarine Research Reserve. Both the refuge and the reserve are located in the horse sanctuary, and the remainder of the sanctuary consists largely of privately owned property. Government officials, like the managers of Back Bay National Wildlife Refuge in Virginia, fear that the horses compete with wildlife for food, cause erosion of environmentally sensitive areas, and trample native plants.[13] In 1997, representatives from these bureaucracies created a management agreement that placed the herd number at 60, a number that members of the CWHF and some veterinarians believe to be too low to maintain genetic diversity.[14] Because of their declining population, the Corolla herd, as well as another herd of wild horses that are located further south in the North Carolina Outer Banks, have been placed in the critical category by the American Livestock Breed Conservancy and the Equus Survival Trust, two more advocacy organizations that are concerned about the welfare of these animals. Dr. Gus Cothran, a Texas A&M University equine geneticist and expert on feral herds, recommended in a 2008 report that the herd size be placed at 110 after DNA samples indicated insufficient genetic diversity.[15] As a result of this study, members of the CWHF requested that the government agencies allow the herd size to increase. The request was denied by both USFWS and NCDENR in April, 2008, and the CWHF issued another request asking for a moratorium on the removal of horses from the sanctuary until studies could be done to assess the impact of the wild horses. That request was also denied.[16] Currently, researchers from North Carolina State University are working with the CWHF and the government agencies to plan a study that will quantify the horses' impact on the environment.

The CWHF and USFWS/NCDENR appear at an impasse and activists continue to rely on future research and increased public interest to resolve the situation and cause a shift in public policy about the herd size of North Carolina's feral horses. However, despite their conflicting policy positions the CWHF and USFWS/NCDENR share a common basis in Christian rhetoric that holds the potential for changing the frame of the debate. The Christian perspectives relevant to the human/nonhuman relationship appear to be general and not specific to any one denomination, and thus we cite both Catholic and Protestant Christian thinkers in this case study. Bacon, a Protestant, shared Aquinas's view that the nonhuman world was intended entirely for human use. St. Francis, however, argued that humans should respect and care for, rather than exploit, animals, and this perspective is shared by both Andrew Linzey, an Anglican priest, and Jack Wintz, a Franciscan friar.[17]

In the following section, we analyze USFWS and NCDENR rhetorics, which reflect Christian theological traditions that assume a hierarchy in the universe that places humans firmly at the top of the physical world, an assumption that is rooted in the creation story from Genesis and in the writings of Aquinas.[18] Under this construction, the nonhuman world is depicted as inert and without intrinsic worth and exists only for human use. USFWS and NCDENR also assume that the physical world is corrupted and in need of careful management by humans, specifically scientists, who act as saviors intent on restoring the world to its uncorrupted state. In a subsequent section, we demonstrate a homological relationship between the rhetoric of the federal and state bureaucrats and the CWHF in their interpretations of the Genesis creation story. We then show how the CWHF articulates an alternative approach to human "dominion" that offers rhetorical resources for advocates of the rights of feral horses.

THE SCIENTIFIC APPROACH: DOMINION AS IMPROVEMENT AND CONSERVATION

Theologians, from Augustine to Aquinas, have maintained that God endowed humans with intelligence and a soul because He had a purpose for them. Nonhumans, including minerals, vegetation, and animals, were seen as inert, irrational, and without intrinsic worth.[19] They lacked a soul or the ability to reason or feel emotions, and, while they were aware of external sense perception, they had no cognitive ability to process the information that they received from their senses.[20] Nonhuman animals, under this construction, were entirely lacking in either intellect or sentiment. The ability to reason and to act with purpose was assigned by God to humans alone, and thus they were granted free will and the dominion of nature in God's place. Moreover, the corporal world was governed by a set of laws put into place by God. Aquinas described these as the "First Cause."[21] According to this narrative, God set all material things in motion and left "man" as His earthly steward. This construction of nature as a rule-governed system, grounded in the creation story and in the hierarchical order of the universe described by Aquinas, reduced nonhuman animals to inert matter that functioned as machines. These theological concepts evolved into the mechanistic view of nature that prevailed among Renaissance philosophers as exemplified by Francis Bacon and René Descartes. Thus Bacon cautioned against the anthropomorphic tendency to assign reason or purpose to the motions of nonhuman animals.[22]

Bacon outlined the scientific methodology of observation and experimentation in *Novum Organum*, and this work's influence on Western science and philosophy persists today.[23] He described "Man" as "the minister and interpreter of Nature" and added that man, through knowledge, could subdue and change nature.[24] By introducing the concept of nature as an economic resource best managed by scientists, Bacon helped establish an ontological and epistemological relationship between humans and nonhuman animals that is reflected in contemporary scientific rhetoric. This relationship was an outgrowth of the hierarchical view of nature established in Aquinas's interpretation of the creation story, which referred to animals as "lesser creatures" and stated that, "all creation is for man."[25] Bacon furthered the utilitarian perspective of nature by suggesting that humans should not only use but also manipulate the nonhuman world to profit humankind and individual humans.[26]

The Renaissance idea of conceiving of nature as a mechanical system was further developed by Descartes.[27] Under his system, nature functioned as a machine, and individual animals were viewed only as parts of that machine, with no consciousness or intrinsic rights. Indeed, Descartes wrote that nonhuman animals were automatons. The construction of nature as both a mechanized system and an economic resource justified colonization of the New World, as advocated by Bacon in his essay "Of Plantations" and in John Locke's description of the New World as *terra nullius*, unoccupied land that begged for European settlement. These theories descended into justifications for the continuing settlement—often called "improvement"—of wild areas in the United States. But it also influenced the conservation movement of the late nineteenth and early twentieth centuries. Gifford Pinchot, who served as the first Chief of the United States Forest Service during the administration of President Theodore Roosevelt, defined conservation as "the use of the natural resources for the greatest good of the greatest number for the longest time."[28] Under the conservation movement, nature came to be defined as pristine wilderness that existed entirely separately from human culture.[29] This definition cemented the bright-line nature/culture dichotomy that was rooted in the Christian belief that humans, unlike animals, were made in God's image and endowed with reason and free will. The definition also fueled an intolerance for non-native animals like the Corolla wild horses, because they were not viewed as part of the natural environment.

The concept of a corrupted physical world that needs a savior to restore it to an original pristine condition is also rooted in the creation story and the curse that God placed on the entire world because of the original sin.[30] While Christian beliefs hold that Jesus is redeemer and savior of the corporeal world, the rhetorical theorist Richard Weaver notes that Western cultures have since the sixteenth century increasingly seen themselves, rather than God, as being in control of nature and responsible for its salvation.[31] This belief is reflected in the conservationists' desire to eradicate feral animals who continue to corrupt the environment because they have been corrupted by their contact with humans. The inconsistency in this construction of nature—improve or conserve—promotes the utilitarian view of nature as a resource to be managed by scientists for the greatest benefit to the most humans. This construction further justifies the eradication of unwanted plant or animal species as "invasive" (as if human intervention is not), and is again reflected in the rhetoric of USFWS and NCDENR. In this view the human/nonhuman animal relationship is based on logical arguments about truth rather than arguments based in ethos or pathos. Through logical analysis and rational practice, wildlife managers reduce corruption and thus conserve nature.

Officials from USFWS and NCDENR state that their purpose is to preserve the natural habitat for the sake of human education, research, and profit. The USFWS mission is "to administer a national network of lands and waters for the conservation, management, and where appropriate, restoration of the fish, wildlife and plant resources and their habitats within the United States for the benefit of present and future generations of Americans."[32] The benefits include the promotion of environmental education and outdoor recreation as well as the enhancement of the local economy from increased nature-based tourism. Similarly, NCDENR officials also state that the reserve exists for "long term research, education and stewardship."[33] The goal, then, is protection of the ecosystem for the purpose of enhancing human profit, pleasure, and knowledge. The goal reflects both Christian rhetoric and Renaissance philosophy, which maintains that nonhumans were created for human use.[34] The concept of nature as a resource that prevails in modern western culture is reflected in USFWS' perceived need to conserve and manage "wildlife and plant resources" "for the benefit of the American people" as well as in its promotion of wildlife oriented recreation for the purpose of enhancing the local economy.[35] Terms such as "management," "research," and "education" reflect Bacon's perspective that the natural world should be carefully manipulated by scientists to enhance research and profit.[36] This bias in favor of management appears in a variety of rhetorical and scientific formulations.

For example, abstract, impersonal terms, such as "fish, wildlife and plant resources" further the concept of nature as inert and lacking free will and intelligence, a concept rooted in Aquinas' rhetoric.[37] Animals are referred to as "pest animals," "furbearers," and "horse herd," for example. Black noted that the rhetorical practice of reducing animals to things through the use of abstract labels, such as "beef" rather than "cow" justifies the use of them for clothing and food.[38] Terms such as "pest animals" and "furbearers" justifies the eradication of animals through trapping, hunting, or other aggressive action. Government officials also posit the horses as "aggressive" and "harmful," which further justifies taking action against them as threats rather than beings. NCDENR officials argue these nonhuman animals are "not part of the natural biota for the island, and their presence has caused problems and interference with the native communities of the reserve."[39] Weaver notes the seeming contradiction in the Christian ideal of altruism and aggressive, competitive behaviors in Western Civilization that are justified by the good/evil duality into which Christians tend to divide the world.[40] By describing the horses as non-native or labeling them as a "nuisance species," government officials employ the use of "devil terms" or terms that connote such extreme evil that aggression against the nuisance is necessary.[41] Thus the horses' behavior, including herding and grazing, is depicted as harmful to native plants and animals: "The action of the horses' hooves can also hasten erosion of island sediment and can cause damage to colonial bird and sea turtle nests."[42] Government officials, with their perceived need to eradicate non-native species, pose themselves as avengers and protectors of the good, the innocent, and the victimized.

While the Corolla wild horses have been objectified and even depicted as evil, they have largely been spared the fate of other herds of feral horses along the Atlantic coast because of public sentiment and local laws. The Mackay Island 2008 Comprehensive Conservation Plan acknowledges the "sentiment attached to the horses," which limits the refuge's "management options," and concedes that the horses attract tourists, thus enhancing the local economy.[43] USFWS officials recognized the conflict between sentiment and science, and have placed their faith in science, which has replaced religion as a foundation for thought about the human relationship to the universe.[44] This "faith" is not surprising. Weaver labels science, which has become synonymous with truth, a "God term" or a term that connotes good to such an extreme that all other terms are subjugated to it, and he further notes that the concept of absolute truth, now associated with science, is rooted in Christianity.[45] The faith that absolute truth can be arrived at through empirical, scientific studies produces skepticism about the physical and emotional experience of animals, which cannot be quantified or observed according to scientific standards of knowing and truth.[46] Charles Darwin, whose theory of evolution was grounded in Aquinas' concept of the first cause, also sought to remove pathos, and in particular the tendency to personify nature, from discussions of the human/nonhuman animal relationship. He defined the word nature as "only the aggregate action and product of many natural laws, and by laws the sequence of events as ascertained by us."[47] Not surprisingly, then, the Corolla horses are treated by scientists and bureaucrats as objects rather than beings.

Even after many pathbreaking studies, contemporary scientists are reluctant to recognize the existence of animal emotions or the kind of experience that would empathetically permit humans to identify with other animals because these qualities—pleasure, pain, happiness, sadness, and so on—are difficult to measure, even in humans.[48] The objectification of the corporeal world, now attributed to science, is rooted in Christian theology, specifically in the writings of Aquinas, who stated that "free will and deliberation and choice and all perfections of this sort" are assigned only to humans, thus distinguishing "man" from other animals.[49] John Passmore, a philosopher and historian of ideas, wrote of the modern construction of nature that, "behind this attitude lies a theology, a theology bitterly opposed to any form of naturalism, determined to insist that between man and beast there is an absolute barrier."[50] Animals are reduced to inert objects in both modern science and medieval theology. The Western construction of the human/nonhuman relationship, which is espoused by members of USFWS and NCDENR, is rooted in the creation story and the interpretation of the word "dominion" as absolute control of nature.

Recently, however, some theologians have arrived at a different interpretation of the creation story and now maintain that God granted intrinsic rights, including rights to the land, to nonhuman animals.[51] This position is reflected in the rhetoric of the activists who advocate for the horses. Like USFWS and NCDENR officials, members of CWHF articulate a worldview that is grounded in the Creation story and the concept of human dominion, but, unlike the government officials, the advocates also assume that animals have intrinsic rights. They also seek to change the human/nonhuman relationship by redefining dominion to mean compassion and caring. In the following pages, we will explore the theological traditions that serve as a foundation for the belief that animals and humans are linked through the creation and that God, in creating the universe, intended for humans and animals to live together and share natural resources. We will then rhetorically analyze the arguments presented by the activists as reflections of this belief system.

ACTIVIST APPROACH: DOMINION, RIGHTS, AND RESPONSIBILITIES

Christian animal rights advocates ground their perspective in the first chapter of Genesis, and point to Genesis 1:29 in particular, which states that God granted the earth, with its bounty of edible plants, to both humans and animals for their use and sustenance. The word "dominion," according to this construction, is a charge to care for and respect nonhuman animals.[52] This interpretation, which can be traced back to St. Francis, grants intrinsic rights to all animals. Furthermore the relationship between humans and nonhuman animals is, according to this definition, one based on respect and compassion rather than control and manipulation. The Christian concept of animal rights dates at least to the twelfth century, when there was a heightened belief in the potential to understand the creator through the created world.[53] The ontological relationship undergirding all of creation was emphasized by St. Bonaventure and was articulated by St. Francis in "The Canticle of the Creatures," written in 1225.[54] St. Francis personified animals and even referred to them as brothers and sisters. He also felt that all animals were a reflection of God's work, and that humans could come closer to God through their relationship with nonhuman animals. Moreover, St. Francis believed that all animals had the ability to recognize and worship God, a belief that was supported by Psalm 148, which commands cattle, creeping things, flying fowl, and other animals to praise God. St. Francis believed that all animals were linked to each other through God and the creation, and that this relationship was a mandate to humans to treat nonhuman animals with compassion. He charged that, "the human race greatly offends its creator" when it misuses "the Lord's creatures," and he chastised children for stealing baby swallows, charging that, "Man is more evil than the birds."[55]

Since the Renaissance, some theologians continued to believe that the human/nonhuman animal relationship should be an empathetic one because humans and other animals were connected through the creation. Martin Luther, George Fox, and John Wesley all assigned immortal souls to animals, and nineteenth-century animal rights movements were spearheaded by Christian groups.[56] Recently, Wintz introduced the term "sacramentality" to express the belief that every creature could be a sign or reflection of the Divine.[57] And Linzey has challenged the very notion of the human/nonhuman animal duality, maintaining that humans are a part of nature. Linzey writes, for example, that, "Man cannot simply take as God's view his own evaluation of himself in the cosmos."[58]

Wintz's and Linzey's views of the human/nonhuman animal relationship can be seen in the rhetoric of the CWHF, and specifically in the activists' views toward their responsibilities to animals. Under Linzey's construction, as the more powerful species humans have not only the right but also the responsibility to care for and in some cases make decisions for animals.[59] Thus members of the CWHF, like Linzey, advocate a managed approach to the nonhuman world. Their mission is "to protect, preserve, and responsibly manage" the horses.[60] They do this by advocating for the animals, administering veterinarian care, assuring that the horses stay within the sanctuary, and controlling the population through gelding or finding adoptive homes for some young horses.[61] This view of management is similar to that of government managers—a homology—in part because both sides have adopted the Bible's injunction: it is humans who exercise dominion. What is dissimilar about the opposing sides' interpretation of dominion is the disagreement over *why* humans exercise dominion. The position of the activists is rooted in the creation story, but unlike Bacon, who advocated management for the benefit of humans, management by the activists is driven by the desire to benefit the horses.[62] Thus, despite the homologies that exist, the two groups, as we will demonstrate in the paragraphs below, diverge on the question of animal rights.

Unlike government officials, the activists contend that animals have certain intrinsic rights, including the intrinsic right of the Corolla horses to exist on the Outer Banks. This belief is illustrated by declarations such as: "This was their land long before it was ours," and "They have shared their land and peacefully coexisted with us."[63] The argument implicitly recognizes that horses can assert title to land by occupation and that horses engage in the humane, not to mention Biblical, activities of sharing and being peaceful. Under this construction, the wild horses have these intrinsic rights primarily because they exist, an argument that Black notes is present in the arguments of both right-to-life groups and animal rights advocates.[64] Christian animal rights advocates, who argue that humans and animals are linked through the creation and their relationship to God, couple "Life" or "created" with "rights," and this perspective is reflected in the rhetoric of secular animal rights groups such as the CWHF.[65] The horses exist not only as sentient creatures but also as citizens of the Outer Banks, and therefore they have a right to be there. This contrasts with the perspective articulated by USFWS and NCDENR that assigns humans the right and responsibility to determine which nonhumans will be allowed to remain in an area.

In fact, advocates depict the horses as not only a part of but also a representation of the Outer Banks. They are described as the embodiment of the Outer Banks "spirit," which is "wild," "free," "untamed," and "rugged."[66] This positing of one concrete part as a representation of the whole is reflected in the writings of St. Francis' "Canticle of the Creatures" as well as in the medieval concept of "microcosm" and "macrocosm," in which the individual is viewed as a microcosm of the entire universe, and the universe exists as a macrocosm of the individual.[67] Under this worldview, the individual and the universe are bound physically and spiritually. The ecofeminist philosopher Carolyn Merchant maintains that this indicates a holistic, organic view of nature in which humans, plants, animals, and minerals are inextricably intertwined; a belief rooted in theology, specifically in the view that the entire corporeal world is linked to God and to each other through the creation.[68]

Thus, the activists attempt to change the human/nonhuman relationship and, by extension, the perceived relationship between nature and human culture, which they see as inextricably related. This holistic view of nature is reflected in the rhetoric employed by the CWHF, wherein horses are depicted as part of the natural environment and God's creation. The CWHF website, for instance, indicates that the horses have survived "nearly 500 years of fierce Nor'easters and hurricanes" and further states: "In order to understand the Banker Horse, one must understand the location and environment from which they developed."[69] The horses are largely linked to local geography, history, and culture through narratives that tell of the horses being shipwrecked and abandoned by early Spanish explorers.[70] During one sixteenth-century shipwreck, for example, "livestock was either lost, or swam ashore," and this shipwreck served as an example "of the dangers which threatened shipping along this most risky stretch of coast."[71] The horses' heroic efforts to survive that shipwreck served as a microcosm of the dangers faced by self-reliant humans and other animals who managed to adapt and survive in a rugged environment. This indicates that, through their ability to adapt and survive, the Corolla horses have not only earned their right to remain on the Outer Banks, they have also come to embody the area's rugged environment; microcosm and macrocosm.

Humans and horses are historically linked through their relationship to the land, but residential development and tourism have created new pressures on the environment and on the horses in recent years. Like USFWS and NCDENR officials, members of the CWHF also believe that humans have corrupted the physical world, a belief that is often found among Christian animal rights activists in general. Horses have been shot to death or have been hit by vehicles and abandoned to suffer and die. Thus the CWHF, echoing St. Francis, chastises humans and labels these acts as "cowardly and cruel."[72] These terms connote evil and fit Weaver's description of "devil terms," or the "counterpart of God terms" in that they are diametrically opposed to altruism, a value rooted in Christianity, and to courage, an American value that is particularly associated with the rugged Outer Banks culture.[73]

Homological analysis of the rhetoric of USFWS/NCDENR and the CWHF, then, indicates both shared traditions and diverging approaches to human "dominion." Both sides of this debate express worldviews grounded in the creation story and in the perception of humans as having authority in the natural world. And, both the government officials and activists view the natural world as a corrupted Garden of Eden that must be restored to its pristine condition by humans. The CWHF diverges from the government perspective, however, in that it grants intrinsic rights to animals and views humans as shepherds who are charged with caring for rather than managing the nonhuman world. They also envision a holistic universe and a link between culture and nature, or, in this case, among humans, horses, and the environment. Because they view the horses as linked to the Outer Banks environment and culture, the CWHF argues for allowing them to remain in their natural habitat. This is evidenced by the advocacy group's website, which depicts horses running along the beach and the banner "Keep them wild and free!" as well as in pleas to "help us save this historically significant dying breed."[74]

The concept that the horses are an integral part of the Outer Banks was also reflected in a letter that McAlpin wrote Hoff, in which she labeled the horses "cultural treasures."[75]

Differing interpretations of the word "dominion" result in different courses of action regarding the wild horses. While government officials posit the horses as inert objects that should be dealt with without emotion, activists argue that the horses should be managed with respect and compassion. These conflicting interpretations are revealed in the adjectives and concrete nouns used by the activists to describe the horses, which contrasts sharply with the objectifying terms used by USFWS and NCDENR officials. Adjectives like "untamed" and "rugged," and active tense verbs imply that the horses have characteristics like rationality and free will conditions—for possessing agency. Unlike government officials, members of the CWHF also speak of the horses as individuals rather than as a collective, and they assign human emotions to them. In an anthropomorphic narrative about a stallion that was euthanized after being hit by an all-terrain vehicle, McAlpin noted that, "Spec did not want to die and fought long and hard."[76] The verbs "want" and "fight" implied that the horse was very much like a human being exercising the desire for life. Notably, the practice of naming animals is rooted in Genesis, when God granted Adam the privilege.[77] In naming the horses, members of the CWHF recognized them as individuals with their own unique charac-teristics rather than as inert objects in a grand system. The horses, then, are presented as rational creatures with a will to survive. Not surprisingly, in her correspondence with Hoff, McAlpin indicated that her organization wanted to alert the public to "the incredible intelligence, athletic ability, trainability, and sensible temperament of the wild horses of the Currituck Outer Banks."[78] Activists claim that the small, hardy horses have adapted to a dry, sandy en-vironment and possess the ability to walk or run for miles through soft sand, scramble up sand dunes, and forage for food in an environment that consists largely of ocean beaches and marshes.[79]

The CWHF's rhetoric is a manifestation of the anthropomorphism that Ba-con sought to eradicate from the human/nonhuman animal relationship. The activists depict their wards as sentient creatures with desires, emotional needs, and the capacity for suffering. The implication that humans should be aware of the horses' sufferings and treat them compassionately is a perspective that Linzey maintains is rooted in the creation story, which he believed established the "generosity paradigm."[80] According to this paradigm, the powerful are mandated by God to care for the weak. While the CWHF also embraces scien-tific research, as evidenced by arguments for a larger herd size that are based on the scientific study conducted by Cothran, it does subscribe to "science in the restricted sense" that reduces nonhuman animals to things.[81] Rather, they see science as a tool that helps fulfill moral responsibilities to the horses. Thus pathos, which Bacon attempted to remove from science, is re-inserted into the human/nonhuman animal relationship. McAlpin, in e-mail correspondence, used the word "love" to describe her affection for all animals.[82]

The activists' narratives and descriptive prose also ascribe moral attributes, including intelligence, courage, love, and a gentle nature, to the horses. For example, the mother of one sick foal was nicknamed "Amarosa" because of the love that she showed to her offspring.[83] Certainly, maternal love, benevolence, and courage are qualities that resonate in American culture, the values of which are influenced by Christian theology. It is also interesting to note that, while government officials rely on purely logical arguments, the CWHF has integrated stories, anecdotes, and narratives into their persuasive communications. The power of narratives to communicate values, beliefs, and attitudes and to create a sense of identification is well-documented by rhetorical scholars.[84] In Western culture, many narratives—even those with secular themes and subjects—are borrowed from Christian myths and have plots and embedded values that resonate deeply.[85] Lessl noted that, "because the theme (*dianoia*) of a narrative derives from the reader's spontaneous decoding of its plot (*mythos*), the secular author who borrows a sacred plot also borrows some of its religious meaning."[86] The narratives that personify the horses and depict them as an integral part of both nature and culture establish an emotional bond between humans and the horses. These narratives, although secular, have borrowed from Christian myth and metaphor, and appeal to values that are embedded in Western culture. And, while storytelling is not unique to Christianity, "didactic stories" are especially important in the Christian tradition and were often employed by Jesus, who used parables as a pedagogical and persuasive tool.[87]

In the activists' narratives, individual horses serve as representations of the entire herd, as well as of the culture, environment, and human/nonhuman relationship. Spec, who represents courage and the will to live, was victimized by a careless or cruel human, and Amarosa, who represents the horses' love and compassion for each other, was aided by a human acting as a shepherd and savior. The narrative discourse posited by the CWHF reframes the creation story, with the horses and the Outer Banks residents serving as a microcosm for the universe. By retelling this story, the activists seek to reframe the human/nonhuman relationship as one of kinship, respect, and caring. The concept of the powerful shepherding the weak is also rooted in Biblical teachings, and specifically in Psalm 23 as well as in the metaphor of Jesus as a shepherd leading his sheep into the fold.

Michael Fox, a doctor and ethologist, notes that one limitation of the animal rights movement, as it is currently intellectually framed, is that it lacks "the dimension of emotion."[88] The worldview of some animal advocates, however, is becoming more holistic as humans establish theologically and philosophically grounded ethical and empathetic relationships with the non-human animal world. This perspective, as we have shown, is reflected in the rhetoric of the CWHF, and, as we discuss in the final section, also holds implications for animal rights groups in general.

CONCLUSION AND IMPLICATIONS

Rhetorical scholars, including Lessl and Black, indicate that new and even seemingly radical ideas are grounded in traditional values that are fundamental to a particular culture. To effect change, rhetoricians must find a common link between traditional beliefs and new ideas.[89] By assigning the horses the moral attributes of love and courage, and by borrowing from Christian narratives in both form and plot, the CWHF members have reframed the concept of human dominion. The holistic worldview and emotive language articulated in the CWHF rhetoric has implications for animal rights groups that find themselves in conflict with conservationists over the management of wild or feral animals. While the stakeholders in this issue disagree about the best course of action, both activists and government officials have adopted the plots and values embedded in Christian beliefs and narratives, including the creation story. Homologies ex-ist in all of the rhetoric of dominion indicating that there is common ground in the philosophy underlying both perspectives. Government officials and activists agree that humans have certain rights and responsibilities toward the environ-ment, and they share a worldview that holds that the physical world has been corrupted by humans and that humans have a responsibility to redeem it.

Perhaps more fundamentally, the stakeholders also agree that nature has value, and both groups seek to protect and preserve the nonhuman world. While the CWHF is focused on preserving a single species, it also argues that the en-vironment must be preserved from overdevelopment and pollution to assure the horses' continued survival.[90] Members of the CWHF advocate for preserving the sanctuary (a term that itself has theological implications) and plead with residents and tourists to respect the land. Their website relates the story of a small foal who was sickened after apparently ingesting poisons, and reminds residents that, "the horses rely on what grows on the land and they drink the water. If it is poisoned – so are they."[91] In a more general sense, however, both animal sanctuaries and wildlife refuges were founded on the premise that some areas should be set aside for use by nonhuman animals. Thus former Currituck County Commissioner Jerry Wright, speaking at an October 2008 meeting of stakeholders, indicated that the horses' presence helped USFWS officials fulfill their mission of preserving the natural environment, because public sentiment discouraged further development within the sanctuary.[92]

The stakeholders involved in this issue have also adopted discursive patterns that are rooted in Biblical tradition and that often appear in American reform rhetoric. Rhetorical scholar James Darsey noted that American reformers, like Old Testament prophets, have a clear sense of their mission, a desire to change public behavior so that it is consistent with a "sacred principle," and an uncompromising stance toward the audience.[93] Clearly, stakeholders involved in this issue are focused on a specific mission, whether it is preservation of native plants and wildlife (USFWS/NCDENR) or protection and conservation of a herd of horses (CWHF). Both government officials and activists are attempting to effect change and to bring public behavior into compliance with their own beliefs and attitudes. The early twentieth-century notion that some wilderness areas should be conserved and that all natural resources should be carefully managed, although anthropocentric, was still a departure from the belief espoused by Bacon that all land should be "improved."[94] Government officials advocate the preservation of wilderness, while the activists attempt to change the human/nature relationship by establishing that animals, like humans, have an intrinsic right to the land. Both groups, then, operate under the "sacred principle" grounded in the creation story: that nonhumans have some value and that humans, as the dominant species, are responsible for maintaining that value.[95] Thus USFWS and NCDENR have set aside tracts of land to be preserved as wilderness and encourage the public to visit these areas for educational and recreational purposes. The CWHF rhetoric also focuses on educating the public to respect both the horses and their environment, and attempts to change specific behaviors, such as careless driving or dumping toxics onto the ground, that violate the basic principle that nature has value.[96] The CWHF mission, then, is linked to that of USFWS and NCDENR. Because all argue against practices that are harmful to the ecosystem, their rhetoric enhances the government agencies' mission of preserving the wildlife, waterways, and wetlands.

The homologies reveal common ground among the stakeholders, as well as among animal rights groups and members of the public, that could serve as a rhetorical tool for activists who are seeking to change beliefs about the human/nonhuman relationship. For example, members of the CWHF, as well as other animal rights advocates, could identify with conservationists by grounding their arguments in three fundamental beliefs that are shared by members of all these groups. First, humans, as the dominant species, are granted certain rights. Second, because rights imply responsibility, humans also are charged with managing nonhumans for the good of the nonhumans and humans as well. Thirdly, nonhumans have worth and should be preserved, and sanctuaries should be established for the purpose of conserving and sharing natural resources. The latter may be the link where stakeholders on both sides of the debate should start from because animals have the ability to arouse public emotion, and this sentiment can be an effective tool for those who argue for preserving natural areas.

Differences remain, however, and negotiations with opponents do not always produce fruitful results. Thus advocacy groups also need to generate support among the general public as the members of the CWHF have done. Though the controversy surrounding the herd size remains unresolved as of this writing, and though we have not attempted to quantify the effectiveness of rhetorical efforts in this study, evidence suggests that the CWHF has achieved some success. By September 2009, 773 concerned citizens had signed a petition, and elected officials and opinion leaders, including U.S. Representative Walter Jones (R-NC) are now advocating for the horses.[97] This support may indicate that an appeal to Christian and American values and human sentiment have resonated with citizens. This is significant because public sentiment results in public policy, as is evidenced by local laws that prohibit harassing or approaching the animals. Concerned citizens have the ability to apply political pressure through their elected officials, and this is an especially effective tactic for animal rights groups who find themselves in opposition to government agencies such as US-FWS and NCDENR. By assigning the horses names and referring to them as individuals, the CWHF has successfully injected the "dimension of emotion" that Fox complained was missing from most discussions about animal rights.[98] Because emotional appeals are an effective technique for persuasion, narratives and vivid language have been helpful in establishing public support.

Due to the Christian narratives, the CWHF and other animal advocates benefit from having pre-established enthymematic connections with larger publics. Thus, the seeds are sown for the enactment of the "sentimental style" to complement logical arguments for animal rights. As rhetorician Stephen Browne defines it, this style includes "familiar emotions linked vicariously with sorrow, pity, sympathy, nostalgia, and their diminutives."[99] The power of the sentimental style is that it communicates the lived experiences of the oppressed to sympathetic audiences with open "hearts and minds" who also happen to have change-making potential as members of the larger dominant public. Nineteenth-century abolitionists were successful, in part, because they appealed overwhelmingly to northern sympathizers who shared common values, but who did not from the outset have a sense for the realities of slavery (aside from the repetitive logical appeals of white activists). Abolitionists found that evocative and imagistic narratives, often grounded in Christian traditions, brought slaves' personal sufferings closer to the masses of sympathizers who, in turn, opted for antislavery positions in lieu of their former complicit attitudes. Soon, these sympathizers began lobbying for policy change to assuage their newfound displeasure.[100] In keeping with the influence of this sentimental style in the U.S. social change tradition, the CWHF and other animal advocates could continue to offer even more responsible accounts of animal life. Advocates should be mindful to couple narratives of animal victimage with narratives of animal survival to both express a need to salve oppression and suffering *and* demonstrate that animals indeed possess agency. Again, the CWHF and animal advocates already have the foundation set for an enthymematic relationship based on shared Christian principles and American values.

This case study reveals simultaneously homologous and disparate perspectives about nonhuman animals that reflect the continuing influence of Christian thought. Even those rhetors who claim to argue from a purely scientific perspective ground their arguments in a faith that humans have dominion over the nonhuman world. Because culturally derived values like the faith in "man's dominion" resonate, they help to determine courses of action appropriate to public policy conflicts.[101] Americans have traditionally justified their behavior toward nonhumans by recalling Aquinas' and Bacon's "logical" assertion that human dominion, granted by God at the creation, meant absolute control. But the alternate reading of Biblical passages about "man's" dominion have begun to resonate emotionally, ethically, and even logically, and are now being used to reframe public policy discussions about the Corolla horses.

The appeal to commonly held values and familiar narratives should become an effective rhetorical tool for animal rights activists seeking to reframe the human/nonhuman animal relationship by introducing the concept that dominion implies care and compassion as well as management and control. The metaphor of the human as shepherd is grounded in Biblical teachings, and therefore is familiar to many Americans, as is the assumption that the physical world is corrupted and must be restored to an uncorrupted state by human saviors. By appealing to commonly held assumptions and beliefs and by employing vivid narratives and concrete language, animal rights advocates can begin to restore pathos to the human/nonhuman relationship.

Notes

CHAPTER ONE

1. See Kenneth Burke, "The Rhetoric of Hitler's 'Battle,'" in *The Philosophy of Literary Form: Studies in Symbolic Action* (1941; Berkeley: University of California Press, 1974): 191–220.

2. Kenneth Burke, *A Rhetoric of Motives* (1950; Berkeley: University of California Press, 1969), 29–30.

3. Charles Patterson, *Eternal Treblinka: Our Treatment of Animals and the Holocaust* (New York: Lantern Books, 2002).

4. Kathryn Olson and Thomas Goodnight, "Entanglements of Consumption Cruelty, Privacy, and Fashion: The Social Controversy Over Fur," *Quarterly Journal of Speech* 80 (1994): 249–276.

5. Peter Simonson, "Social Noise and Segmented Rhythms: News, Entertainment, and Celebrity in the Crusade for Animal Rights," *The Communication Review* 4, no. 3 (2001): 399–420.

6. Lesli Pace, "Image Events and PETA's Anti Fur Campaign," *Women and Language* 28, no. 2 (2005): 33–41.

7. See Kevin DeLuca, *Image Politics: The New Rhetoric of Environmental Activism* (New York: Guilford Press, 1999).

8. Jason Edward Black, "Extending the Rights of Personhood, Voice, and Life to Sensate Others," *Communication Quarterly* 51, no. 3 (2003): 312–31; and Jason Edward Black "SLAPPs and Social Activism: Free Speech Struggles in Grey2K's Campaign to Ban Dog Racing," *Free Speech Yearbook* 40 (2003): 70–82.

9. Wendy Atkins-Sayre, "Articulating Identity: People for the Ethical Treatment of Animals and the Animal/Human Divide," *Western Journal of Communication* (forthcoming).

10. Mary Trachsel, "Husserl's Intersubjectivity and the Possibility of Living with Nonhuman Persons," *Phenomenology of Life from the Animal Soul to the Human Mind* 93 (2007): 33–52.

11. Patricia Malesh, "Sharing Our Recipes: Vegan Conversion Narratives as Social Praxis," in *Active Voices: Composing A Rhetoric of Social Movements*, ed. Sharon McKenzie Stevens and Patricia Malesh (Albany: State University of New York Press, 2009): 131–48.

12. Carrie Packwood Freeman, "This Little Piggy Went to Press: The American News Media's Construction of Animals in Agriculture," *The Communication Review* 12, no. 1 (2009): 78–103; and Carrie Packwood Freeman and Debra Merskin, "Having It His Way: The Construction of Masculinity in Fast-Food TV Advertising," in *Essays on Eating and Culture*, ed. Lawrence C. Rubin (Jefferson, NC: McFarland, 2008): 277–93.

13. Burke, *A Rhetoric of Motives*, 41, 43.

14. Kenneth Burke, "Dramatism," in *International Encyclopedia of the Social Sciences*, ed. David L. Sills (New York: Free Press, 1968): 445.

15. Sonja K. Foss, Karen A. Foss, and Robert Trapp, *Contemporary Perspectives on Rhetoric* (Prospect Heights, IL: Waveland Press, 1985), 182.

16. Edward Schiappa, *Protagoras and Logos: A Study in Greek Philosophy and Rhetoric* (2nd ed.; Columbia: University of South Carolina Press, 2003), 49, 227; and Randy Allen Harris, *Rhetoric and Incommensurability* (West Lafayette, IN: Parlor Press 2005), 8–9.

17. Aristotle, *The History of Animals*, trans. Richard Cresswell (London: George Bell, 1897), 250; Aristotle, *On the Parts of Animals*, trans. W. Ogle (London: Kegan Paul, Trench & Co., 1882), 54, 185, fn. 5 and 188, fn. 14; and Aristotle, *On the Parts of Animals*, trans. A. L. Peck (Cambridge, MA: Harvard University Press, 1955), 201–203.

18. Leland M. Griffin, "The Rhetoric of Historical Movements," *Quarterly Journal of Speech* 38 (April 1952): 184–188.

19. For instance, a debate about social movement study involving essays by Michael Calvin McGee, David Zarefsky, Stephen E. Lucas, James R. Andrews, and Charles J. Stewart was published in *Central States Speech Journal* 31 (Winter 1980). The forum ranged from the functionality of a modernist/sociological approach to the study of movement leaders, internal strategies, external strategies, and organizational structure to the efficacy and need of a theory altogether.

20. Christine Oravec, "John Muir, Yosemite, and the Sublime Response: A Study in the Rhetoric of Preservationism," *Quarterly Journal of Speech* 67 (1981): 245–258.

21. See Jonathan Lange, "Refusal to Compromise: The Case Study of Earth First!," *Western Journal of Communication* 54 (1990): 473–494; M. Jimmie Killingsworth and Jacqueline S. Palmer, *Ecospeak: Rhetoric and Environmental Politics* (Carbondale: Southern Illinois University Press, 1992); Tarla Rai Peterson, *Sharing the Earth: The Rhetoric of Sustainable Development* (Columbia: University of South Carolina Press, 1992); Phaedra Pezzullo, "Performing Critical Interruptions: Stories, Rhetorical Invention, and the Environmental Justice Movement," *Western Journal of Communication* 65 (2001): 1–25; and DeLuca, *Image Politics*. Bear in mind that there have been scores of essays and books since.

22. Raymie E. McKerrow, "Critical Rhetoric: Theory and *Praxis*," *Communication Monographs* 56 (1989): 91–111.

CHAPTER TWO

1. Jacques Derrida, "The Animal that Therefore I Am (More to Follow)," trans. David Willis, *Critical Inquiry,* 28 (2002): 372.

2. I choose to use the term *nonhuman animal* (NHA) instead of the more common term *animal* as a way to avoid the implication that "animal" is a separate category in which humans do not belong. Therefore, when I just say *animal(s),* it includes humans too. This is part of my attempt to embrace humanimality (a sense of human's innate animality). I acknowledge the limitations of the term NHA later in this chapter.

3. I define "animal rights" as an anti-exploitation movement for the abolition of animal slavery. Since the goal is liberation, I could use the term "animal liberation" to describe the movement. However, I choose to employ "animal rights," because it is the label by which the movement is more commonly known. For distinctions between animal welfare and rights ideologies, see Gary Francione, *Rain without Thunder* (Philadelphia: Temple University, 1996), 1–20.

4. Carrie P. Freeman, "Struggling for Ideological Integrity in the Social Movement Framing Process: How U.S. Animal Rights Organizations Frame Values and Ethical Ideology in Food Advocacy Communication." PhD Diss., University of Oregon, 2008. Abstract in *Dissertation Abstracts International*, publ. nr. AAT 3325661 (2008), iv–v.

5. I define "posthuman" as a way of thinking that envisions the human as an animal in a larger ecological community where humans no longer privilege their own species as a wholly separate and superior category and begin to include themselves as one among other animated subjects. Posthumanism incorporates the human rights goals of humanism and blends them with concerns for animal rights and environmentalism. For more information see Cary Wolfe, "posthumanities," http://www.carywolfe.com/post.html.

6. Mary Midgley, "Beasts, Brutes and Monsters," in *What is an Animal?* ed. Tim Ingold (London: Unwin Hyman, 1988), 35.

7. Tim Ingold, "Introduction," in *What is an Animal?* ed. Tim Ingold (London: Unwin Hyman, 1988), 4.

8. Joan Dunayer, *Animal Equality: Language and Liberation* (Derwood, MD: Ryce Publishing, 2001), 2.

9. Dunayer, *Animal Equality,* 11.

10. See Carol Adams, *The Sexual Politics of Meat: A Feminist-Vegetarian Critical Theory* (New York: Continuum, 1990); and Marjorie Spiegel, *The Dreaded Comparison: Human & Animal Slavery* (New York: Mirror Books, 1996).

11. But *human animal* is awkward and inconsistent in the sense that we do not refer to other specific species by adding the term *animal* to their name (i.e., we do not say *dog animals*).

12. Jacques Derrida, *For What Tomorrow: A Dialogue (Cultural Memory in the Present)*, trans. Jeff Fort (Stanford, CA: Stanford University Press, 2004), 63.

13. The term "infra-human" is used by Derrida and Wolfe; William J. T. Mitchell also used the term "humanimal" in the foreword to Wolfe's book. See William J. T. Mitchell, "The Rights of Things" in *Animal Rites: American Culture, the Discourse of Species, and Posthumanist Theory*, by Cary Wolfe (Chicago: University of Chicago Press, 2003), xiii; and Jacques Derrida, "Eating Well, or the Calculation of the Subject," in *Points . . . Interviews, 1974–1994, Jacques Derrida*, ed. Elisabeth Weber, trans. Peter Conner and Avital Ronell (Stanford, CA: Stanford University Press, 1995), 255–287.

14. Consider how the women's movement has combated the patriarchy inherent to terms like *mankind* or *chairman*. See Cheris Kramarae and Paula A. Treichler, *A Feminist Dictionary* (Boston: Pandora Press, 1985), s.v. "Chairman," "Mankind."

15. Derrida, *For What Tomorrow*, 66.

16. P. J. Ucko, "Foreword," in *What is an Animal?* ed. Tim Ingold (London: Unwin Hyman, 1988), ix-xvi.

17. Derrida, *For What Tomorrow*, 66.

18. Peter Singer, *Animal Liberation* (2nd ed.; London: Random House, 1990), 18.

19. Elizabeth A. Lawrence, "Cultural Perceptions of Differences Between People and Animals: A Key to Understanding Human-Animal Relationships," *Journal of American Culture* 18 (1995): 75–82.

20. Derrida, "Eating Well," 284–5.

21. Mary Midgley, "The Lure of the Simple Distinction," in *Animal Rights: A Historical Anthology*, ed. Andrew Linzey and Paul Barry Clarke (New York: Columbia University Press, 2004), 48–50.

22. Daniel Elstein, "Species as a Social Construction: Is Species Morally Relevant?" *Animal Liberation Philosophy & Policy Journal* 1 (2003): 1–19.

23. Elstein, "Species as a Social Construction," 1.

24. Elstein, "Species as a Social Construction," 16.

25. Singer, *Animal Liberation*, 1–23; Tom Regan, *The Case for Animal Rights* (Berkeley, CA: University of California Press, 1983), 185.

26. See Michel Foucault, *Power/Knowledge* (Harvester: Brighton, 1980).

27. Dunayer, *Animal Equality*, 11.

28. Derrida, *For What Tomorrow*, 64.

29. Derrida, *For What Tomorrow*, 64.

30. Derrida, *For What Tomorrow*, 71.

31. Derrida, "The Animal that Therefore I Am," 394.

32. Dunayer, *Animal Equality*, 4.

33. Adams, *Sexual Politics of Meat*, 42.

34. Dunayer, *Animal Equality*, ix.

35. Marc Bekoff and Jessica Pierce, *Wild Justice: The Moral Lives of Animals* (Chicago: University of Chicago Press, 2009), 1–23. The authors provide examples about cooperation, empathy, and justice, such as an African elephant who rescues a trapped group of antelope and rats who refuse to administer shocks to other rats, eschewing the food rewards.

36. This is a term coined by Herbert Spencer, *Principles of Biology* (1864; Honolulu, HI: University Press of the Pacific, 2002), 444.

37. Aristotle, "Animals are Not Political," in *Animal Rights: A Historical Anthology*, ed. Andrew Linzey and Paul B. Clarke (New York: Columbia University Press, 2004), 7.

38. Porphyry, "On the Eating of Flesh," in *Ethical Vegetarianism: From Pythagoras to Peter Singer*, ed. Kerry S. Walters and Lisa Portmess (New York: SUNY Press, 1999), 39.

39. Thomas Hobbes, "Animals Have No Language," in *Animal Rights: A Historical Anthology*, ed. Andrew Linzey and Paul B. Clarke (New York: Columbia University Press, 2004), 19.

40. Michel de Montaigne, "Exclusion from Friendship is Not Rational," in *Animal Rights: A Historical Anthology*, eds. Andrew Linzey and Paul B. Clarke (New York: Columbia University Press, 2004), 106.

41. Johann G. Herder, "Organic Difference," in *Animal Rights: A Historical Anthology*, ed. Andrew Linzey and Paul B. Clarke (New York: Columbia University Press, 2004), 35.

42. Jean-Jacques Rousseau, "Freedom of the Will," in *Animal Rights: A Historical Anthology*, ed. Andrew Linzey and Paul B. Clarke (New York: Columbia University Press, 2004), 33.

43. Cited in Foss, Foss, and Trapp, *Contemporary Perspectives on Rhetoric*, 207.

44. Rosalind Coward, "Dominion is Social," in *Animal Rights: A Historical Anthology*, ed. Andrew Linzey and Paul B. Clarke (New York: Columbia University Press, 2004), 96.

45. Jim Mason, *An Unnatural Order: Why We Are Destroying the Animals and Each Other* (New York: Continuum, 1997), 118–157.

46. See previous references to Montaigne, Herder, and Rousseau in Linzey and Clarke, *Animal Rights*.

47. Peter Singer and Jim Mason, *The Ethics of What We Eat: Why our Food Choices Matter* (Emmaus, PA: Rodale, 2006), 3.

48. J. Baird Callicott, "The Conceptual Foundations of the Land Ethic," in *Environmental Philosophy: From Animal Rights to Radical Ecology*, ed. M. E. Zimmerman (Englewood Cliffs, NJ: Prentice Hall, 1993), 110–134; and Michael Pollan, *The Omnivore's Dilemma: A Natural History of Four Meals* (New York: Penguin Press, 2006), 214 (original term credited to Wes Jackson).

49. Aldo Leopold, "The Land Ethic," in *The Environmental Ethics and Policy Book*, ed. Donald Van de Veer and Christine Pierce (Belmont, CA: Wadsworth, 2003), 215.

50. See Callicott, "The Land Ethic," 110–134.

51. See Matt Ridley, *The Origins of Virtue* (London: Viking, 1996); and Peter Kropotkin, "Nature Teaches Mutual Aid," in *Animal Rights: A Historical Anthology* (1939), ed. Andrew Linzey and Paul Barry Clarke (New York: Columbia University Press, 2004), 88–90.

52. Callicott, "The Land Ethic," 129.

53. Holmes Rolston, "Challenges in Environmental Ethics," in *Environmental Philosophy: From Animal Rights to Radical Ecology*, ed. M. E. Zimmerman (Englewood Cliffs, NJ: Prentice Hall, 1993), 135–157.

54. See Bill Devall and George Sessions, *Deep Ecology: Living as if Nature Mattered* (Salt Lake City: Peregrine Smith Books, 1985).

55. Mitchell, "The Rights of Things," xiv.

56. Derrida, *For What Tomorrow*, 64, 65.

57. Derrida, *For What Tomorrow*, 67.

58. See Singer, *Animal Liberation*; and Regan, *Case for Animal Rights*.

59. Wolfe, *Animal Rites*, 8.

60. Lynda Birke and Luciana Parisi, "Animals Becoming," in *Animal Others: On Ethics, Ontology, and Animal Life*, ed. H. Peter Steeves (Albany, NY: State University of New York Press, 1999), 57.

61. See Introduction in Ingold, *What is an Animal?* 1–15; and Josephine Donovan and Carol J. Adams, "Introduction," in *The Feminist Care Tradition in Animal Ethics*, ed. Josephine Donovan and Carol J. Adams (New York: Columbia University Press, 2007), 1–20.

62. Paola Cavalieri and Peter Singer, "A Declaration on Great Apes," in *The Great Ape Project: Equality Beyond Humanity*, ed. Paola Cavalieri and Peter Singer (New York: St. Martin's Press, 1993), 1–7.

63. See Stephen R. L. Clark, "Is Humanity a Natural Kind?" in *What is an Animal?* ed. Ingold, 17–34; and refer back to previous citations of Derrida, *For What Tomorrow*, 66; and Lawrence, "Cultural Perceptions," 75–82.

64. Giorgio Agamben, *The Open: Man and Animal*, trans. Kevin Attell (Stanford, CA: Stanford University Press, 2004).

65. David Wood, "Thinking with Cats (A Response to Derrida)," in *Animal Philosophy: Ethics and Identity*, ed. Matthew Calarco and Peter Atterton (New York: Continuum, 2004), 128–144.

66. Lee Hall, *Capers in the Churchyard: Animal Rights Activism in the Age of Terror* (Darien, CT: Nectar Bat Press, 2006), 89.

67. Gary Steiner, *Animals and the Moral Community: Mental Life, Moral Status, and Kinship* (New York: Columbia University Press, 2008), ix–xii.

68. Steiner, *Animals and the Moral Community*, 125.

69. See David Abram, *The Spell of the Sensuous: Perception and Language in a More-than-Human World* (New York: Vintage Books, 1997), 78–79.

70. See Mary Trachsel, "How to Do Things Without Words: Whisperers as Rustic Authorities on Interspecies Dialogue," in this volume.

71. See Jonathan Balcombe, *Pleasurable Kingdom: Animals and the Nature of Feeling Good* (New York: Palgrave, 2006); Roger Fouts, *Next of Kin: My Conversations with Chimpanzees* (New York: Avon Books, 1997); Tim Friend, *Animal Talk: Breaking the Codes of Animal Language* (New York: Free Press, 2004); Jeffrey M. Masson and Susan McCarthy, *When Elephants Weep: The Emotional Lives of Animals* (New York: Dell Publishing, 1995); George Page, *Inside the Animal Mind: A Groundbreaking Exploration of Animal Intelligence* (New York: Doubleday, 1999); and Bekoff and Pierce, *Wild Justice*.

72. Wolfe, *Animal Rites*, 53.

73. Thomas Laquer, *Making Sex: Body and Gender from the Greeks to Freud* (Cambridge, MA: Harvard University Press, 1990), 149.

74. Dunayer, *Animal Equality*, 13.

75. Ingold, *What is an Animal?* 10.

76. See Stephen R. L. Clark, "Apes and the Idea of Kindred," in *The Great Ape Project: Equality Beyond Humanity*, ed. Paola Cavalieri and Peter Singer (New York: St. Martin's Press, 1993), 113–125.

77. Steiner, *Animals and the Moral Community*, 137.

78. Foss, Foss, and Trapp, *Perspectives on Rhetoric*, 192.

79. Gilles Deleuze and Félix Guattari, "Becoming Animal," in *Animal Philosophy: Ethics and Identity*, ed. Matt Calarco and Peter Atterton (New York: Continuum, 2004), 87–100.

80. Donna J. Haraway, *When Species Meet* (Minneapolis, MN: University of Minnesota Press, 2008), 19.

CHAPTER THREE

Acknowledgments. I wish to acknowledge the University of Iowa's generous support for this project in the form of a Career Development Award from the College of Liberal Arts and Sciences and a faculty fellowship with the Obermann Center for Advanced Studies at the University of Iowa's Research Park.

1. J. L. Austin, *How to Do Things with Words: The William James Lectures Delivered at Harvard in 1955* (Oxford: Clarendon, 1962).

2. Kenneth Burke, *Language as Symbolic Action* (Los Angeles & Berkeley: University of California Press, 1966), 3–9.

3. Daniel Dennett, *Kinds of Minds* (New York: Basic Books, 1996), 139.

4. Dennett, *Kinds of Minds*, 23.

5. Daniel Dennett, "Animal Consciousness: What Matters and Why," in *Brain Children: Essays on Designing Minds* (Boston: MIT Press, 1998) 339.

6. Stephen Anderson, *Dr. Doolittle's Delusion: Animals and the Uniqueness of Human Language* (New Hartford, CT: Yale University Press, 2004).

7. Henry Wadsworth Longfellow, "Hiawatha's Childhood" in *The Song of Hiawatha*, http://etext.lib.virginia.edu/modeng/modengL.browse.html.

8. Josephine Donovan, "Caring to Dialogue," in *The Feminist Care Tradition in Animal Ethics*, ed. Josephine Donovan and Carol J. Adams (New York: Columbia, 2007), 360–369.

9. Eric King Watts, "'Voice' and 'Voicelessness' in Rhetorical Studies," *Quarterly Journal of Speech* 87, no. 2 (2001): 180.

10. Watts, "Voice," 192.

11. Michael J. Hyde, *The Call of Conscience: Heidegger and Levinas, Rhetoric and the Euthanasia Debate* (Columbia: University of South Carolina, 2001), 94.

12. Donovan, "Caring to Dialogue," 362.

13. Donovan, "Caring to Dialogue," 362, 363.

14. Donovan, "Caring to Dialogue," 364.

15. Donovan, "Caring to Dialogue," 363.

16. Donovan, "Caring to Dialogue," 363.

17. Peter Singer, *Animal Liberation* (New York: Avon Books, 1973).

18. Singer, *Animal Liberation*, ii. Donovan points out in "Animal Rights and Feminist Theory" that Singer is concerned in this scene to distance himself from the trivializing force of "womanish sentiment." Josephine Donovan, "Animal Rights and Feminist Theory," in *Beyond Animal Rights: A Feminist Caring Ethic for the Treatment of Animals*, ed. Carol J. Adams and Josephine Donovan (New York: Continuum, 1996), 34–35.

19. Burke, *Language as Symbolic Action*, 5.

20. Singer, *Animal Liberation*, ii.

21. Donovan, "Caring to Dialogue," 365.

22. Donovan, "Caring to Dialogue," 365.

23. Konrad Lorenz, *The Foundations of Ethology* (New York: Simon & Schuster, 1982).

24. Konrad Lorenz, *On Aggression* (San Diego: Harcourt Brace, 1963).

25. Margaret Urban Walker, *Moral Understandings* (New York: Routledge, 1998).

26. Konrad Lorenz, *King Solomon's Ring*, trans. Marjorie Kerr Wilson (New York: Thomas Y. Crowell, 1952), xiii, xvi.

27. Lorenz, *King Solomon's Ring*, xviii.

28. Colin Allen and Marc Bekoff, *Species of Mind: The Philosophy and Biology of Cognitive Ethology* (Cambridge, MA: MIT Press, 1997), xvi.

29. Zhanna Reznikova, "Dialogue with Black Box: Using Information Theory to Study Animal Language Behavior," *ACTA Ethologica* 10, no. 1 (2007): 1–12.

30. Hayden Lorimer, "Herding Memories of Humans and Animals," *Environment and Planning D: Society and Space* 24 (2006): 501.

31. Lorimer, "Herding Memories of Humans and Animals," 497.

32. Lorimer, "Herding Memories of Humans and Animals," 517.

33. Graham Harvey, *Animism: Respecting the Living World* (New York: Columbia University Press, 2005).

34. Graham Harvey, "Animals, Animists, and Academics," *Zygon* 41 no. 1 (March 2006): 10.

35. Harvey, "Animals, Animists, and Academics," 10.

36. Harvey, "Animals, Animists, and Academics," 17.

37. Allen and Bekoff, *Species of Mind*, 73.

38. Valeri A. Farmer-Dougan and James D. Dougan, "The Man Who Listens to Behavior: Folk Wisdom and Behavior Analysis from a Real Horse Whisperer," *Journal of the Experimental Analysis of Behavior* 72, no. 1 (July 1999): 143.

39. Farmer-Dougan and Dougan, "The Man Who Listens to Behavior," 146.

40. Farmer-Dougan and Dougan, "The Man Who Listens to Behavior," 147.

41. Farmer-Dougan and Dougan, "The Man Who Listens to Behavior," 149.

42. Nicholas Evans, *The Horse Whisperer* (New York: Dell, 1995); and Monty Roberts, *The Man Who Listens to Horses* (New York: Ballantine Books, 1996), 53.

43. Paul Owens (with Norma Eckroate), *The Dog Whisperer: A Compassionate, Nonviolent Approach to Dog Training* (Avon, MA: Adams Media Corporation, 1999); Cesar Millan (with Melissa Jo Peltier), *Be the Pack Leader* (New York: Three Rivers Press, 2007); Cesar Millan, *Cesar's Way* (New York: Three Rivers Press, 2006); and Temple Grandin, *Animals Make Us Human* (New York: Houghton-Mifflin Harcourt: 2009), 79.

44. Grandin, *Animals Make Us Human*, 149.

45. Roberts, *The Man Who Listens to Horses;* Henry Blake, *Talking to Horses* (London: Trafalgar Square Publishers, 1975); Jan Fennel, *The Dog Listener* (New York: Harper Collins, 2000); Barbara Woodhouse, *Talking to Animals* (New York: Stein and Day, 1974); Stanley Coren, *How to Speak Dog* (New York: Simon and Schuster, 2000); Bash Dibra, *Catspeak* (New York: G.P. Putnam's Sons, 2001); and Temple Grandin, *Animals in Translation* (New York: Scribner, 2005).

46. Hyde, *The Call of Conscience*, 95–96.

47. Robert Miller and Rick Lamb, *The Revolution in Horsemanship* (Guilford, CT: Lyons Press, 2005), 118–119.

48. Blake, *Talking to Horses*, 41.

49. Blake, *Talking to Horses*, 41.

50. Miller and Lamb, *The Revolution in Horsemanship*.

51. Miller and Lamb, *The Revolution in Horsemanship*, 33.

52. Woodhouse, *Talking to Animals*, 208.

53. Owens, *The Dog Whisperer*, xvi.

54. Owens, *The Dog Whisperer*, xv.

55. Owens, *The Dog Whisperer*, xvi.

56. Russell Lyon, *The Quest for the Original Horse Whisperers* (Edinburgh, UK: Luath Press, 2003); Miller and Lamb, *The Revolution in Horsemanship*, 184–190; Blake, *Talking to Horses*, 30.

57. Lyon, *The Quest for the Original Horse Whisperers*, 32.

58. Lyon, *The Quest for the Original Horse Whisperers*, 7.

59. Lyon, *The Quest for the Original Horse Whisperers*, 10, 165.

60. Lyon, *The Quest for the Original Horse Whisperers*, 24.

61. Lyon, *The Quest for the Original Horse Whisperers*, 24.

62. Lyon, *The Quest for the Original Horse Whisperers*, 42.

63. Dennett, *Kinds of Minds*, 35.

64. Grandin, *Animals Make Us Human*, 166.

65. Grandin, *Animals Make Us Human*, 166.

66. Roberts, *The Man Who Listens to Horses*, 62.

67. Roberts, *The Man Who Listens to Horses*, 40.

68. Woodhouse, *Talking to Animals*, 15.

69. Blake, *Talking to Horses*, 136.

70. Millan, *Cesar's Way*, 15.

71. Roberts, *The Man Who Listens to Horses*, 24.

72. Roberts, *The Man Who Listens to Horses*, 27.

73. Roberts, *The Man Who Listens to Horses*, 77.

74. Blake, *Talking to Horses*, 9.

75. Fennel, *The Dog Listener*, 58.

76. Malcolm Gladwell, "What the Dog Saw," *New Yorker* 82, no. 14 (May 22, 2006): 51. Dibra advises that the degree of perlocutionary force behind a request depends upon the species being trained, and he is famous in the animal-training world for coining the phrase, "To get a *dog* to do what you want, you give it a *command*. To get a *cat* to do what you want, you give it a *suggestion*." Dibra, *Catspeak*, 4.

77. Yi-Fu Tuan, *Dominance and Affection: The Making of Pets* (New Haven, CT: Yale University Press, 1984), 176.

78. Leslie Irvine, *If You Tame Me: Understanding Our Connection with Animals* (Philadelphia: Temple University Press, 2004), 28.

79. Meg Daley Olmert, *Made for Each Other: The Biology of the Human-Animal Bond* (Cambridge, MA: DaCapo Press, 2009), 78, 85.

80. Here again, cats seem to be an exception. Dibra maintains that because cats are not pack animals and are not particularly interested in leadership, a human who occupies the "top cat" position does so as a "caring companion" rather than a leader. Dibra, *Catspeak*, 8.

81. Miller and Lamb, *The Revolution in Horsemanship*, 119. Whisperers generally agree that freedom from fear is the defining goal of whispered dialogues and therefore advocate cooperative rather than coercive or competitive human-animal relationships. Woodhouse writes that any conversation with another animal should foster "complete freedom from fear." Miller and Lamb, *The Revolution in Horsemanship*, 208. While Millan insists that using punishment to make animals behave through fear is both cruel and ineffective. Millan, *Cesar's Way*, 218. In the same vein, Owens disparages "antagonistic" training methods in which humans "win" by making dogs perform as they're told. Owens, *The Dog Whisperer*, 79. And Fennel explains that her dog-training approach employs the lesson she learned from Roberts: "If you did not get the animal on your side, then anything you did was an act of violation, you were imposing your will on an unwilling being." Fennel, *The Dog Listener*, 22.

82. Miller and Lamb, *The Revolution in Horsemanship*, 119.

83. Millan, *Cesar's Way*.

84. Woodhouse, *Talking to Animals*, 11.

85. Roberts, *The Man Who Listens to Horses*, 110.

86. Fennel, *The Dog Listener*, 89.

87. Miller and Lamb credit this cultural change for the "revolution in horsemanship." For a detailed account of the position of dogs in contemporary American culture, see Michael Schaffer's *One Nation Under Dog: Adventures in the New World of Prozac-Popping Puppies, Dog-Park Politics, and Organic Pet Food* (New York: Henry Holt, 2009).

88. Roberts, *The Man Who Listens to Horses*, np.

89. Roberts, *The Man Who Listens to Horses*, 31.

90. Coren, *How to Speak Dog*, xi.

91. Blake, *Talking to Horses*, 70–82; and Dibra, *Catspeak*, 133.

CHAPTER FOUR

1. Peter Singer, *Animal Liberation* (New York: Avon Books, 1977); Carol J. Adams, *Living Among Meat Eaters: The Vegetarian's Survival Handbook* (New York: Continuum International Publishing Group, 2001); Carol J. Adams, *The Sexual Politics of Meat: A Feminist-Vegetarian Critical Theory* (New York: Continuum, 1990); Erik Marcus, *Vegan: The New Ethics of Eating* (Ithica: McBooks Press, 1998); Donna Maurer, *Vegetarianism: Movement or Moment?* (Philadelphia: Temple UP, 2002); Barbara Willard, "The American Story of Meat: Discursive Influences on Cultural Eating Practices," *Journal of Popular Culture* 36 (2002): 105–118; Gregory James Flail, "The Sexual Politics of Meat Substitutes." PhD diss., Georgia State University, 2006; C. Wesley Buerkle, "Metrosexuality Can Stuff It: Beef Consumption as (Heteromasculine) Fortification," *Text and Performance Quarterly* 29 (2009): 77–93; Patricia Malesh, "Sharing Our Recipes: Vegan Conversion Narratives as Social Praxis," in *Active Voices: Composing a Rhetoric of Social Movements*, ed. Sharon McKenzie Stevens and Patricia Malesh (Albany: State University of New York Press, 2009), 131–145.

2. Parke G. Burgess, "The Rhetoric of Black Power: A Moral Demand?" *Quarterly Journal of Speech* 54 (1968): 190.

3. Jean Nienkamp, *Internal Rhetorics: Toward a History and Theory of Self-Persuasion* (Carbondale: Southern Illinois University Press, 2001), 136.

4. Michael Warner argues that state-sanctioned and supported heteronormativity politicizes and demoralizes queer intimacies. When the personal becomes political in this way, queer agency and collectivity form a counterpublic born of "a sense of belonging" that is "self-organized through discourse" and in "tension with" *the* public sphere. Michael Warner, *Publics and Counterpublics* (New York: Zone Books, 2002), 70, 56. Similarly Charles Stewart extends Richard Gregg's argument that protest rhetoric is essentially a "self-directed" means of "constituting [positive] self-hood through expression." Stewart argues that, "protest songs enable protesters to identify against others and thus locate themselves positively within the social hierarchy yet away from symbolically defensive positions." Charles Stewart, "The Ego Function of Protest Songs: An Application of Gregg's Theory of Protest Rhetoric," *Communication Studies* 42, no. 3 (1991): 240, 241. For Alberto Melucci, collective identity is a product of self-reflection, through which individuals recognize and shape the symbolic and relational dimensions of autonomous action. Alberto Melucci, *Challenging Codes* (New York: Cambridge University Press, 1996), 73. Through this process of self-reflection, individuals recognize their post-structural agency, which then allows them to auto-identify with multiple and morphing collectivities simultaneously.

5. See note 1 above.

6. Nienkamp, *Internal Rhetorics*, 136.

7. See also Charles Stewart, "Championing the Rights of Others and Challenging Evil: The Ego Function of the Rhetoric of Other-Directed Social Movements," *Southern Communication Journal* 64 (1999): 91–105.

8. Michel Foucault, *Fearless Speech* (Los Angeles: Semiotext(e), 2001), 106.

9. Nienkamp, *Internal Rhetorics*, ix.

10. See Nienkamp *Internal Rhetorics*, 128–31.

11. See Stewart, *Championing the Rights of Others*.

12. Kenneth Burke, *A Rhetoric of Motives* (1950; Berkeley: University of California Press, 1969), 19–29; Nienkamp, *Internal Rhetorics*, 126; and Plato, "Theaetetus," *Complete Works*, ed. John M. Cooper (Indianapolis: Hackett, 1997), 189e. Burke "describe[s] the function of rhetoric as identification rather than persuasion because identification emphasizes the positive connecting and cooperative aspects of language use over the 'presence of strife, enmity, faction as a characteristic motive of rhetorical expression' whereas "persuasion is "often adversarial" (quoted in Nienkamp, *Internal Rhetorics*, 93). Identification, then, is an instrument that shows "how rhetorical motive is often present where it is not usually recognized" as well as "the way that language users assert mutual interests or 'consubstantiality' with their listeners." Quoted in Nienkamp, *Internal Rhetorics*, 92. Burke also refers to socialization as the rhetorical pressures that "are internalized, actively working to continuously shape and reshape a person's sense of self." Quoted in Nienkamp, *Internal Rhetorics*, 109.

13. Nienkamp, *Internal Rhetorics*, 2, 126.

14. Nienkamp, *Internal Rhetorics*, 120. For the ancient Greeks, thought "[took] on the characteristics of a dialogue with internally persuasive characteristics" whereby the ideal effect was the "successful coercion of the 'lower' parts of the soul [emotion] by the 'higher' [reason]." See Nienkamp, *Internal Rhetorics*, 37, 38. The moral philosophers located this internal dialogue across appetites, imagination, reason and will as faculties of the mind. They sustained the belief of ancient rhetoricians that rhetoric should be guided by reason rather than emotions, which were "lesser" and/or impure in comparison. Modern rhetoricians establish continuity with their predecessors in that they "regain [internal rhetoric's] status as an epistemic as well as an ethical tool, a way of attaining and testing knowledge as well as a way of making moral decisions and actions." Nienkamp, *Internal Rhetorics*, 82. However, they filter their perceptions through psychology to explain postmodern fragmentation of self.

15. Kenneth Burke, *Language as Symbolic Action* (Berkeley: University of California Press, 1966), 44–55; and Nienkamp, *Internal Rhetorics*, ix.

16. Foucault describes *parrhesia* as non-rhetorical in that those who use it declare their words frankly as their opinion—as their thoughts laid bare unencumbered or altered by techne. If parrhesistic speech moves audiences to adjust their praxis, it is because the courage to be transparent that the *parrhesiastes* embodies is as persuasive as his/her unadorned beliefs are true. However, the Greco-Roman assumption that frankness and ethos can somehow lie outside the domain of rhetoric has been displaced in contemporary social thought. Foucault, *Fearless Speech*.

17. Foucault, *Fearless Speech*, 108.

18. Nienkamp, *Internal Rhetorics*, ix, 34.

19. Nienkamp, *Internal Rhetorics*, 4.

20. Among the most widely recognized New Social Movement scholars are Italian sociologist Alberto Melucci, Spanish sociologist Manuel Castells, French sociologist Alain Touraine, and German philosopher and sociologist Jürgen Habermas.

21. Alberto Melucci, "The Symbolic Challenge of Contemporary Movements," *Social Research* 52 (1985): 800.

22. Melucci, "The Symbolic Challenge of Contemporary Movements," 800.

23. Richard Gregg, "The Ego-Function of the Rhetoric of Protest," *Philosophy and Rhetoric* 4 (1971): 74.

24. Charles Stewart, "The Rights of Others."

25. Stewart, "The Rights of Others," 97.

26. Stewart, "The Rights of Others," 91.

27. Stewart, "The Rights of Others," 103.

28. Nienkamp, *Internal Rhetorics*, 120.

29. Nienkamp, *Internal Rhetorics*, 131, 127.

30. Nienkamp, *Internal Rhetorics*, 129.

31. Nienkamp draws on Perelman and Olbrechts-Tyteca's postmodern perception of facts and truths as "statuses attributed by a 'community of minds' to constructs that the community is willing to treat as premises for argumentation." As historically and culturally situated norms that differ across time and space (communities), facts and truths, as well as the ethics that flow from them, can change over time. Ethical and moral norms, then, are both born of internal rhetoric and inherently rhetorical in nature.

32. Nienkamp, *Internal Rhetorics*, 112.

33. Nienkamp, *Internal Rhetorics*, 111.

34. Nienkamp, *Internal Rhetorics*, 88.

35. Nienkamp, *Internal Rhetorics*, 50.

36. Foucault, *Fearless Speech*, 101.

37. Nienkamp, *Internal Rhetorics*, 5, xiii.

38. See note 1.

39. Adams, *Sexual Politics of Meat*, 40.

40. Adams, *Sexual Politics of Meat*, 47.

41. Adams, *Sexual Politics of Meat*, 40–8.

42. Jennie Taylor Martin, "A Field of Grazing Cows," *Voices from the Garden: Stories of Becoming a Vegetarian*, ed. Sharon and Daniel Towns (New York: Lantern Books, 2001), 52 (emphasis mine).

43. Diana Engoron, *Voices from the Garden: Stories of Becoming a Vegetarian*, ed. Sharon and Daniel Towns (New York: Lantern Books, 2001), 82 (emphasis mine).

44. Erik Marcus, *Vegan: The New Ethics of Eating* (Ithaca: McBooks Press, 1998), 186.

45. Paul McCartney, quoted in People for the Ethical Treatment of Animals, UK (PETA), Poster, 2008.

46. "Lisa the Vegetarian," *The Simpsons*, FOX, October 15, 1995.

47. Nienkamp, *Internal Rhetorics*, 131.

48. Nienkamp, *Internal Rhetorics*, xii, 19.

49. Using George Herbert Mead's theory of the mind and Freudian psychoanalysis, Nienkamp frames internal rhetorics as activities through which internalized social attitudes engage pre-cultural bio-emotive responses. Mead separates the rhetorical self into an "I" comprised of the "biological individual" who responds organically to

the attitudes of others and multiple "Me's" as "internalized social attitudes [that can conflict] with one another at any given time." Quoted in Nienkamp, *Internal Rhetorics*, 121. The aspects of the rhetorical self that Mead describes as "me's" parallel what Freud terms the superego or the "internalized voice of parental and societal norms," while the "I" is an "unpredictable and creative . . . agent" that interrogates the "me's" against one another, placing emergent "me's" or "new voices" on equal footing with familiar ones. Nienkamp, *Internal Rhetorics*, 96, 122. Examples of encounters during which humans ascribe animals' rhetorical agency, despite antithetical socio-cultural conditioning, illustrate how internal rhetorics cause vegetarian/vegan converts to modify their personal and collective identity. Nienkamp credits these internal dialogues as thought processes that make possible individual agency within a social continuum that terminates with norming on one end and reinvention on the other: "The rhetorical power of existing voices may strengthen or weaken, depending on how the new voice fits into the existing rhetorical self." Nienkamp, *Internal Rhetorics*, 129. Human-animal encounters that make overt animals as the referent of meat can be powerful enough to undo the semantic and cultural representations that hide this fact.

50. Jeremy Bentham, *An Introduction to the Principles of Morals and Legislation* (New York: Oxford University Press, 1970), xvii.

51. Quoted in Joanne Stepaniak, *The Vegan Sourcebook* (Los Angeles: Lowell House, 1998), 31.

52. Charles Patterson, *Eternal Treblinka: Our Treatment of Animals and the Holocaust* (New York: Lantern Books, 2002).

53. Upton Sinclair, *The Jungle* (Columbia: University of Missouri Press, 1906).

54. Kerry McCarthy, entry on "How I became a vegetarian," . . . Shot By Both Sides Blog, posted August 18, 2009, http://kerry-mccarthy.blogspot.com/2009/08/how-i-became-vegetarian.html (accessed August 21, 2009).

55. GoVeg.com, "Downed Cow: This Story Will Change Your Life," http://www.goveg.com/downedcow.asp.

56. Robert Pulcini and Shari Springer Berman (Dir.), *American Splendor*, (Universal City: Fine Line Features, 2003).

57. Foucault, *Fearless Speech*, 119.

58. In Nienkamp, *Internal Rhetorics*, 87.

59. Nienkamp, *Internal Rhetorics*, 87.

60. Talk of the Nation, "A Conversation with Temple Grandin," NPR, January 20, 2006, http://www.npr.org/templates/story/story.php?storyId=5165123 (accessed August 12, 2009).

61. Temple Grandin, "Thinking in Pictures," http://www.spinninglobe.net/cowlady.htm (accessed August 12, 2009).

62. Maru Vigo, "How I Became a Vegetarian," *Voices from the Garden: Stories of Becoming a Vegetarian*, ed. Sharon and Daniel Towns (New York: Lantern Books, 2001), 17 (emphasis mine).

63. Alexis Preisser, "Cinderella," *Voices from the Garden: Stories of Becoming a Vegetarian*, ed. Sharon and Daniel Towns (New York: Lantern Books, 2001), 95 (emphasis mine).

64. Elizabeth Ferrari, "Why I Became a Vegetarian," *American Chronicles*, posted January 25, 2007, http://www.americanchronicle.com/articles/view/19670 (accessed August 21, 2009) (emphasis mine). Elizabeth Ferrari is the director of the Chattanooga, TN chapter of non-profit organization Saving Animals Via Education (SAVE).

65. Quoted in Nienkamp, *Internal Rhetorics*, 69.

66. Nienkamp, *Internal Rhetorics*, 2.

67. See note 1 above.

68. Bjorn-Magne Stuestol, "Cows with Guns," YouTube http://www.youtube.com/watch?v=FQMbXvn2RNl (accessed August 12, 2009).

69. "Cows with Guns."

70. Tom McKeon, *MadCow*, Totally Tom, http://www.totallytom.com/MadCow.html (accessed September 16, 2009).

71. *The Meatrix*, http://www.themeatrix.com (accessed May 18, 2007).

72. *The Matrix* is the story of Neo, a computer hacker turned hero of humanity, who joins a group of renegade humans in the fight between humans and the cognate machines that enslave them. When Neo joins the resistance, he discovers that life on earth is an artificial reality that occupies the minds of humans who exist as "factory-farmed" bio-sources for energy.

73. *The Meatrix*.

74. Nienkamp, *Internal Rhetorics*, 101.

75. Nienkamp, *Internal Rhetorics*, 101.

CHAPTER FIVE

1. Katha Pollitt, "The Solipsisters," *New York Times*, April 18, 1999.

2. Americans' love affair with food coincided with the sexual revolution and the women's movement. Leslie Brenner, *American Appetite: The Coming of Age of a National Cuisine* (New York: Perennial, 1999), 299.

3. Michael Pollan, *The Omnivore's Dilemma: A Natural History of Four Meals* (New York: Penguin, 2006), 143.

4. Erik Marcus, *Meat Market: Animals, Ethics & Money* (Boston: Brio Press, 2005), 83.

5. Nicholas Kristof, "Humanity even for Nonhumans," *New York Times*, April 8, 2009.

6. Harold D. Guither, *Animal Rights: History and Scope of a Radical Social Movement* (Carbondale, IL: Southern Illinois University Press, 1998), 9.

7. John W. Bowers et al., *The Rhetoric of Agitation and Control* (Prospect Heights, IL: Waveland, 2010), 7.

8. Bowers et al., *Rhetoric of Agitation and Control*, 7.

9. Donna Maurer, *Vegetarianism: Movement or Moment* (Philadelphia: Temple Univ. Press, 2002), 14–18.

10. "Vegetarianism in America," *vegetariantimes.com*, http://vegetariantimes.com/features/archiv_of_editorial/667 (accessed July 21, 2009).

11. Mat Thomas, "The Road to Vegetopia; (Re)Imaging the Future of Food," *VegNews*, March/April 2009, 36.

12. See Maurer, *Vegetarianism*, 8–14; and Thomas, "The Road to Vegetopia."

13. "Vegetarianism in America."

14. Maurer, *Vegetarianism*, 3–4.

15. Maurer, *Vegetarianism*, 20–21.

16. Maurer, *Vegetarianism*, 8.

17. Maurer, *Vegetarianism*, 8.

18. Kurt Back and Margaret Glasgow, "Social Networks and Psychological Conditions in Dietary Preferences: Gourmets and Vegetarians," *Basic and Applied Social Psychology* 2 (1981): 9.

19. Maurer, *Vegetarianism*, 9.

20. Maurer, *Vegetarianism*, 8.

21. Margaret Visser, "The Sins of the Flesh," *Granta* 1 (Winter 1995): 129.

22. Eugene N. Anderson, *Everyone Eats: Understanding Food and Culture* (New York: New York University Press, 2005), 125.

23. Maurer, *Vegetarianism*, 2.

24. Nanette Hansen, "Organic Food Sales See Healthy Growth," MSNBC, http://www.msnbc.msn.com/id/6638417 (accessed July 21, 2009).

25. Melanie Warner, "What is Organic? Powerful Players Want a Say," *New York Times*, November 1, 2005.

26. Catherine Greene and Carolyn Dimitri, "Organic Agriculture: Gaining Ground," USDA Economic Research Service, September 2002, http://www.ers.usda.gov/Publications/AIB777 (accessed June 30, 2009).

27. In fact we're eating more of everything. According to a report published in the *Journal of the American Medical Association*, Americans had "collectively gained more than a billion pounds in just 10 years." Elizabeth Kolbert, "XXXL: Why are we so fat?" *New Yorker*, July 20, 2009, 73.

28. Marcus, *Meat Market*, 5.

29. Marcus, *Meat Market*, 66.

30. Guither, *Animal Rights*, 49.

31. See United States Department of Labor, Bureau of Labor Statistics, http://www.bls.gov/news.release/atus2.t01.htm (accessed September 11, 2009); and Pauline Oo, "Grocery Stores: Trends and Tips," http://www1.umn.edu/umnnews/Feature_Stories/Grocery_stores3A_trends_and_tips.html (accessed September 11, 2009).

32. Brett Lunceford, "PETA and the Rhetoric of Nude Protest," in this volume.

33. For a commercially successful example of this strategy see Rory Freedman and Kim Barnouin, *Skinny Bitch!* (Philadelphia: Running Press, 2006).

34. Bowers et al., *The Rhetoric of Agitation and Control*, 29.

35. PETA "About peta2," http://peta2/about_peta2.asp (accessed September 9, 2009).

36. PETA, "'Breasts, Not Animal Tests' Tunic Tank," https://www.petacatalog.org/prodinfo.asp?number=TS272 (accessed September 9, 2009).

37. Animal Rights Stuff, www.AnimalRightsStuff.com (accessed September 5, 2009).

38. PETA, "Cruelty Doesn't Fly," http://www.peta.org/crueltydoesntfly/contest.asp (accessed September 9, 2009).

39. PETA, "Tofu Wrestling," http://www.petatv.com/tvpopup/Prefs.asp?video=tofu_wrestling (accessed September 7, 2009).

40. PETA, "Veggie Love," http://www.peta.org/content/standalone/VeggieLove/Default.aspx (accessed September 11, 2009).

41. Beth A. Eck, "Men are Much Harder: Gendered Viewing of Nude Images," *Gender and Society* 17, no. 5 (2003): 706.

42. Center for Communication and Civic Engagement, "Culture Jamming and Meme-based Communication," http://depts.washington.edu/ccce/polcomm campaigns/CultureJamming.htm (accessed September 11, 2009).

43. See Irving Goffman, *Frame Analysis: An Essay on the Organization of Experience* (New York: Harper and Row, 1974).

44. Robert L. Scott, "The Conservative Voice in Radical Rhetoric: A Common Response to Division," in *Readings on the Rhetoric of Social Protest*, ed. Charles E. Morris III and Stephen H. Browne (State College, PA: Strata Publishing, 2001), 83.

45. Scott, "The Conservative Voice in Radical Rhetoric," 83.

46. Tanner Stransky, "Burger King's Super Seven Incher ad: Subtlety is Dead," Popwatch, http://popwatch.ew.com/2009/06/24/burger-kings-super-seven-incher (accessed September 12, 2009).

47. Carol J. Adams, *The Sexual Politics of Meat: A Feminist Vegetarian Critical Theory* (New York: Continuum Publishing Company, 1990), 43.

48. Scott, "The Conservative Voice in Radical Rhetoric," 83.

49. Robert S. Cathcart, "Movements: Confrontation as Rhetorical Form," in *Readings on the Rhetoric of Social Protest*, ed. Charles E. Morris III and Stephen H. Browne (State College, PA: Strata Publishing, 2001), 107.

50. See Maneesha Deckha, "Disturbing Images: PETA and the Feminist Ethics of Animal Advocacy," *Ethics and the Environment* 13, no. 2 (2008): 35–76; and Lunceford, "PETA and the Rhetoric of Nude Protest."

51. Cathcart, "Movements," 105.

52. Cathcart, "Movements," 105.

53. Bowers et al., *The Rhetoric of Social Agitation and Control*, 23.

54. Sandor Ellix Katz, *The Revolution Will Not Be Microwaved: Inside America's Underground Food Movement* (White River Junction, VT: Chelsea Green Publishing, 2006), 255.

55. World Vegetarian Day, "Have Fun and Make the World a Better Place," http://www.worldvegetarianday.org (accessed September 9, 2009).

56. Torres, *Making a Killing*, 136.

57. *VegNews*, "About Us," http://www.vegnews.com/web/pages/page.do?pageId=9 (accessed September 7, 2009).

58. *Vegetarian Times*, "About Us," http://www.vegetariantimes.com/about_us (accessed September 7, 2009).

59. The GirlieGirl Army, http://girliegirlarmy.com (accessed September 14, 2009.)

60. Maurer, *Vegetarianism*, 117–118.

61. See Kathryn Paxton George, *Animal, Vegetable, or Woman? A Feminist Critique of Ethical Vegetarianism* (Albany: State University of New York Press, 2000), 7–10.

62. Matt Flanzer, "Dream a Little Dream (& Save the World Too)," *VegNews*, July/August 2009, 38.

63. Colleen Patrick-Goudreau, "Rhetoric Revolution," *VegNews*, March/April 2009, 62.

64. Michael Pollan, *In Defense of Food: An Eater's Manifesto* (New York: Penguin, 2008), 34.

65. Patrick-Goudreau, "Rhetoric Revolution,"62.

66. Bowers et al., *The Rhetoric of Social Agitation and Control*, 24.

67. bell hooks, *Feminist Theory: From Margin to Center* (Boston: South End Press, 1994), 17.

68. Kenneth Burke, *A Rhetoric of Motives* (New York: Prentice Hall, 1950), 27.

69. Burke, *A Rhetoric of Motives*, 27.

70. Vetra Taylor and Nancy E. Whittier, "Collective Identity in Social Movement Communities: Lesbian Feminist Mobilization," in *Waves of Protest: Social Movements from the Sixties*, ed. Jo Freeman and Victoria Johnson (Lanham, MD: Rowan and Littlefield, 1999), 170.

71. Taylor and Whitter, "Collective Identity," 174–5.

72. Taylor and Whitter, "Collective Identity," 175.

73. Taylor and Whitter, "Collective Identity," 175.

74. hooks, *Feminist Theory*, 31.

CHAPTER SIX

1. Like all folklore, the story of Lady Godiva is a pastiche of fact and fiction with no authoritative account. According to legend, Lady Godiva rode through the streets of Coventry, England as a means of persuading her husband, Leofric, Earl of Mercia, to stop taxing his subjects oppressively. He issued the challenge that if she would ride through the streets of Coventry naked, he would relent, believing that her piousness would prevent her from performing such an act. After issuing a proclamation that everyone should remain in their houses with the shutters and doors closed, she embarked on her ride. Because of this act, Coventry was freed from paying the tax. According to some versions of the legend, one person, a tailor named Tom, looked out and was struck blind, which spawned the notion of "peeping Tom." See Dorothy Appleton, "Lady Godiva," *Dawn*, no. 36 (2000): 12; H. R. Ellis Davidson, "The Legend of Lady Godiva," *Folklore* 80, no. 2 (1969): 107–21; and E. Sidney Hartland, "Peeping Tom and Lady Godiva," *Folklore* 1, no. 2 (1890): 207–26.

2. Bare Witness, "Bare Witness Peace," 2003, http://www.barewitness.org (accessed March 23, 2007).

3. World Naked Bike Ride, "World Naked Bike Ride (WNBR)—I See Painted Naked People on Bicycles!" December 22, 2006, http://www.worldnakedbikeride .org (accessed March 23, 2007).

4. Anthony Ramirez, "War Protester in Village Takes Her Cue from Lady Godiva," *New York Times*, August 10, 2005.

5. Terisa E. Turner and Leigh S. Brownhill, "Why Women Are at War with Chevron: Nigerian Subsistence Struggles against the International Oil Industry," *Journal of Asian and African Studies* 39, no. 1–2 (2004): 67. Although not explicitly defined in the article, "male dealers" seem to be the local Nigerians that were complicit in oil company operations.

6. Turner and Brownhill, "Why Women Are at War," 71. See also Phillips Stevens Jr., "Women's Aggressive Use of Genital Power in Africa," *Transcultural Psychiatry* 43, no. 4 (2006): 592–99.

7. See Cathryn Bailey, "We Are What We Eat: Feminist Vegetarianism and the Reproduction of Racial Identity," *Hypatia* 22, no. 2 (2007): 41; Brian Delevie and Isshaela Ingham, "Unconscionable or Communicable: The Transference of Holocaust Photography in Cyber Space," *Afterimage* 31, no. 6 (2004): 7.

8. See Lesli Pace, "Image Events and PETA's Anti Fur Campaign," *Women & Language* 28, no. 2 (2005): 33–41.

9. Maneesha Deckha, "Disturbing Images: PETA and the Feminist Ethics of Animal Advocacy," *Ethics & the Environment* 13, no. 2 (2008): 55. See also Laura K. Hahn, "I'm Too Sexy for Your Movement: An Analysis of the Failure of the Animal Rights Movement to Promote Vegetarianism," in this volume; and Wendy Atkins-Sayre, "Protection from 'Animal Rights Lunatics': The Center for Consumer Freedom and Animal Rights Rhetoric," in this volume.

10. People for the Ethical Treatment of Animals, "PETA's State of the Union Undress," http://www.peta.org/feat/stateoftheunion/f-stateoftheunion.asp (accessed January 16, 2008).

11. People for the Ethical Treatment of Animals, "PETA's State of the Union Undress."

12. Jill Howard Church, "A Whopper of a Campaign," *The Animals' Agenda* 21, no. 3 (2001): 10; Merle Hoffman, "Do Feminists Need to Liberate Animals, Too? Carol Adams Sees Feminism as a Visionary Philosophy That Includes Stewardship of the Earth," *On The Issues* 4, no. 2 (1995): 18–24, 54–56; Mark Hudis, "PETA Picks a Pic of Naked Pop Star," *MediaWeek* 5, no. 13 (1995): 44; Andrew Linzey, "Good Causes Do Not Need Exaggeration," *The Animals' Agenda* 20, no. 1 (2000): 24–25; and Peter Simonson, "Social Noise and Segmented Rhythms: News, Entertainment, and Celebrity in the Crusade for Animal Rights," *Communication Review* 4, no. 3 (2001): 399–420.

13. Guy Debord, *The Society of the Spectacle*, trans. Donald Nicholson-Smith (New York: Zone Books, 1994), 151.

14. Todd C. Frankel, "Activists, Circus Take Wraps Off Feud over Animals' Treatment," *St. Louis Post Dispatch*, November 17, 2005.

15. Frankel, "Activists, Circus Take Wraps Off Feud over Animals' Treatment."

16. Richard B. Gregg, "The Ego-Function of the Rhetoric of Protest," *Philosophy & Rhetoric* 4, no. 2 (1971): 74.

17. J. Michael Hogan, *The Nuclear Freeze Campaign: Rhetoric and Foreign Policy in the Telepolitical Age* (East Lansing: Michigan State University Press, 1994), 187.

18. Debord, *The Society of the Spectacle*, 15.

19. Dan Barry, "In Times Sq. These Days, Naked Ladies Have Causes," *New York Times*, November 23, 2005.

20. Simonson, "Social Noise and Segmented Rhythms," 402.

21. Simonson, "Social Noise and Segmented Rhythms," 416.

22. John Elvin, "Tough Times for Buff Protests," *Insight on the News* 19, no. 5 (2003): 17.

23. Edwin Black, "The Second Persona," *Quarterly Journal of Speech* 56, no. 2 (1970): 112.

24. Frankel, "Activists, Circus Take Wraps Off Feud over Animals' Treatment."

25. For more on the "women in prison" genre of movies, see Suzanna Danuta Walters, "Caged Heat: The (R)Evolution of Women-in-Prison Films," in *Reel Knockouts: Violent Women in the Movies*, ed. Martha McCaughey and Neal King (Austin, TX: University of Texas Press, 2001): 106–23.

26. In this section, I will review several studies concerning sex and/or nudity in advertising, but for a meta-analysis of this literature, see Tom Reichert, "Sex in Advertising Research: A Review of Content, Effects, and Functions of Sexual Information in Consumer Advertising," *Annual Review of Sex Research* 13 (2002): 241–73.

27. Jessica Severn, George E. Belch, and Michael A. Belch, "The Effects of Sexual and Non-Sexual Advertising Appeals and Information Level on Cognitive Processing and Communication Effectiveness," *Journal of Advertising* 19, no. 1 (1990): 22.

28. Severn, Belch and Belch, "The Effects of Sexual and Non-Sexual Advertising," 21.

29. Frankel, "Activists, Circus Take Wraps Off Feud over Animals' Treatment."

30. Claire Sherman and Pascale Quester, "The Influence of Product/Nudity Congruence on Advertising Effectiveness," *Journal of Promotion Management* 11, no. 2/3 (2005): 80.

31. Jaideep Sengupta and Darren W. Dahl, "Gender-Related Reactions to Gratuitous Sex Appeals in Advertising," *Journal of Consumer Psychology* 18, no. 1 (2008): 73. For the most part Americans in particular have a love/hate relationship with nudity and sexuality. In a study that used in advertisements a woman in a swimsuit, a topless model, and a nude model, Sid Dudley found that "the advertisement featuring the nude model was viewed as the most offensive, immoral, unethical, and exploitative." Such an attitude would affect how the observer views the display. Sid C. Dudley, "Consumer Attitudes toward Nudity in Advertising," *Journal of Marketing Theory and Practice* 7, no. 4 (1999): 92.

32. Michael S. LaTour, "Female Nudity in Print Advertising: An Analysis of Gender Differences in Arousal and Ad Response," *Psychology & Marketing* 7, no. 1 (1990): 78.

33. Beth A. Eck, "Men Are Much Harder: Gendered Viewing of Nude Images," *Gender & Society* 17, no. 5 (2003): 706. For more on the impact of gender on the viewing of sexual advertising, see Richard Elliott and others, "Overt Sexuality in Advertising: A Discourse Analysis of Gender Responses," *Journal of Consumer Policy* 18, no. 2/3 (1995): 187–217; Marilyn Y. Jones, Andrea J. S. Stanaland, and Betsy D.

Gelb, "Beefcake and Cheesecake: Insights for Advertisers," *Journal of Advertising* 27, no. 2 (1998): 33–51.

34. Eck, "Men Are Much Harder," 698.

35. See Nikki Craft, "PETA: Where Only Women Are Treated Like Meat," 2001, http://www.nostatusquo.com/ACLU/PETA/peta.html (accessed January 18, 2008); kitchenMage, "Dear PETA, Women Are Animals Too . . . ," October 22, 2007, http://blog.kitchenmage.com/2007/10/dear-peta-women.html (accessed January 18, 2008); Pace, "Image Events and PETA's Anti Fur Campaign."

36. Joseph Libertson, *Proximity, Levinas, Blanchot, Bataille, and Communication* (The Hague: Martinus Nijhoff, 1982), 223.

37. Gregg, "The Ego-Function of the Rhetoric of Protest," 74.

38. Debord, *The Society of the Spectacle*, 39.

39. See Donnovan Andrews, "Bullish Steps," *Black Enterprise* 32, no. 10 (2002): 114.

40. Timothy J. Mitchell, "Bullfighting: The Ritual Origin of Scholarly Myths," *The Journal of American Folklore* 99, no. 394 (1986): 405.

41. People for the Ethical Treatment of Animals, "Running of the Nudes: Out with the Old—in with the Nude!" http://www.runningofthenudes.com (accessed January 18, 2008).

42. Hilliard Lackey, "Running of the Bulls and Running of the Nudes, Intriguing Options," *Mississippi Link*, July 6–12, 2006.

43. People for the Ethical Treatment of Animals, "Running of the Nudes: Out with the Old—in with the Nude! // Next Year's Race // Look Who's Running," http://www.runningofthenudes.com/look_whos_running.asp (accessed January 18, 2008).

44. I use the term "carnival" much as literary critic Mikhail Bakhtin does: "Because of their obvious sensuous character and their strong element of play, carnival images closely resemble certain artistic forms, namely the spectacle." Mikhail M. Bakhtin, *Rabelais and His World*, trans. Hélène Iswolsky (Bloomington: Indiana University Press, 1984), 7.

45. Lackey, "Running of the Bulls and Running of the Nudes, Intriguing Options."

46. "All the Nudes That's Fit to Print," *Coventry Evening Telegraph*, June 23, 2006.

47. Bill Radford, "Bullfight Protester Goes Bare; Woman with Local Ties Works for PETA," *The Gazette* (Colorado Springs), June 25, 2005.

48. "Emma to Bare All for Naked Truth over Cruelty to Bulls," *Journal* (Newcastle-upon-Tyne, UK), June 19, 2006.

49. Andrew Sterling, "Director Offers Version of the Hole Truth," *Columbus Dispatch*, May 20, 2005.

50. Pamela E. Oliver and Daniel J. Myers, "How Events Enter the Public Sphere: Conflict, Location, and Sponsorship in Local Newspaper Coverage of Public Events," *American Journal of Sociology* 105, no. 1 (1999): 38, 39.

51. Kevin Michael DeLuca, *Image Politics: The New Rhetoric of Environmental Activism* (Mahwah, NJ: Lawrence Erlbaum Associates, 1999), 21–22.

52. Deckha, "Disturbing Images," 60. Pace also notes that "PETA's ads work simultaneously with and against the system." Pace, "Image Events and PETA's Anti Fur Campaign," 38.

53. Deckha, "Disturbing Images," 59.

54. Deckha, "Disturbing Images," 55.

55. Deckha, "Disturbing Images," 55.

56. Deckha, "Disturbing Images," 51.

57. Joseph N. Scudder and Carol Bishop Mills, "The Credibility of Shock Advocacy: Animal Rights Attack Messages," *Public Relations Review* 35, no. 2 (2009): 162–64.

58. Jacques Ellul, *Propaganda: The Formation of Men's Attitudes*, trans. Konrad Kellen and Jean Lerner (New York: Knopf, 1965), 28.

59. "Emma to Bare All for Naked Truth over Cruelty to Bulls."

60. Franklyn S. Haiman, "The Rhetoric of the Streets: Some Legal and Ethical Considerations," *Quarterly Journal of Speech* 53, no. 2 (1967): 114.

61. M. Kent Jennings and Ellen Ann Andersen, "Support for Confrontational Tactics among AIDS Activists: A Study of Intra-Movement Divisions," *American Journal of Political Science* 40, no. 2 (1996): 331.

62. Jennings and Anderson, "Support for Confrontational Tactics," 331.

63. Haig A. Bosmajian, "Obscenity and Protest," *Today's Speech* 18 (1970): 11.

64. Theodore Otto Windt Jr., "The Diatribe: Last Resort for Protest," *Quarterly Journal of Speech* 58, no. 1 (1972): 8.

65. Chantal Conneller, "Becoming Deer: Corporeal Transformations at Star Carr," *Archaeological Dialogues* 11, no. 1 (2004): 43.

66. Kevin Michael DeLuca, "Unruly Arguments: The Body Rhetoric of Earth First!, ACT UP, and Queer Nation," *Argumentation & Advocacy* 36, no. 1 (1999): 13.

67. Gilles Deleuze and Félix Guattari, *A Thousand Plateaus: Capitalism and Schizophrenia*, trans. Brian Massumi (Minneapolis: University of Minnesota Press, 1987), 275.

68. Maurice Charland, "Constitutive Rhetoric: The Case of the *Peuple Quebecois*," *Quarterly Journal of Speech* 73, no. 2 (1987): 143.

69. For more on the idea of PETA serving as a voice in defense of (and in place of) animals, see Jason Edward Black, "Extending the Rights of Personhood, Voice, and Life to Sensate Others: A Homology of Right to Life and Animal Rights Rhetoric," *Communication Quarterly* 51, no. 3 (2003): 323, 327.

70. Baruch Spinoza, *The Ethics; Treatise on the Emendation of the Intellect; Selected Letters*, ed. Seymour Feldman (2nd ed.; Indianapolis, IN: Hackett, 1992), 105.

71. Gilles Deleuze, "Ethology: Spinoza and Us," in *The Body: A Reader*, ed. Mariam Fraser and Monica Greco (New York: Routledge, 2005), 58.

72. Although I could find no studies that measured physiological response to the unexpected viewing of a live, nude body, in Western culture it is difficult to separate nudity from the erotic. Thus, I make this claim based on studies conducted by cognitive scientists and psychologists that suggest that erotic stimuli have a variety of possible effects on the viewer. Some of these researchers also note that intervening variables can affect how one responds to erotic stimuli. See Giulia Buodo, Michela Sarlo, and Daniela Palomba, "Attentional Resources Measured by Reaction Times Highlight Differences within Pleasant and Unpleasant, High Arousing Stimuli," *Motivation & Emotion* 26, no. 2 (2002): 123–38; C. Jiao et al., "Alterations in Grip Strength During Male Sexual Arousal," *International Journal of Impotence Research* 18, no. 2 (2006): 206–09; S. W. Kim et al., "Brain Activation by Visual Erotic Stimuli

in Healthy Middle Aged Males," *International Journal of Impotence Research* 18, no. 5 (2006): 452–57; Cindy M. Meston and Boris B. Gorzalka, "Differential Effects of Sympathetic Activation on Sexual Arousal in Sexually Dysfunctional and Functional Women," *Journal of Abnormal Psychology* 105, no. 4 (1996): 582–91; Ion G. Motofel and David L. Rowland, "The Physiological Basis of Human Sexual Arousal: Neuroendocrine Sexual Asymmetry," *International Journal of Andrology* 28, no. 2 (2005): 78–87; Harald T. Schupp and others, "Brain Processes in Emotional Perception: Motivated Attention," *Cognition & Emotion* 18, no. 5 (2004): 593–611; and Mark Spiering, Walter Everaerd, and Erick Janssen, "Priming the Sexual System: Implicit Versus Explicit Activation," *Journal of Sex Research* 40, no. 2 (2003): 134–45.

73. Kenneth Burke, *A Rhetoric of Motives* (New York: Prentice-Hall, 1952), 43, 38.

CHAPTER SEVEN

Acknowledgments. This essay was inspired and motivated by the activist efforts of Grey2K USA, Christine Dorchak, the Greyhound Protection League, and Susan Netboy.

1. Massachusetts Secretary of State Office website, "Ballot Questions," found at http:/www.sec.state.ma.us/ele/ele08/ballot_questions_08. Last accessed on September 12, 2008.

2. Jason Edward Black, "SLAPPS and Social Activism: The *Wonderland v. Grey2K* Case," *Free Speech Yearbook* 40 (2002–2003): 70.

3. Grey2K USA, "Greyhounds Win Landslide Victory" (November 5, 2008), http://www.grey2kusa.org/news/110508.html.

4. Greyhound Protection League, "The Difference Between Greyhound Racing's Propaganda and Reality is Like Night and Day," http://www.greyhounds.org/gpl/contents/nightday.html (accessed on March 20, 2007).

5. Stuart Hall, "Editor's Introduction—Cultural Studies and Its Theoretical Legacies" in *The Cultural Studies Reader*, ed. Simon During (3rd ed.; London: Routledge, 2007), 43.

6. See Mark Bernstein, "Legitimizing Liberation," in *Terrorists or Freedom Fighters—Reflections on the Liberation of Animals*, ed. Steve Best and Anthony Nocella (New York: Lantern, 2004), 93–105; Charles Patterson, *Eternal Treblinka—Our Treatment of Animals and the Holocaust* (New York: Lantern Press, 2003); Richard D. Ryder, *Animal Revolution—Changing Attitudes Towards Speciesism* (New York: Berg, 2000); and H. Peter Steeves, *Animal Others—On Ethics, Ontology, and Animal Life* (Albany: State University of New York Press, 1999).

7. Charles Stewart, "Championing the Rights of Others and Challenging Evil: The Ego Function in the Rhetoric of Other-Directed Social Movements," *Southern Communication Journal* 64 (1999): 97.

8. Karyn Olson, "Detecting a Common Interpretive Framework for Impersonal Violence: The Homology in Participants' Rhetoric on Sport Hunting, 'Hate Crimes,' and Stranger Rape," *Southern Communication Journal* 67 (2002): 217.

9. Raka Shome, "Postcolonial Interventions in the Rhetorical Canon: An 'Other' View," *Communication Theory* 6, no. 1 (1996): 41.

10. Derek Buescher and Kent A. Ono, "Civilized Colonialism: Pocahontas as Neocolonial Rhetoric," *Women's Studies in Communication* 19 (1996): 131.

11. Raka Shome and Radha S. Hegde, "Postcolonial Approaches to Communication: Charting the Terrain, Engaging the Intersections," *Communication Theory* 12 (2002): 258.

12. Though some ideological scholars in rhetorical studies, such as Michael Calvin McGee, see little division between the material and symbolic. Michael Calvin McGee, "The Ideograph: A Link Between Rhetoric and Ideology," *Quarterly Journal of Speech* 66 (1980): 1–16.

13. Stuart Hall, "Cultural Identity and Diaspora," in *Identity: Community, Culture, Difference*, ed. John Rutherford (London: Lawrence and Wishart, 1990), 222–237; Gayatri Spivak, *In Other Worlds* (New York: Routledge, 1988); Gayatri Spivak, "Can the Subaltern Speak?," in *Marxism and the Interpretation of Culture*, ed. Lawrence Grossberg and Cary Nelson (Urbana: University of Illinois Press, 1988), 271–313; Homi Bhabha, "The Other Question: Difference, Discrimination, and the Discourse of Colonialism," in *Literature, Politics, and Theory: Papers from the Essex Conference, 1976–1984*, ed. Francis Barker (London: Metheun, 1986), 148–172; Homi Bhabha, *The Location of Culture* (New York: Routledge, 1994); Edward Said, *Orientalism* (New York: Random House, 1978); and Edward Said, *Culture and Imperialism* (New York: Knopf, 1993).

14. Laurence Finsen and Susan Finsen, *The Animal Rights Movement in America: From Compassion to Respect* (New York: Twayne Publishers, 1994), 25.

15. Though many examples exist, perhaps the most popular, controversial, and simultaneously timely is Patterson's homological analysis of the U.S. factory farm and the European Holocaust, though he also draws comparisons between animal containment and American Indian reservations. See Patterson, *Eternal Treblinka*. A similar comparison is offered in Karen Davis, *The Holocaust and the Henmaid's Tale: A Case for Comparing Atrocities* (New York: Lantern Books, 2005).

16. Susan Silbey, "'Let Them Eat Cake': Globalization, Postmodern Colonialism, and the Possibilities of Justice," *Law and Society Review* 31 (1997): 210.

17. Said, *Orientalism*, 44.

18. Stewart, "Championing the Rights," 97.

19. Greyhound Protection League, "Greyhound Protection League," http://www.greyhounds.org (accessed on March 20, 2007).

20. Harold D. Guither, *Animal Rights: History and Scope of a Radical Social Movement* (Carbondale: Southern Illinois University Press, 1998), 9.

21. Marouf Hasian, Jr., "Rhetorical Studies and the Future of Postcolonial Theories and Practices," *Rhetoric Review* 20 (2001): 25.

22. Raymie McKerrow, "Critical Rhetoric: Theory and Praxis," *Communication Monographs* 56 (1989): 91.

23. Greyhound Protection League, "Answers to Commonly Asked Questions," http://www.greyhounds.org/gpl/contents/common.html (accessed on March 20, 2007).

24. Grey2K USA, "About Dog Racing Economics," http://www.grey2kusa.org/racing/economics.html.

25. Greyhound Protection League, "Answers to Commonly Asked Questions," http://www.greyhounds.org/gpl/contents/common.html (accessed on March 20, 2007).

26. Grey2K USA, "Greyhounds Need Your Help Now!" pamphlet, mailed to members, May 2008.

27. Greyhound Protection League, "Entry Page," http://www.greyhounds.org/gpl/contents/entry.html (accessed on March 20, 2007).

28. Grey2K USA, "About Dog Racing Economics," http://www.grey2kusa.org/racing/economics.html.

29. Raka Shome, "Caught in the Term Postcolonial and Why It Still Matters," *Critical Studies in Mass Communication* 15 no. 2 (1998): 206.

30. Greyhound Protection League, "Answers to Commonly Asked Questions," found at http://www.greyhounds.org/gpl/contents/common.html. Last accessed on March 20, 2007. The GPM's use of words like "man" and "[in]human[e]" indicates a centering of humans as active agents in the anti-racing enterprise. Such use might underscore how the GPM views itself as a *decolonial* agent and, thus, by extension, how it conceives of its (human) members as *colonized* alongside their greyhound wards.

31. Grey2K USA, "Will the Cruelty of Massachusetts Dog Racing Finally End? The Answer Depends on You!," pamphlet, mailed to members, April 2008.

32. Stuart Hall, "Editor's Introduction," 40.

33. Olga Gershenson, "Postcolonial Discourse Analysis and Intercultural Communication: Building a New Model," *The Intercultural and International Communication Annual* (2005), 28, 128.

34. Gershenson, "Postcolonial Discourse Analysis and Intercultural Communication," 128.

35. Grey2K USA, "About Dog Racing Economics," http://www.grey2kusa.org/racing/economics.html.

36. Grey2K USA, "About Dog Racing Economics," http://www.grey2kusa.org/racing/economics.html.

37. The report can be found at Greyhound Protection League, "An Industry in Decline," http://www.greyhounds.org/gpl/contents/decline.html (accessed on March 20, 2007).

38. Grey2K USA, "Help End the Killing," pamphlet, mailed to members, June 2008.

39. See, in particular, Charles J. Stewart, Craig Allen Smith, and Robert E. Denton, *Persuasion and Social Movements* (5th ed.; Long Grove, IL: Waveland, 2004), 61–78.

40. See Theodore Otto Windt, "Diatribe: Last Resort for Protest," *Quarterly Journal of Speech* 58 (1972): 1–14.

41. There is not space in this essay to examine visual images of greyhound suffering as they fold into this decolonizing strategy to reveal the murderousness of the colonizing racing industry, but the images are nonetheless stark. A representation of these types of images can be found at Greyhound Protection League, "Proof is in the Pictures," http://www.greyhounds.org/gpl/contents/proof.html (accessed on October 30, 2008).

42. Greyhound Protection League, "What They Have to Say About Greyhound Racing," http://www.greyhounds.org/gpl/contents/testimony.html (accessed on March 20, 2007).

43. Greyhound Protection League, "The Difference Between Greyhound Racing's Propaganda and Reality is Like Night and Day," http://www.greyhounds.org/gpl/contents/nightday.html (accessed on March 20, 2007).

44. Stephen Browne, "'Like Gory Spectres' Representing Evil in Theodore Weld's *American Slavery As It Is*," *Quarterly Journal of Speech* 80 (1994): 277–292.

45. Grey2K USA, "Help End the Killing," pamphlet, mailed to members, June 2008.

46. "Grey2K bests tracks; Court: Ban on dog racing fir for ballot box," *Boston Herald*, July 16, 2008.

47. Greyhound Protection League, "The Difference Between Greyhound Racing's Propaganda and Reality is Like Night and Day," http://www.greyhounds.org/gpl/contents/nightday.html (accessed on March 20, 2007).

48. Greyhound Protection League, "Entry Page," http://www.greyhounds.org/gpl/contents/entry.html (accessed on March 20, 2007).

49. Arnold Krupat, *Ethnocriticism: Ethnography, History, Literature* (Berkeley: University of California Press, 1991), 156.

50. Jason Edward Black, "Extending the Rights of Personhood, Voice, and Life to Sensate Others: A Homology of Right to Life and Animal Rights Rhetoric," *Communication Quarterly* 51, no. 3 (2003): 327.

51. Patterson, *Eternal Treblinka*, 27.

52. See Haig Bosmajian, *The Language of Oppression* (Lanham, MD: University Press of America, 1983).

53. Postcolonial scholars have worked from the other direction to show how human beings are reduced to so-called animalism. See Ward Churchill, *Kill the Indian, Save the Man: The Genocidal Impact of American Indian Residential Schools* (San Francisco: City Lights Books, 2004).

54. Lynda Birke and Luciana Parisi, "Animals, Becoming," in *Animal Others: On Ethics, Ontology, and Animal Life*, ed. H. Peter Steeves (Albany: State University of New York Press, 1999), 61.

55. Birke and Parisi, "Animals Becoming," 61.

56. Anti-Defamation League, "ADL Denounces PETA for its 'Holocaust On Your Plate' Campaign; Calls Appeal for Jewish Community Support 'The Height Of Chutzpah,'" February 24, 2003; updated May 5, 2005, http://www.adl.org/PresRele/HolNa_52/4235_52.htm.

57. Grey2K USA, "Greyhounds Win Landslide Victory," press release, e-mailed to members, November 5, 2008.

CHAPTER EIGHT

1. William James, *William James: Pragmatism, in Focus*, ed. Doris Olin (New York: Routledge, 1992), 99.

2. A. Z. Akhtar, "Flaws With Animal Research a Deep-Rooted Problem," *British Medical Journal* February 9, 2007, http://www.bmj.com/cgi/eletters/334/7586/163F.K (accessed May 10, 2009); Fanny K. Ennever and Lester B. Lave, "Implications of the

Lack of Accuracy of the Lifetime Rodent Bioassay for Predicting Human Carcinogenicity," *Regulatory Toxicology and Pharmacology* 38 (2003): 52–57; J. Bailey, A. Knight, and J. Balcombe, "The Future of Teratology Research is in Vitro," *Biogenic Amines* 19 (2005): 97–145; L. B. Lave et al., "Information Value of the Rodent Bioassay," *Nature* 336 (1988): 631–633; E.J. Topol, "Failing the Public Health—Rofecoxib, Merck, and the FDA," *New England Journal of Medicine* 351 (2004): 1707–9; D. J. Graham et al., "Risk of Acute Myocardial Infarction and Sudden Cardiac Death in Patients Treated with Cyclo-Oxygenase 2 Selective and Non-Selective Non-Steroidal Anti-Inflammatory Drugs: Nested Case-Control Study," *Lancet* 365 (2005): 475–81; R. S. Bresalier et al., "For the Adenomatous Polyp Prevention on Vioxx (APPROVe) Trial Investigators: Cardiovascular Events Associated with Rofecoxib in a Colorectal Adenoma Chemoprevention Trial," *New England Journal of Medicine* 352 (2005): 1092–1102; and A. Z. Akhtar, J. J. Pippin, and C. B. Sandusky, "Animal Models in Spinal Cord Injury: A Review," *Reviews in the Neurosciences* 19, no. 1 (2008): 47–60.

3. John Waite Bowers and Donovan J. Ochs, *The Rhetoric of Agitation and Control* (Reading, MA: Addison-Wesley, 1971), 41–50.

4. Leah Ceccarelli, "Rhetorical Criticism and the Rhetoric of Science," *Western Journal of Communication* 65, no. 3 (Summer 2001): 321.

5. Thomas Kuhn, *The Structure of Scientific Revolutions* (3rd ed., Chicago: University of Chicago Press, 1996), 66–76.

6. See Dava Sobel, *Galileo's Daughter: A Historical Memoir of Science, Faith, and Love* (New York: Walker, 1999).

7. Kuhn, *The Structure of Scientific Revolutions*, 64.

8. Bruno Latour, *Science in Action: How to Follow Scientists and Engineers through Society* (Cambridge, MA: Harvard University Press, 1987), 25.

9. Latour, *Science in Action*, 29, 43. Latour derives the concept of tacit knowledge from Michael Polanyi, *The Tacit Dimension*, (New York: Anchor Books, 1967), 4.

10. *Innovation or Stagnation: Challenge and Opportunity on the Critical Path to New Medical Products* (Washington: U.S. Department of Health and Human Services, Food and Drug Administration, 2005), 8; Lester M. Crawford, "Presentation to the Global Pharmaceutical Strategies Seminar," May 25, 2004, http://www.fda.gov/oc/speeches/2004/gpss0525.html (accessed October 14, 2007); Lester M. Crawford, "Presentation to PhRMA," April 3, 2004, http://www.fda.gov/oc/speeches/2004/phrma0403.html (accessed October 14, 2007); U.S. Food and Drug Administration, "FDA Issues Advice to Make Earliest Stages Of Clinical Drug Development More Efficient," http://www.fda.gov/bbs/topics/news/2006/NEW01296.html (accessed October 15, 2007). The 95 percent figure for "major" discoveries is in S. Claiborne Johnston, "Translation: Case Study in Failure," *Annals of Neurology* 59, no. 3 (March 2006): 447.

11. See e.g. [U.S. General Accounting Office], *FDA Drug Review: Postapproval Risks 1976–1985* (Washington: General Accounting Office, 1990); "Drug Testing Labyrinth," *Cleveland Plain Dealer*, January 10, 1995; Despina G. Contopoulos-Ioannidis, Evangelia E. Ntzani, and John P. A. Ioannidis, "Translation of Highly Promising Basic Science Research into Clinical Applications," *American Journal of Medicine* 114 (April 15, 2003): 477. Because the introduction of new drugs has

slowed considerably in the past 15 years, their contribution to the number of adverse drug events has only produced a moderate increase in the number of these cases. See Thomas J. Moore, Michael R. Cohen, and Curt D. Furberg, "Serious Adverse Drug Events Reported to the Food and Drug Administration, 1998–2005," *Archives of Internal Medicine* 167, no. 16 (2007): 1757.

12. Simon Festing & Robin Wilkinson, "The Ethics of Animal Research: Talking Points on the Use of Animals in Scientific Research," *Embo Reports* 8, no. 6 (2007): 526.

13. Penny Hawkins, *Recognizing and Assessing Pain, Suffering, and Distress in Laboratory Animals: A Survey of Current Practice in the UK with Recommendations* (West Sussex: Research Animals Department, 2002), 8.

14. See Bernard E. Rollin, *Science and Ethics* (New York: Cambridge University Press, 2006), 6–9.

15. José Luiz Telles de Almeida and Fermin Roland Schramm, "Paradigm Shift, Metamorphosis of Medical Ethics, and the Rise of Bioethics" *Cadernos de Saúde Pública* 15, no. 1 (1999), http://www.scielo.br/scielo.php?pid=S0102–311X1999000500003&script=sci_arttext&tlng= (accessed, September 16, 2007).

16. "Einstein Deplores Use of Atom Bomb," *New York Times* August 19, 1946.

17. I acknowledge that vivisection is increasingly employed for veterinary purposes, the ethicality of which reminds me of Nazi experiments on humans to improve human medical practices.

18. Elizabeth A. Lawrence, "Cultural Perceptions of Differences between People and Animals: A Key to Understanding Human-Animal Relationships," *Journal of American Culture* 18, no. 3 (1995): 75–82; Gregory Radick, *The Simian Tongue: The Long Debate about Animal Language* (Chicago: University of Chicago Press, 2008), 16, 218–19; and Karen Dawn, *Thanking the Monkey: Rethinking the Way We Treat Animals* (New York: Harper, 2008), 14–15. Because of Jane Goodall's chimpanzee research in the 1960s and 1970s, the paradigm has been challenged from multiple angles. Jane Goodale, "The Dragonfly's Gift," in *Kinship with Animals*, ed. Michael Tobias and Kate Solisti (rev. ed.; San Fransisco: Council Bluffs, 2006), 6. See Carrie Packwood Freeman, "Embracing Humanimality: Deconstructing the Human/Animal Dichotomy," in this volume.

19. Christopher Baber, *Cognition and Tool Use: Forms of Engagement in Human and Animal Use of Tools* (New York: Taylor & Francis, 2003), 42.

20. I recognize more recent discoveries like the purification of insulin (1923) but even these are dated and increasingly rare.

21. See Anita Guerrini, *Experimenting with Humans and Animals: From Galen to Animal Rights* (Baltimore: Johns Hopkins University Press, 2003), 151.

22. Pandora Pound et al., "Where is the Evidence that Animal Research Benefits Humans," *British Medical Journal* 328 (February 28, 2004): 514. For an example of a researcher who argues without evidence that primate-testing is of "enormous value," see Jon Cohen, "The Endangered Lab Chimp," *Science* 315 (January 26, 2007), 451. See also Johnston, "Translation: Case Study in Failure," 448. The article in question is J. H. Comroe, Jr., and R. D. Dripps, "Scientific Basis for the Support of Biomedical Science," *Science* 192 (1976): 105–111.

23. See esp. Jane Qiu, "Mighty Mouse," *Nature* 444 (December 14, 2006): 816.

24. Over Cabrera et al., "The Unique Cytoarchitecture of Human Pancreatic Islets has Implications for Islet Cell Function," *Proceedings of the National Academy of Science* 103 (February 6, 2006): 2334.

25. Kevin Dolan, *Ethics, Animals, and Science* (Malden, MA: Blackwell, 1999), 176–79.

26. Ray Moynihan, "Who Pays for the Pizza? Redefining the Relationship Between Doctors and Drug Companies," *British Medical Journal* 326 (May 31, 2003): 1195. See also Anna Wilde Mathews and Stephanie Kang, "Media Industry Helped Drug Firms Fight Ad Restraints," *Wall Street Journal*, September 21, 2007.

27. See e.g. Bill Hogan, "Pulling Strings from Afar: Drug Industry Finances Nonprofit Groups that Claim to Speak for Older Americans," *AARP Bulletin* (February 2003), http://www.aarp.org/bulletin/consumer/Articles/a2003–06–30–pullingstrings.html (accessed October 9, 2007).

28. Many advocates for patient groups find themselves on the gravy train to pharmaceutical company headquarters to beg for a little money in exchange for promoting that pharmaceutical company's products to the relevant patient groups. In addition to performing this unpleasant chore, as a lobbyist I was once asked by legislators in Washington, DC (who in turn were being lobbied by the pharmaceutical corporations) to trade my association's position on reforming the Food and Drug Administration for assistance in passing a non-related bill to benefit people with brain injuries. I announced the shift in a letter to the editor published in the *Washington Post*. See Gregory S. Goodale, "Approval Process for Pharmaceuticals," *Washington Post*, March 23, 1996. Three months later the United States Congress passed the Traumatic Brain Injury Act.

29. See, e.g., John Morgan and Stephen A. Shoop, "Katie Couric Reports on Colorectal Cancer," *USA Today*, June 24, 2004.

30. Marcia Angell, "The Truth About the Drug Companies," *New York Review of Books* 51, no. 12 (July 15, 2004), http://www.nybooks.com/articles/17244. See also Rollin, *Science and Ethics*, 4.

31. The international BRI is so complex it would be impossible to provide an exact figure. Given one agency's budget in one country (the United States' National Institutes of Health) of $30 billion for FY2008 and global pharmaceutical sales of $602 billion in 2005, I am confident of this figure given projections of sales growth of between 5 percent–8 percent per year. See "Global Pharmaceutical Sales Grew 7 percent to cross $600 Billion in 2005," *Metrics 2.0: Business and Market Intelligence*, http://www.metrics2.com/blog/2006/06/13/global_pharmaceutical_sales_grew_7_to_cross_600_bi.html (accessed October 27, 2007).

32. Rhetorical critic Richard Harvey Brown recognizes that, "As the scale of science increases, traditional epistemology no longer offers guidance in evaluating knowledge claims. This is because the huge number of such claims that are produced today, and the even greater number of plausible contexts for assessing them makes it impossible and irrational to assess each of them on its particular epistemological merits." Richard Harvey Brown, "New Roles for Rhetoric: From Academic Critique to Civic Affirmation," *Argumentation* 11, no. 1 (1997): 19.

33. Ioannidis, "Why Most Published Research Findings are False."

34. John P. Gluck and Steven R. Kubacki, "Animals in Biomedical Research: The Undermining Effect of the Rhetoric of the Besieged," *Ethics & Behavior* 1, no. 3 (1991): 164–65.

35. Andrea Gawrylewski, "The Trouble with Animal Models: Why Did Human Trials Fail?" *The Scientist* 21, no. 7 (2006): 44.

36. John P. A. Ioannidis, "Evolution and Translation of Research Findings: From Bench to Where?" *Public Library of Science: Clinical Trials* 1, no. 7 (November 2006), http://www.pubmedcentral.nih.gov/articlerender.fcgi?artid=1851723 (accessed September 1, 2009).

37. See, e.g., Daniel G. Hackam, "Translating Animal Research into Clinical Benefit," *British Medical Journal* 334 (2007): 163–64.

38. Peter Greaves, Andrew Williams, and Malcolm Eve, "First Dose Of Potential New Medicines To Humans: How Animals Help," *Nature* (March 2004): 234.

39. Kanwaljeet S. Anand, "Anesthetic Neurotoxicity in Newborns: Should We Change Clinical Practice?" *Anesthesiology* 107, no. 1 (July 2006): 2–4.

40. Jean Dietz Moss and William A. Wallace, *Rhetoric & Dialectic in the Time of Galileo* (Washington: Catholic University of America Press, 2003), 12.

41. Latour, *Science in Action*, 44.

42. Dale L. Sullivan, "Keeping the Rhetoric Orthodox: Forum Control in Science," *Technical Communication Quarterly* 9, no. 2 (Spring 2000): 125–46.

43. Personal correspondence. It is remarkable how similar the explanation is to the explanation Celeste Condit received when she had a letter to the editor rejected (see below). Bowers and Ochs term this the denial of means. Bowers and Ochs, *The Rhetoric of Agitation and Control*, 45. See also Herbert W. Simons, "The Rhetoric of the Scientific Research Report: 'Drug-pushing' in a Medical Journal Article," in *The Recovery of Rhetoric: Persuasive Discourse and Disciplinarity in the Human Sciences*, ed. R. H. Roberts and J. M. M Good (Charlottesville, VA: University of Virginia Press, 1993): 152; and Gluck and Kubacki, "Animals in Biomedical Research," 160.

44. Bowers and Ochs call this harassment and banishment. Bowers and Ochs, *The Rhetoric of Agitation and Control*, 47–50.

45. John P. A. Ioannidis, "Why Most Published Research Findings are False," *Public Library of Science: Medicine* 2, no. 8 (2005), http://medicine. plosjournals.org/perlserv/?request=get-document&doi=10.1371 percent2Fjournal. pmed.0020124&ct=1 (accessed September 29, 2007). See also Pablo Perel et al., "Comparison of Treatment Effects Between Animal Experiments and Clinical Trials: Systematic Review," *British Medical Journal* 333 (December 16, 2006), http://www .bmj.com/cgi/content/full/334/7586/197 (accessed, September 21, 2007); Pound et al., "Where is the Evidence that Animal Research Benefits Humans," 515.

46. Alan G. Gross, *The Rhetoric of Science* (Cambridge, MA: Harvard University Press, 1990), 84. See also Linda Birke and Jane Smith, "Animals in Experimental Reports: The Rhetoric of Science," *Society & Animals* 3, no. 1 (1995), http://www .psyeta.org/sa/sa3.1/birke.html (accessed, September 29, 2007).

47. Simons, "The Rhetoric of the Scientific Research Report," 148, 153.

48. Perel et al., "Comparison of Treatment Effects Between Animal Experiments and Clinical Trials."

49. Robert Freedman et al. "Conflict of Interest—An Issue for Every Psychiatrist," *American Journal of Psychiatry* 166 (2009): 274; Shankar Vedantam, "A Silenced Drug Study Creates An Uproar," *Washington Post*, March 18, 2009.

50. See e.g., Andrew Pollack, "Avastin Falls Short in Test as Colon Cancer Medicine," *New York Times* April 22, 2009.

51. Celeste Condit, "How Bad Science Stays That Way: Brain Sex, Demarcation, and the Status of Truth in the Rhetoric of Science," *Rhetoric Society Quarterly* 26, no. 4 (Fall 1996): 93, 96. See also Celeste M. Condit, "Hegemony in a Mass Mediated Society: Concordance About 'Reproductive Technologies,'" *Critical Studies in Mass Communication* 11, no. 3 (September 1994): 205–230; and James Darsey, A Conspiracy of Science," *Western Journal of Communication* 66, no. 4 (Fall 2002): 469–91. On the nastiness of HIV/AIDS scientists' attacks, see Brian Martin, "The Politics of a Scientific Meeting: The Origin-of-AIDS Debate at the Royal Society," *Politics and Life Sciences* 20, no. 2 (September 2001): 128; and Brian Martin, "Peer Review and the Origin of AIDS: A Case Study in Rejected Ideas," *BioScience* 43, no. 9 (October 1993): 624–627.

52. Personal correspondence with Jarrod Bailey; Stephen Pincock, "Scientists Call for Retractions: Animal Research Supporters Say Journal Published 'Propaganda' while an Antivivisectionist was on Editorial Board," *The Scientist* (March 2, 2006), http://www.the-scientist.com/news/display/23184/ (accessed, January 4, 2007); and "House of Commons Debate," *Europeans for Medical Progress Newsletter* (Winter 2005/2006), 1.

53. See, e.g., Bernard E. Rollin, "The Regulation of Animal Research and the Emergence of Animal Ethics: A Conceptual History," *Theoretical Medicine and Bioethics* 27 (2006): 285–304.

54. David Benatar, "Unscientific Ethics: Science and Selective Ethics," *Hastings Center Report* 37, no. 1 (2007): 31.

55. Benatar, "Unscientific Ethics: Science and Selective Ethics," 32.

56. Latour, *Science in Action*, 33.

57. See, e.g. Jason Edward Black, "SLAPPs and Social Activism: Free Speech Struggles in Grey2K's Campaign to Ban Dog Racing," *Free Speech Yearbook* 40 (2002–03): 70–82.

58. Lewis Carroll, "Some Popular Fallacies about Vivisection," in *The Complete Works of Lewis Carroll* (New York: Modern Library, n.d.): 1189–1201.

59. Michael Balls, "Advocates of Animal Experimentation: What's in a Name?" *ATLA* 36, no. 4 (September 2008): 371.

60. "Overview," *Americans for Medical Progress*, http://www.amprogress.org/site/c.jrLUK0PDLoF/b.933817/k.D675/OVERVIEW.htm (accessed, May 10, 2009).

61. "About," *Speaking of Research*, http://www.speakingofresearch.org (accessed, May 10, 2009).

62. National Institutes of Health, "NIEHS Kid's Pages," http://kids.niehs.nih.gov (accessed, May 10, 2009).

63. *The Lucky Puppy: A Coloring Workbook* (4th ed., Raleigh, NC: North Carolina Association for Biomedical Research 2008), 6–7. My thanks to Maxim Fetissenko for bringing this to my attention.

64. *The Lucky Puppy: A Coloring Workbook*, 20.

65. *The Lucky Puppy: A Coloring Workbook*, 10.

66. See e.g. *The Oxford English Dictionary* (2nd ed. rev.; New York: Oxford University Press, 2005), s.v. "Vivisection;" and Lewis Carroll, "Through the Looking Glass," in *The Complete Works of Lewis Carroll* (New York: Modern Library, n.d.), 214.

67. Festing and Wilkinson, "The Ethics of Animal Research," 526–30.

68. Research Defence Society, "Frequently Asked Questions," http://www.rds-online.org.uk/pages/faq.asp?i_ToolbarID=8&i_PageID=82 (accessed September 28, 2007).

69. See e.g. "What's at Stake?" *Americans for Medical Progress*, http://www.amprogress.org/site/c.jrLUK0PDLoF/b.1147215/k.9FC3/WHATS_AT_STAKE.htm (accessed, May 10, 2009).

70. Festing and Wilkinson, "The Ethics of Animal Research," 530.

71. On the importance of drawing attention to enthymemes in arguments about animal ethics, see Kathryn M. Olson and G. Thomas Goodnight, "Entanglements of Consumption, Cruelty, Privacy, and Fashion: The Social Controversy Over Fur," in *Readings in the Rhetoric of Social Protest*, ed. Charles E. Morris, III and Stephen H. Browne (State College, PA: Strata, 2001), 354–58.

72. Angell, "The Truth About the Drug Companies;" and Rollin, *Science and Ethics*, 4.

CHAPTER NINE

1. People for the Ethical Treatment of Animals, "PETA's History: Compassion in Action," http://www.peta.org/mc/factsheet_display.asp?ID=107 (accessed May 10, 2005); Although it is true, as Peter Simonson points out, that PETA depends heavily on the use of celebrities spreading the group's message, I argue that PETA continues to use news-based controversy to create an audience for its message. Peter Simonson, "Social Noise and Segmented Rhythms: News, Entertainment, and Celebrity in the Crusade for Animal Rights," *Communication Review* 4 (2001): 399–420.

2. The majority of CCF's anti–animal rights advertisements specifically mention PETA. In some cases, the ads broaden the condemnation to "food police" or "animal rights extremists." In this chapter, I have tried to use CCF's exact wording when discussing the advertisement. In general, however, although the group occasionally talks about the animal rights movement as a whole, it also directs all viewers to their website. On the website, almost every page that discusses animal rights or "food radicals" mentions PETA. Thus, although viewers might draw conclusions about the animal rights movement more broadly, PETA is a central component of that image as constructed by CCF.

3. Center for Consumer Freedom, *Your Kids, PETA's Pawns: How the Animal "Rights" Movement Hurts Children* (Washington, DC: Center for Consumer Freedom, n.d.); Center for Consumer Freedom, "Animal Scam.com," http://www.animalscam.com (accessed March 17, 2008).

4. Center for Consumer Freedom, "Animal Scam.com."

5. PETA has, for example, been successful at changing the behavior of many corporations and research institutions. With over 1.8 million members and a $31 million budget, the group has the means to attract attention to the animal rights message. Larry Copeland, "Animal Rights Fight Gains Momentum; Groups Report Increase in Membership as High-Profile Incidents Make Headlines," *USA Today*, January 28, 2008; Allison Enright, "PETA's PR has Claws," *Marketing News*, October 1, 2005; People for the Ethical Treatment of Animals, "Annual Review 2006: The Year in Numbers," http://www.peta.com/feat/annualreview06/numbers.asp (accessed March 20, 2007).

6. People for the Ethical Treatment of Animals, "About PETA," http://www.peta. org/about/faq.asp (accessed September 5, 2009).

7. For example, a 2000 Gallup poll found that 61 percent of respondents supported the goals of the animal rights movement. Mahalley D. Allen, "Animal Rights," in *Polling America: An Encyclopedia of Public Opinion*, ed. Samuel J. Best and Benjamin Radcliff (Westport, CT: Greenwood Press, 2005), 23.

8. Copeland, "Animal Rights Fight Gains Momentum."

9. Center for Consumer Freedom, "About us: What is the Center for Consumer Freedom?" http://www.consumerfreedom.com/about.cfm (accessed February 7, 2008).

10. Sourcewatch, "Center for Consumer Freedom," Center for Media and Democracy, http://www.sourcewatch.org/index.php?title=Center_for_Consumer_Freedom (accessed February 18, 2008).

11. Sourcewatch, "Center for Consumer Freedom."

12. Melanie Warner, "Striking Back at the Food Police," *New York Times*, June 12, 2005.

13. Sourcewatch, "Center for Consumer Freedom"; Warner, "Striking Back at the Food Police."

14. Sourcewatch, "Center for Consumer Freedom."

15. A social movement can be defined as a bottom-up, grassroots organization, while an organization exists in a top-down structure. Additionally, social movement organizations (such as PETA) are defined separately from a larger social movement (such as the animal rights movement). See, for example, Charles J. Stewart, Craig Allen Smith, and Robert E. Denton, Jr., *Persuasion and Social Movements* (5th ed.; Long Grove, IL: Waveland Press, 2007). For an example of the use of the term "astroturf organization," see Phaedra C. Pezzullo, "Resisting 'National Breast Cancer Awareness Month': The Rhetoric of Counterpublics and their Cultural Performances," *Quarterly Journal of Speech* 89 (2003): 345–65.

16. Center for Consumer Freedom, "About Us: What is the Center for Consumer Freedom?" http://www.consumerfreedom.com/about.cfm (accessed September 3, 2009).

17. Sourcewatch, "Center for Consumer Freedom."

18. Center for Consumer Freedom, "Animal Scam.com."

19. All CCF advertisements are available on the group's website: http://www .consumerfreedom.org. The advertisements examined in this chapter were taken from the website and from a packet sent to the author by the organization.

20. Kevin DeLuca and Jennifer Peeples, "From Public Sphere to Public Screen: Democracy, Activism, and the 'Violence' of Seattle," *Critical Studies in Media Communication* 19 (2002): 125–51.

21. DeLuca and Peeples, "From Public Sphere to Public Screen," 125–31.

22. Jürgen Habermas, *The Structural Transformation of the Public Sphere: An Inquiry into a Category of Bourgeois Society*, trans. Thomas Burger and Frederick Lawrence (1962; Cambridge, MA: MIT Press, 1989).

23. DeLuca and Peeples, "From Public Sphere to Public Screen," 128.

24. DeLuca and Peeples, "From Public Sphere to Public Screen," 131.

25. DeLuca and Peeples, "From Public Sphere to Public Screen," 134.

26. John W. Delicath and Kevin Michael DeLuca, "Image Events, the Public Sphere, and Argumentative Practice: The Case of Radical Environmental Groups," *Argumentation* 17 (2003): 315.

27. Delicath and DeLuca, "Image Events," 326. See also Michael Calvin McGee, "Text, Context, and the Fragmentation of Contemporary Culture," *Western Journal of Speech Communication* 54 (1990): 274–89.

28. Delicath and DeLuca, "Image Events," 327.

29. Davi Johnson, "Martin Luther King Jr's 1963 Birmingham Campaign as Image Event," *Rhetoric & Public Affairs* 10 (2007): 20.

30. DeLuca and Peeples, "From Public Sphere to Public Screen," 145.

31. Lesli Pace, "Image Events and PETA's Anti Fur Campaign," *Women and Language* 28 (2005): 33–41.

32. Jeff McDonald, "PETA Campaign Quickly Draws Ire; Jewish Leaders Decry Holocaust References," *New York Times*, March 1, 2003; C. Richard King, "Troubling Images: PETA's 'Holocaust on Your Plate' and the Limits of Image Events," *Enculturation* 6, no. 2 (2009), http://enculturation.gmu.edu/6.2/king.

33. People for the Ethical Treatment of Animals, "Got Beer? Better Than Milk," http://www.milksucks.com/beersurvey.asp (accessed September 6, 2009); People for the Ethical Treatment of Animals, "J. Lo and the Lowdown on Fur: Animals Skinned Alive," http://www.jlodown.com (accessed September 6, 2009); People for the Ethical Treatment of Animals, "Vogue Sucks.com," http://www.voguesucks.com/action.html (accessed September 6, 2009).

34. Michael Specter, "The Extremist: The Woman Behind the Most Successful Radical Group in America," *The New Yorker* (April 14, 2003): 52–67.

35. Christine Harold, "Pranking Rhetoric: 'Culture Jamming' as Media Activism," *Critical Studies in Media Communication* 21 (2004): 191.

36. Warner, "Striking Back at the Food Police"; Seth Lubove, "Food Fight," *Forbes.com*, September 23, 2005, http://www.forbes.com/business/2005/09/23/obesity-lobbying-ccf-cz_sl_0923ccf.html (accessed March 16, 2008); Verlyn Klinkenborg, "The Story Behind a New York Billboard and the Interests it Serves," *New York Times*, July 24, 2005.

37. Joe Sharkey, "Perennial Foes Meet Again in a Battle of the Snack Bar," *New York Times*, November 23, 2004; Lubove, "Food Fight."

38. Klinkenborg, "The Story Behind a New York Billboard."

39. Julie K. Shutten, "Invoking *Practical Magic*: New Social Movements, Hidden Populations, and the Public Screen," *Western Journal of Communication* 70 (2006): 351.

40. DeLuca and Peeples, "From Public Sphere to Public Screen."

41. Center for Consumer Freedom, "You are Too Stupid," http://www.consumer-freedom.com/advertisements_detail.cfm/ad/7 (accessed March 5, 2008). No specific organizations are named, but one can assume from the message that they are referring to animal rights groups, anti-obesity campaigns, and anti-drinking and driving campaigns.

42. Center for Consumer Freedom, "Radio Ads," http://www.consumerfreedom .com/advertisements_radio.cfm (accessed August 10, 2009).

43. Center for Consumer Freedom, "Food Police Smashing your Choices?" http:// www.consumerfreedom.com/advertisements_detail.cfm?ad=38 (accessed March 5, 2008). Once viewers visit the website and click on the "Food Radicals" section, animal rights groups (and PETA in particular) are included in this section.

44. Sherry B. Ortner, *Making Gender: The Politics and Erotics of Culture* (Boston: Beacon Press, 1996).

45. Center for Consumer Freedom, "Lab Rats or Sick Kids," http://www .consumerfreedom.com/advertisements_detail.cfm/ad/19 (accessed March 5, 2008).

46. Center for Consumer Freedom, "Rats vs. Sick Kids," http://www.consumer freedom.com/advertisements_detail.cfm/ad/8 (accessed March 5, 2008).

47. Ortner, *Making Gender*.

48. Wendy Atkins-Sayre, "Articulating Identity: People for the Ethical Treatment of Animals and the Animal/Human Divide," *Western Journal of Communication* (forthcoming).

49. Center for Consumer Freedom, "Hey PETA, Mind your own Business."

50. Center for Consumer Freedom, "What is PETA Teaching your Kids?" http:// www.consumerfreedom.com/advertisements_detail.cfm/ad/28 (accessed March 5, 2008).

51. Center for Consumer Freedom, "PETA's Explosive Rhetoric," http://www .consumerfreedom.com/advertisements_detail.cfm/ad/16 (accessed March 5, 2008).

52. Center for Consumer Freedom, "PETA's Foot-in-mouth Disease," http://www .consumerfreedom.com/advertisements_detail.cfm/ad/17 (accessed March 5, 2008).

53. Center for Consumer Freedom, "A Mother's Concern about PETA," http:// www.consumerfreedom.com/advertisements_detail.cfm?ad=1 (accessed March 5, 2008).

54. Center for Consumer Freedom, "Hey PETA, Mind your own Business," http:// www.consumerfreedom.com/advertisements_detail.cfm?ad=48 (accessed March 5, 2008).

55. Center for Consumer Freedom, "Hey PETA, Mind your own Business."

56. Center for Consumer Freedom, "PETA Leader Wants to Blow Stuff Up," http://www.consumerfreedom.com/advertisements_detail.cfm/ad/2 (accessed March 5, 2008).

57. DeLuca and Peeples, "From Public Sphere to Public Screen," 131.

58. DeLuca and Peeples, "From Public Sphere to Public Screen," 144.

59. Kevin M. DeLuca, *Image Politics: The New Rhetoric of Environmental Activism* (New York: Guilford Press, 1999).

60. Delicath and DeLuca, "Image Events, the Public Sphere, and Argumentative Practice," 328.

61. DeLuca and Peeples, "From Public Sphere to Public Screen."

62. Delicath and DeLuca, "Image Events, the Public Sphere, and Argumentative Practice," 322.

63. Chaim Perelman and Lucie Olbrechts-Tyteca, *The New Rhetoric: A Treatise on Argumentation* (Notre Dame: Notre Dame Press, 1969).

64. Stewart, Smith, and Denton, *Persuasion and Social Movements*.

65. Jo Littler, "Corporate Involvement in Image Events: Media Stunts, Guerilla Marketing and the Problem of Political Interpretation," *Enculturation* 6, no. 2 (2009), http://enculturation.gmu.edu/6.2/littler.

66. DeLuca and Peeples, "From Public Sphere to Public Screen."

67. Lubove, "Food Fight."

68. Lubove, "Food Fight."

69. DeLuca and Peeples, "From Public Sphere to Public Screen," 146.

CHAPTER TEN

1. "Needle in a Haystack," *Whale Wars*, DVD, produced by River Media (Santa Monica, CA: River Media, 2009).

2. Sea Shepherd Conservation Society, "Who We Are," http://www.seashepherd .org/who-we-are (accessed August 15, 2009).

3. Kevin M. DeLuca, *Image Politics: The New Rhetoric of Environmental Activism* (New York: Guilford Press, 1999).

4. Daniel Pace, "Whale War Battles . . . Over Best Protest Method," *Hobart Mercury*, December 1, 2008.

5. Mike Flaherty, "Controversy Buoys 'Whale Wars': Hit Show's Extreme Tactics Come Under Fire" *Daily Variety*, November 19, 2008.

6. Flaherty, "Controversy Buoys 'Whale Wars.'"

7. Gary Strauss, "'Whale' Saviors on Warpath; Series' Team Chases Japanese Hunters," *USA Today*, November 7, 2008.

8. Sea Shepherd Conservation Society, "'Whale Wars' Season 1 a Big Hit for Animal Planet and Sea Shepherd," http://66.17.141.136/whales/whale-wars.html (accessed August 15, 2009).

9. Christopher Bantick, "Risking Life in Whale Wars," *Hobart Mercury*, December 1, 2008.

10. Quoted in Kevin M. DeLuca and Jennifer Peeples, "From Public Sphere to Public Screen: Democracy, Activism, and the 'Violence' of Seattle," *Critical Studies in Media Communication* 19 (2002): 127.

11. Jürgen Habermas, "The Public Sphere: An Encyclopedia Article (1964)," *New German Critique* 3 (1974): 49–55; Jürgen Habermas, *The Structural Transformation*

of the Public Sphere: An Inquiry into a Category of Bourgeois Society, trans. Thomas Burger and Frederick Lawrence (1962; Cambridge, MA: MIT Press, 1991).

12. David Zarefsky, "The Decline of Public Debate," *USA Today (Magazine)*, March 1998, 59.

13. Christopher Lasch, "The Lost Art of Political Argument," *Harper's Magazine*, September 1990, 17–22.

14. Neil Postman, *Amusing Ourselves to Death: Public Discourse in the Age of Show Business* (New York: Penguin Books, 1985).

15. Nancy Fraser, "Rethinking the Public Sphere: A Contribution to the Critique of Actually Existing Democracy," in *Habermas and the Public Sphere*, ed. Craig Calhoun (Cambridge: MIT Press, 1991), 109–142.

16. Fraser, "Rethinking the Public Sphere," 111.

17. Michael Schudson, "Was There Ever a Public Sphere? If So, When? Reflections on the American Case," in *Habermas and the Public Sphere*, ed. Craig Calhoun (Cambridge: MIT Press, 1991), 143–163.

18. Cara A. Finnegan and Jiyeon Kang, "'Sighting' the Public: Iconoclasm and Public Sphere Theory," *Quarterly Journal of Speech* 90 (2004): 377–402.

19. DeLuca, *Image Politics*, 1.

20. John W. Delicath and Kevin Michael DeLuca, "Image Events, the Public Sphere, and Argumentative Practice: The Case of Radical Environmental Groups," *Argumentation* 17 (2003): 315.

21. Davi Johnson, "Martin Luther King Jr.'s 1963 Birmingham Campaign as Image Event," *Rhetoric & Pubic Affairs* 10 (2007): 2.

22. Delicath and DeLuca, "Image Events, the Public Sphere, and Argumentative Practice," 318.

23. DeLuca and Peeples, "From Public Sphere to Public Screen," 133.

24. DeLuca and Peeples, "From Public Sphere to Public Screen," 127.

25. DeLuca and Peeples, "From Public Sphere to Public Screen," 131.

26. Delicath and DeLuca, "Image Events, the Public Sphere, and Argumentative Practice," 320.

27. DeLuca and Peeples, "From Public Sphere to Public Screen," 134.

28. Delicath and DeLuca, "Image Events, the Public Sphere, and Argumentative Practice," 324.

29. Michael Spangler and David Knapp, "Ways We Talk About the Earth: An Exploration of Persuasive Tactics and Appeals in Environmental Discourse," in *Earthtalk: Communication Empowerment for Environmental Action*, ed. Star A. Muir and Thomas L. Veenendall (Wesport, CT: Praeger, 1996); Jonathan Gray, "Striking Social Dramas, Image Events, and Meme Warfare: Performance and Social Activism—Past, Present, and Future," *Text & Performance Quarterly* 21 (2001): 67–68.

30. A notable exception is the recent special issue of *Enculturation*. For a brief summary of the issues, see Kevin M. DeLuca and Joe Wilferth, "Foreword," *Enculturation: A Journal of Rhetoric, Writing, and Culture* 6 (2009), http://enculturation .gmu.edu/node/102/pdf (accessed August 31, 2009).

31. Lesli Pace, "Image Events and PETA's Anti Fur Campaign," *Women and Language* 28 (2005): 33–41; C. Richard King, "Troubling Images: PETA's 'Holocaust

on Your Plate' and Image Events," *Enculturation: A Journal of Rhetoric, Writing, and Culture* 6 (2009), http://enculturation.gmu.edu/node/118/pdf (accessed August 31, 2009); Hunter Stephenson, "(Re)claiming the Ground: Image Events, Kairos, and Discourse," *Enculturation: A Journal of Rhetoric, Writing, and Culture* 6 (2009), http://enculturation.gmu.edu/node/107/pdf (accessed August 31, 2009); Brett Lunceford, "PETA and the Rhetoric of Nude Protest," in this volume.

32. Lydia Bell, "Many Whales Ago," *Natural History* 117 (2008): 10.

33. Eric Jay Dolin, "A Glimpse into Whaling History," *The Boston Globe*, July 6, 2007.

34. Michael Easterbrook, "The Great Big Sea: A Whaler's Lament," *The Globe and Mail*, January 30, 2007.

35. Dolin, "A Glimpse into Whaling History," A11.

36. "Don't Resurrect This Cruel Trade," *Western Daily Press*, March 30, 2007.

37. International Whaling Commission, "IWC Information," http://www.iwcoffice.org/commission/iwcmain.htm (accessed November 20, 2008).

38. Sean Lengell, "Whaling Ban Strains U.S.-Japan Relations; Tokyo Seeks to End Moratorium," *The Washington Times* April 26, 2007.

39. International Whaling Commission, "Scientific Permit Whaling," http://www.iwcoffice.org/conservation/permits.htm (accessed November 20, 2008).

40. International Whaling Commission, "Catches Taken: Under Scientific Permit," http://www.iwcoffice.org/conservation/table_permit.htm (accessed November 20, 2008).

41. Ben Haywood, "Beastly Motives," *The Age*, November 26, 2007.

42. Haywood, "Beastly Motives."

43. "Boiling Point," *Whale Wars*, DVD, produced by River Media (Santa Monica, CA: River Media, 2009).

44. Charles J. Stewart, "Championing the Rights of Others and Challenging Evil: The Ego Function in the Rhetoric of Other-Directed Social Movements," *Southern Communication Journal* 64 (1999): 91–105.

45. Jason E. Black, "Extending the Rights of Personhood, Voice, and Life to Sensate Others: A Homology of Right to Life and Animal Rights Rhetoric," *Communication Quarterly* 51 (2003): 312–331.

46. "Needle in a Haystack."

47. "Nothing's Ideal," *Whale Wars*, DVD, produced by River Media (Santa Monica, CA: River Media, 2009).

48. "International Incidents R Us," *Whale Wars*, DVD, produced by River Media (Santa Monica, CA: River Media, 2009).

49. Flaherty, "Controversy buoys 'Whale,'" 20.

50. "Nothing's Ideal."

51. "International Incidents R Us."

52. "We Are Hooligans," *Whale Wars*, DVD, produced by River Media (Santa Monica, CA: River Media, 2009).

53. "Doors Slamming and Things Breaking," *Whale Wars*, DVD, produced by River Media (Santa Monica, CA: River Media, 2009).

54. "Doors Slamming."

55. "Ladies First," *Whale Wars*, DVD, produced by River Media (Santa Monica, CA: River Media, 2009).

56. "Boiling Point."

57. "Boiling Point."

58. "Boiling Point."

59. David Hinckley, "'Whale' of a Reality A Show Gets a Sea-plus," *Daily News*, November 6, 2008.

60. Jo Littler, "Corporate Involvement in Image Events: Media Stunts, Guerrilla Marketing and the Problem of Political Imagination," *Enculturation: A Journal of Rhetoric, Writing, and Culture* 6 (2009), http://enculturation.gmu.edu/node/105/pdf (accessed August 31, 2009).

CHAPTER ELEVEN

1. People for the Ethical Treatment of Animals, "Why Animal Rights," http://www.peta.org/about/WhyAnimalRights.asp (accessed September 8, 2009); and Bureau of Land Management, "Wilderness," http://www.blm.gov/wo/st/en/prog/blm_special_areas/NLCS/Wilderness.html (accessed September 8, 2009).

2. Corolla Wild Horse Fund, "Shackleford 127–Corolla 60," *Wild and Free Newsletter* 1, no. 7 (November 2008).

3. Genesis 1: 26, *Bible: New Revised Standard Version* (henceforth *NRSV*).

4. Francis Bacon, "Novum Organum," in *Great Books of the Western World Series*, ed. Robert Maynard Hutchins (Chicago: Benton, 1955), 50: 107–195; and Thomas Aquinas, *Aquinas's Shorter Summa* (Manchester, N.H.: Sophia Institute Press, 1993), 190.

5. Rod Preece, "Darwinism, Christianity, and the Great Vivisection Debate," *Journal of the History of Ideas* 64 (2003): 399–419; and Jack Wintz, *Will I See My Dog in Heaven?* (n.p.: Paraclete Press, 2009), 12–13.

6. Thomas Lessl, "The Culture of Science and the Rhetoric of Scientism: From Francis Bacon to the Darwin Fish," *Quarterly Journal of Speech* 93 (2007): 123–149.

7. Bacon, "Novum Organum," 50:107–195

8. Elizabeth Walker Mechling and Jay Mechling, "Sweet Talk: The Moral Rhetoric Against Sugar," *Central States Speech Journal* 34, no. 1 (1983): 19–32.

9. James McDaniel, "Figures of Evil: A Triad of Rhetorical Strategies for Theo-Politics," *Rhetoric and Public Affairs* 6, no. 3 (2003): 539–550.

10. Jason Edward Black, "Extending the Rights of Personhood, Voice, and Life to Sensate Others: A Homology of Right to Life and Animal Rights Rhetoric," *Communication Quarterly* 51, no. 3 (2003): 312–331.

11. Black, "Extending the Rights," 314.

12. Corolla Wild Horse Fund, http://www.corollawildhorses.com (accessed August 15, 2009).

13. North Carolina Department of Environment and Natural Resources, "The North Carolina Coastal Reserve & National Estuarine Research Center, Rachel Carson Component," http://www.nccoastalreserve.net (accessed August 15, 2009);

and U.S. Fish and Wildlife Service, Mackay Island National Wildlife Refuge 2008 Comprehensive Conservation Plan, http://www.fws.gov/southeast/planning/PDF documents/Mackay/MackayIslandCCPEA.pdf126 (accessed July 15, 2009), 126.

14. Corolla Wild Horse Fund, "Shackleford 127–Corolla 60," 1.

15. Gus E. Cothran, "Analysis of Gentic Diversity in the Corolla Feral Horse Herd of North Carolina," http://www.corollawildhorses.com/Images/News/genetic -diversity-analysis.pdf (accessed September 9, 2009), 2.

16. Corolla Wild Horse Fund, "Denial of Request to Allow Corolla Wild Colonial Spanish Mustangs to Remain at a Genetically Healthy Level," http://www.corolla wildhorses.com/Images/News/genetic-crisis-rev.pdf (accessed September 9, 2009).

17. Andrew Linzey, *Animal Theology* (Chicago: University of Illinois Press, 1995), 13; and Wintz, *Will I See My Dog in Heaven*, 12–13.

18. Aquinas, *Aquinas's Shorter Summa*, 136

19. Aquinas, *Aquinas's Shorter Summa*, 76–77; and Frederick Coppleston, *A History of Philosophy* (New York: Doubleday, 1963), 2:388–389.

20. Aquinas, *Aquinas's Shorter Summa*, 77.

21. Aquinas, *Aquinas's Shorter Summa*, 63.

22. Coppleston, *A History of Philosophy*, 3:303.

23. Coppleston, *A History of Philosophy*, 3:308.

24. Bacon, "Novum Organum," 1:107.

25. Aquinas, *Aquinas's Shorter Summa*, 166.

26. Bacon, "Of Gardens," in *The Harvard Classics*, ed. Charles W. Eliot (New York: P. F. Collier, 1909), 112–117.

27. Coppleston, *A History of Philosophy* 3:252, 290; René Descartes, "Discourse on Method," in *Classics of Western Thought: The Modern World*, ed. Charles Hirschfeld and Edgar E. Knoebel (3rd ed.; San Diego: Harcourt Brace Jovanovich, 1980), 3:15–27; and Tom Regan, *The Case for Animal Rights* (Berkeley: University of California Press, 1983), 25.

28. Gifford Pinchot, *Breaking New Ground* (Seattle: University of Washington Press), 326.

29. Kevin Michael DeLuca and Anne Teresa Demo, "Imaging Nature: Watkins, Yosemite, and the Birth of Environmentalism," *Critical Studies in Media Communication* 17 (2000): 241.

30. Genesis 3:17, *NRSV*.

31. Richard M. Weaver, "Ultimate Terms in Contemporary Rhetoric," in *The Ethics of Rhetoric* (1953; Davis, CA: Hermorgoras Press, 1985), 213.

32. U.S. Fish and Wildlife Service, *Mackay Island National Wildlife Refuge 2008 Comprehensive Conservation Plan*, http://www.fws.gov/southeast/planning/ PDFdocuments/Mackay/MackayIslandCCPEA.pdf126 (accessed July 15, 2009), 126.

33. The North Carolina Coastal Reserve & National Estuarine Research Center, http://www.nccoastalreserve.net (accessed August 15, 2009).

34. Aquinas, *Aquinas's Shorter Summa*, 190

35. Carolyn Merchant, *The Death of Nature: Women, Ecology and the Scientific Revolution* (San Francisco: Harper & Row, 1980), 1–41; and U.S. Fish and Wildlife Service, *Comprehensive Conservation Plan*, 116.

36. U.S. Fish and Wildlife Service, *Comprehensive Conservation Plan*, 12; and The North Carolina Coastal Reserve & National Estuarine Research Center, http://www.nccoastalreserve.net (accessed August 15, 2009).

37. US Fish and Wildlife, *Comprehensive Conservation Plan*, 12; and Aquinas, *Aquinas's Shorter Summa*, 142.

38. Black, "Extending the Rights," 316; and U.S. Fish and Wildlife Service, *Comprehensive Conservation Plan*, 126.

39. The North Carolina Coastal Reserve & National Estuarine Research Center, "Rachel Carson Component," http://www.nccoastalreserve.net (accessed August 15, 2009), 22.

40. Weaver, "Ultimate Terms in Contemporary Rhetoric," 222.

41. U.S. Fish and Wildlife Service, "Currituck National Wildlife Refuge," http://www.fws.gov/currituck (accessed August 15, 2009); and Weaver, "Ultimate Terms," 226.

42. "Rachel Carson Component," 73.

43. U.S. Fish and Wildlife Service, *Comprehensive Conservation Plan*, http://www.fws.gov/southeast/planning/PDFdocuments/Mackay/MackayIslandCCPEA.pdf126 (accessed July 15, 2009), 57.

44. Kenneth Burke, *Counter-Statement* (Los Altos: Hermes Publications, 1953), 162–163.

45. Weaver, "Ultimate Terms," 214.

46. Coppleston, *A History of Philosophy*, 3:292–303.

47. Charles Darwin, "The Origin of the Species," in *Great Books of the Western World Series*, ed. Robert Hutchins (Chicago: Benton, 1952), 49:40.

48. Marc Bekoff, *The Emotional Lives of Animals* (Novato, CA: New World Library, 2007), 118.

49. Aquinas, *Aquinas's Shorter Summa*, 142.

50. John Passmore, "The Treatment of Animals," *Journal of the History of Ideas* 36 (1975): 213.

51. Andrew Linzey, "The Place of Animals in Creation: A Christian View," in *Animal Sacrifices: Religious Perspectives on the Use of Animals in Science*, ed. Tom Regan (Philadelphia: Temple University Press, 1986): 115–148.

52. Preece, "Darwinism, Christianity and the Great Vivisection Debate," 400.

53. Michael Fox, *St. Francis of Assisi, Animals and Nature* (Washington: Center for Respect of Life and Environment, 1989), 1–2.

54. Coppleston, *A History of Philosophy*, 3:258–277; and Francis of Assisi, "The Canticle of the Creatures," quoted in Fox, *St. Francis of Assisi*, 9.

55. Francis of Assisi, quoted in Fox, *St. Francis of Assisi*, 10, 3.

56. Preece, "Darwinism, Christianity and the Great Vivisection Debate," 400–401; and Linzey, *Animal Theology*, 20–36.

57. Wintz, *Will I See My Dog in Heaven?* 85.

58. Linzey, *Animal Theology*, 123.

59. Linzey, *Animal Theology*, 37.

60. Corolla Wild Horse Fund, http://www.corollawildhorses.com (accessed August 15, 2009).

61. Corolla Wild Horse Fund, http://www.corollawildhorses.com (accessed August 15, 2009).

62. See Corolla Wild Horse Fund, "Luck, Love, and Toxins," *Wild and Free Weekly*, blogpost August 5, 2009, http://corollawildhorses.blogspot.com (accessed August 10, 2009).

63. See Corolla Wild Horse Fund, "Luck, Love, and Toxins," *Wild and Free Weekly*, blogpost August 5, 2009, http://corollawildhorses.blogspot.com (accessed August 10, 2009).

64. Black, "Extending the Rights," 313.

65. Linzey, *Animal Theology*, 24.

66. See Corolla Wild Horse Fund, "Luck, Love, and Toxins," *Wild and Free Weekly*, blogpost August 5, 2009, http://corollawildhorses.blogspot.com, (accessed August 10, 2009).

67. Kenneth Burke, *A Grammar of Motives* (Berkeley: University of California Press, 1969), 508; Coppleston, *A History of Philosophy*, 3:265; and Merchant, *The Death of Nature*, 1–41.

68. Merchant, *The Death of Nature*, 1–41. See also Linzey, *Animal Theology*, 59, 68.

69. Corolla Wild Horse Fund, http://www.corollawildhorses.com (accessed September 14, 2009).

70. Corolla Wild Horse Fund, http://www.corollawildhorses.com (accessed August 15, 2009).

71. Corolla Wild Horse Fund, "History," http://www.corollawildhorses.com/history.html (accessed September 14, 2009).

72. Corolla Wild Horse Fund, "Luck, Love, and Toxins."

73. Weaver, "Ultimate Terms," 222.

74. Corolla Wild Horse Fund, http://www.corollawildhorses.com (accessed September 22, 2009); and Corolla Wild Horse Fund, "Critically Endangerd/Nearly Extinct," http://www.corollawildhorses.com/index.html (accessed September 22, 2009), 1.

75. Karen McAlpin to Mike Hoff (shared with author), August 5, 2008.

76. Corolla Wild Horse Fund, "Luck, Love, and Toxins."

77. Genesis 2:19–20, *NRSV*.

78. Karen McAlpin to Mike Hoff, August 5, 2008 (shared with author).

79. Corolla Wild Horse Fund, "The 'Happily Adopted' Ones," http://www.corolla wildhorses.com/happily_adopted.html (accessed September 13, 2009).

80. Linzey, *Animal Theology*, 49.

81. Burke, *A Grammar of Motives*, 510.

82. Karen McAlpin, e-mail message to author, June 16, 2009.

83. Corolla Wild Horse Fund, "Luck, Love, and Toxins."

84. Walter R. Fisher, "Narration as a Human Communication Paradigm: The Case of Public Moral Argument," *Communication Monographs* 51 (1984): 1–22; and Robert C. Rowland, "Narrative: Mode of Discourse or Paradigm?" *Communication Monographs* 54 (1987): 264–275.

85. Andrew Greeley, "Religion and Attitudes toward the Environment," *Journal for the Scientific Study of Religion* 32 (1993): 19; and Lessl, "The Culture of Science and the Rhetoric of Scientism," 131.

86. Lessl, "The Culture of Science and the Rhetoric of Scientism," 131.

87. Amos Wilder, *Early Christian Rhetoric: The Language of the Gospel* (Cambridge: Harvard University Press, 1971), 55–56.

88. Fox, *St. Francis of Assisi*, 24.

89. Lessl, "The Culture of Science and the Rhetoric of Scientism," 131; and Black, "Extending the Rights," 314.

90. Corolla Wild Horse Fund, "Luck, Love, and Toxins."

91. Corolla Wild Horse Fund, "Luck, Love, and Toxins."

92. Jerry Wright, quoted in Corolla Wild Horse Fund, "Update on Genetic Crisis," http://www.corollawildhorses.com/Images/News/genetic-update-nov21.pdf (accessed September 15, 2009).

93. James Darsey, *The Prophetic Tradition and Radical Rhetoric in America* (New York: New York University Press, 1997).

94. Bacon, "Of Plantations," *The Harvard Classics*, ed. Charles W. Eliot (New York: P. F. Collier, 1909), 85–87.

95. Darsey, *The Prophetic Tradition and Radical Rhetoric in America*, 16.

96. Corolla Wild Horse Fund, "Luck, Love, and Toxins."

97. Corolla Wild Horse Fund, "Save the Wild Horses of Corolla from Genetic Collapse," http://www.ipetitions.com/petition/SaveTheWildHorsesOfCorolla/index.html (accessed September 17, 2009); and Corolla Wild Horse Fund, "Update on Genetic Crisis."

98. Fox, *St. Francis of Assisi*, 24.

99. Stephen Browne, "'Like Gory Spectres': Representing Evil in Theodore Weld's *American Slavery As It Is*," *Quarterly Journal of Speech* 80 (1994): 278.

100. Browne, "'Like Gory Spectres,'" 278.

101. Kenneth Burke, *The Philosophy of Literary Form: Studies in Symbolic Action* (1941; Berkeley: University of California Press, 1973), 109.

Index

About the Contributors

Wendy Atkins-Sayre (Ph.D., University of Georgia) is assistant professor of communication studies and director of the Speaking Center at the University of Southern Mississippi. Her research interests center on issues of identity as constructed through discourse. Her research has appeared in *Women and Language*, and her reviews have appeared in *Women's Studies in Communication*, *Southern Communication Journal*, and *Quarterly Journal of Speech*. Her article "Articulating Identity: People for the Ethical Treatment of Animals and the Animal/Human Divide" is forthcoming in the *Western Journal of Communication*.

Renee S. Besel is currently a graduate student in the English department at Roosevelt University. A devout vegetarian, she is currently pursuing her M.F.A. in creative writing. Her research and writing interests focus on animal rights, environmental fiction, family relationships, and mediated discourse.

Richard D. Besel (Ph.D., University of Illinois) is an assistant professor in the communication studies department at California Polytechnic State University, San Luis Obispo. His primary research interests focus on rhetorical studies, science studies, and environmental communication. He has been a vegetarian for seven years.

Jason Edward Black (Ph.D., Maryland) is an assistant professor at the University of Alabama. His research program is located at the juncture of rhetorical studies and cultural studies, with an emphasis on social change. His specific topical interests include American Indian, GLBT-Q, and animal protection discourses. His work in these areas has appeared in *Quarterly Journal* *of Speech*, *Southern Communication Journal*, *Communication Quarterly*, *American Indian Quarterly*, *Kenneth Burke Journal*, *Journal of Media and Cultural Politics*, and numerous book chapters. Black has been the recipient of the Rushing Early Career Award and the Owen Peterson Award from the Southern States Communication Association, and the Wrage-Baskerville Award from the National Communication Association.

Carrie Packwood Freeman (Ph.D., University of Oregon) is an assistant professor of communication at Georgia State University. She researches media ethics, communication strategies for social movements, and media coverage of nonhuman animal and environmental issues, specializing in animal agribusiness and veganism. Her research on national news construction of farmed animals appears in *The Communication Review*. She has authored book chapters on the connection between meat and masculinity in fast-food advertising and on *South Park*'s use of comedy as a social corrective in addressing nonhuman animal issues. She's been active in the animal rights movement for almost two decades, running local grassroots groups in three states.

Greg Goodale (J.D., University of Virginia School of Law; Ph.D., University of Illinois) is assistant professor in the Department of Communication Studies and the Law, Policy & Society Program at Northeastern University. As an attorney, lobbyist, and congressional aide in Washington, D.C., Dr. Goodale developed an interest in the limits and rights of citizenship, and the power of lobby organizations to distort the truth and warp policy-making decisions. At Northeastern University, he was tasked with developing a new curriculum titled "Public Advocacy & Rhetoric" in addition to a minor in oratory and an interdisciplinary minor in rhetoric. Beyond his interest in animal ethics, Dr. Goodale also researches in early republican mythologies and in the persuasive effects of sound. He has recently published essays in *American Quarterly* (with Jeremy Engels) and *Communication and Critical/Cultural Studies* (also with Jeremy Engels) and chapters in two scholarly volumes.

Laura K. Hahn (Ph.D., Ohio State University) is an associate professor, University ombudsperson, and the coordinator of the Social Advocacy Program in the Department of Communication at Humboldt State University. She is the coauthor of a recent essay, "Accessible Artifact for Community Discussion About Anarchy and Education" (Routledge, 2009) and a forthcoming textbook on communication. Her interests include social advocacy, rhetorical criticism, and gender and communication.

Brett Lunceford (Ph.D., The Pennsylvania State University) is assistant professor of communication at the University of South Alabama, where he serves as the head of the Interpersonal/Rhetoric track. His research focuses on social movements, technology, and democratic practice. His current research examines the use of nudity in protest action. His work has appeared in *Review of Communication, Northwestern Journal of Technology and Intellectual Property, Theology and Sexuality, ETC: A Review of General Semantics, Explorations in Media Ecology,* and *American Communication Journal,* and *Media History Monographs.* Forthcoming articles will appear in *Communication Teacher and Explorations in Media Ecology.*

Patricia Malesh (Ph.D., University of Arizona) is an assistant professor of communication and the associate director of the Program for Writing and Rhetoric at the University of Colorado–Boulder. Her research examines the intersections of personal agency and social change. In particular, she focuses on movement studies as rhetorical-critical theory by blending performance studies, public/counterpublics theory, ethnography/auto-ethnography, and narrative theory with sociological and psychological insight. She recently coedited the collection *Active Voices: Composing a Rhetoric of Social Movements* (SUNY Press) with Sharon Stevens and is currently working on a manuscript that extends the scholarship on rhetorics of consumption (vegetarianism/veganism as socio-cultural movements) that she began in her dissertation "Rhetorics of Consumptions: Identity, Confrontation, and Corporatization in the American Vegetarian Movement," which won the Rhetoric Society of America's Dissertation of the Year award in 2006.

Sabrina Marsh is a Ph.D. student in communication at the University of Illinois Urbana-Champaign. Her research focuses on American social reform movements and gender in public address. Her dissertation research will explore the rhetoric of Christian organizations addressing emergent social crises during the interwar years.

Jane Bloodworth Rowe has a Ph.D. from Regent University. She is currently an adjunct assistant professor at Old Dominion University, where she teaches rhetorical criticism, media analysis and criticism, and public speaking. Her research interests include environmental communication, environmental justice, and animal rights issues, and she has published articles in *Environmental Communication: A Journal of Nature and Culture* as well as in the *Environmental Communication Yearbook.*

Mary Trachsel (Ph.D., University of Texas) is an associate professor and former chair of the Department of Rhetoric at the University of Iowa, where she teaches rhetoric and composition, feminist pedagogy, feminist ethics, and animal studies courses. Her recent scholarship has examined human/

nonhuman animal relationships, particularly those between scientists and animal research subjects in the field of ape language research. She lives in Iowa City, Iowa, with her husband, three cats, and two dogs. She volunteers at two local animal shelters and serves on the board of the Iowa Humane Alliance, an organization dedicated to providing low-cost, high-quality, high-volume spay and neuter services in eastern Iowa.

Lightning Source UK Ltd.
Milton Keynes UK
175961UK00001B/143/P